# Praise for
# *Negotiating with Iran*
# *Wrestling the Ghosts of History*

"Negotiating with Iran *should be read not just by foreign service officials but also by academics and general readers interested in U.S.-Iran relations.*"

—**Ervand Abrahamian,** Baruch College, CUNY

"*This is an excellent book and an important contribution to what is rapidly becoming the central issue in American foreign policy. Limbert draws on years of professional and personal experience to explore and explain the problematic nature of Iran-U.S. relations and to offer coherent and constructive solutions for the future. Limbert is in the enviable position of being able to combine the perspective of a historian with the immediacy of a diplomat who has been at the forefront of America's tragic relationship with Iran, to provide a penetrating yet accessible account of the relationship. This book should be essential reading for students and practitioners alike.*"

—**Ali M. Ansari,** University of St. Andrews

"*Drawing on his personal observations, interviews with key players, and the historical record, John Limbert has written a thought-provoking study on the experience of negotiating with Iran in the recent past and the lessons the past provides for negotiating with Iran today. This carefully documented essay is both handbook and history—a must-read for both government officials who intend to sit at the negotiating table with Iran and all those interested in the tangled record of Iran relations with the West and Russia.*"

—**Shaul Bakhash,** George Mason University

"*A must-read for anyone who hopes for (or fears) an American reengagement with Iran. Superb diplomatic history focused on lessons learned rather than festering grievances. I hope Iranians read this as well as Americans. Limbert is one of our few genuine Iran experts.*"

—**Richard W. Bulliet,** Columbia University

"*Well conceived and organized, a major addition to the study of contemporary Iran, this book is compelling reading and is comprehensive in its historical and political reach. The author provides a welcome resource as the United States and other countries begin to consider expanded discussions with the Iranian leadership.*"

—**Nicholas Burns,** Harvard University

# Negotiating with Iran

# NEGOTIATING WITH IRAN

Wrestling the Ghosts of History

JOHN W. LIMBERT

UNITED STATES INSTITUTE OF PEACE PRESS

Washington, D.C.

UNITED STATES INSTITUTE OF PEACE
1200 17th Street, NW, Suite 200
Washington, DC 20036-3011
www.usip.org

First published 2009

Printed in the United States of America

The paper used in this publication meets the minimum requirements of American National Standards for Information Science—Permanence of Paper for Printed Library Materials, ANSI Z39.48-1984.

**Library of Congress Cataloging-in-Publication Data**

Limbert, John W.
Negotiating with Iran : wrestling the ghosts of history / John W. Limbert.
    p. cm.
Includes bibliographical references and index.
ISBN 978-1-60127-043-6 (pbk. : alk. paper)—ISBN 978-1-60127-044-3 (cloth)
1. United States—Foreign relations—Iran. 2. Iran—Foreign relations—United States. I. Title.
E183.8.I55L55 2009
327.73055—dc22

2009015716

*To Parvaneh, my beloved wife and companion of forty-three years.
She has taught me many lessons in the art of negotiation.*

# Contents

Foreword            ix

Introduction            1

1. Historical and Cultural Constants            15

2. The Azerbaijan Crisis of 1945–47            35

3. The Oil Nationalization Crisis of 1951–53            59

4. The Embassy Hostage Crisis of 1979–81            87

5. Freeing the Lebanon Hostages            121

6. The Lessons: Fourteen Steps to Success            153

7. Overcoming Mutual Myth-Perceptions            179

Bibliography            196

Appendix            201

Index            206

About the Author            217

# Foreword

Thirty years ago, after a group of zealous Islamist students invaded the U.S. embassy in Tehran for a "set-in," the nations of Iran and the United States came to an impasse. Seeing opportunity in the confusion, powerful mullahs turned the planned demonstration into a fulcrum, from which they leveraged revolutionary Iran into an Islamist theocracy. America found itself powerless to rescue the fifty-two captive members of its diplomatic mission, and equally incapable of bargaining for their release. The students who would hold the Americans hostage for more than a year were, in a sense, captives themselves.

One of the chief ironies of the crisis was this: If there was one person in the world ideally suited to steer both sides out of the mess, it was John Limbert. Unfortunately, the students had tied him to a chair.

Here was the best American friend Iran had. Limbert was that rare American who understood and loved the ancient near-Eastern nation. He had first visited as a college student almost two decades earlier, and had returned as a Peace Corps volunteer. In those years he met and married his Iranian wife, Parvaneh. Their children were natives of both countries. Limbert had a doctorate in history from Harvard University, was fluent in Farsi, had taught in Iranian universities, and in the months prior to being taken hostage, had been second secretary in the embassy's political section. Few Americans knew as much or cared as much about Iran's long, rich history and culture as he did, and no one better understood the violent currents of change buffeting that country in 1979.

Each of the captive Americans responded differently to captivity. Some became meditative and found solace in religion. Some tried to escape. Some became depressed. Embassy political officer Michael Metrinko, who also spoke fluent Farsi, responded with anger. He fought back with unrelenting fury, right up until the day of his release, when he picked a fight with guards on the bus to the Tehran airport. Limbert's response was the opposite. Locked in various basement rooms for months on end, he clung to his role as diplomat. He gently reasoned with his captors. He listened to them and patiently corrected their grammar—in English and Farsi—and their understanding of history—American and Iranian. He looked unceasingly for common ground.

His captivity perfectly encapsulated the students' dilemma. Without diplomats, there was no way to engage in serious dialogue. In striking a symbolic blow against the United States, the students had, in effect, burned the only bridge between our nations. It has been down ever since.

As I write this in 2009, Iran and the United States are still eyeing each other warily across an abyss. The ruling mullahs' pursuit of a nuclear arsenal and President Obama's determination to stop them is just the latest twist in an ongoing saga of discord. Much of the anger and distrust that separates us is valid, but much is also rooted in misunderstanding. Iranian true-believers see the United States as The Great Satan, a "world-devouring," godless force bent on dismantling Islam and reducing their country to its former vassal status. Patriotic Americans see Iran as champion of the great backward movement of the twenty-first century, a powerful enemy of liberal western values, a sponsor of terror attacks, and increasingly as a direct mortal threat to Israel.

Getting past these competing caricatures, both of which have elements of truth, will require skilled diplomacy. Obama has been criticized in this country just for being willing to try, and it remains to be seen if Iran will meet him halfway. If and when a formal dialogue resumes, sorting our way back to mutuality won't be easy. Many of the differences between Iran and America are fundamental, and the stakes are high on both sides.

In *Negotiating with Iran*, Limbert decries the "downward spiral" that has defined U.S.-Iran relations for a half-century. "Each side sees every move of the other in the worst light possible, and responds accordingly," he writes. "That view—assuming the worst about the other—has also driven both Iranians and Americans to acts that create self-fulfilling prophesies. Assumptions about hostility create more hostility. . . . Hostile intent is assumed, and both sides find the evidence to fit their assumptions."

America is not a nineteenth-century-style imperial power bent on colonizing smaller nations, and Iran is not a theocratic monolith. It is a nation with a surprisingly vibrant political life. The things an American president says about Iran have tremendous impact within that country. When President Bush referred to Iran as part of the "axis of evil," he played into the hands of hard-liners who rely on fear of America for domestic popularity. Obama's approach could deflate the appeal of the aging religious regime and boost reformers in Iran who may be capable of edging their country away from religious zealotry and international confrontation.

Limbert examines Iran's major collisions with the western world in modern times, taking us beyond the evil caricatures. He notes the "mental traps" that prevent successful negotiation, such as simplistic, xenophobic assumptions about "national character," and warns his American colleagues, "such labeling and mental shortcuts…guarantee the failure of negotiations by eliminating nuance, hard questions, and exploration of what may lie behind the apparently inexplicable actions of Iranians." He provides a nuanced understanding of the struggle for Iranian independence after World War II, and shows that U.S. involvement in the overthrow of Prime Minister Mohammed Mossadeq in 1953, while deplorable, was not as straightfor- wardly imperial as the official Iranian version would have it. Simplistic and often propagandistic accounts of modern history blind us to mutual self- interest. *Negotiating With Iran* maps an escape from the downward spiral.

Despite being one of the primary victims of Iran's assault on international civility, Limbert has long advocated renewed dialogue. Anyone making this argument has encountered the sentiment that negotiation, in itself, amounts to capitulation. Why waste time talking to a regime that, in one of its founding acts, so famously repudiated diplomacy?

This question has an easy answer. Merely talking to Iran, or to any enemy for that matter, has no downside, particularly in an age where appearances frequently count for more than reality. Opening a dialogue doesn't mean capitulation or even significant concession. Success would back both nations away from economic or military confrontation, something any sensible person would desire. And even if we fail utterly to dissuade the mullahs from building atomic weapons, which we may, making the effort affords us significant international leverage, which we will need if further sanctions or force become necessary. Just by trying to resolve the standoff peacefully, the United States steps away from the image created by Tehran's propagandists. Iran, on the other hand, becomes less a hero of the Islamist cause than a dangerous and warlike state putting its own ambitions before the larger interests of mankind.

Can a government that sees itself as divinely inspired compromise on anything? Given Iran's historical slipperiness and fanaticism, the old rug- merchant stereotype, aren't we setting ourselves up to be taken?

As Limbert makes clear, Americans are just as capable of clever, tough bargaining as Iranians. Understanding the country's history and politics is a critical step in that direction, as is a deep appreciation for what skillful negotiation can accomplish.

Mark Bowden

# Introduction

*Any proponents [of seeking areas of agreement with Iran]—in some cases diplomats who had been held hostage in 1979—were treated like the thesis they espoused, as delusional.*

—Ali Ansari, *Confronting Iran*

## A Personal Note

This story begins with a failure. In Tehran on the wet and overcast morning of November 4, 1979, as a political officer assigned to the American Embassy, I took part in a catastrophic breakdown of negotiations with some very unhappy Iranians. What happened was this. About two weeks after our government announced it was admitting the shah of Iran to the United States for medical treatment, several hundred young Iranians, calling themselves Moslem Student Followers of the Imam's Path, stormed the 30-acre U.S. Embassy compound in downtown Tehran. The attackers found a vulnerable spot at the basement level of our two-story chancery (main office), broke into the building, and occupied the basement and first floor. With about a hundred other staff members, both Iranian and American, I found myself barricaded behind a steel door on the second floor. Telephone calls to what passed for Iranian government offices at the time (officially known as the provisional government) brought no help.[1] From that quarter, we heard only evasive responses and vague promises from officials unwilling or unable to act. In the meantime, we knew that some of our colleagues—including our security officer, our press officer, and others outside the steel door—were in serious danger from the attacking crowd.

What could we do? Our appeals to officials at the Iranian Foreign Ministry and the prime minister's office had elicited only questions about when their American visas would be ready. (Obviously they were hedging their bets on the outcome of Iran's ongoing political turmoil.) Our chargé d'affaires, Ambassador Bruce Laingen, along with political chief Victor Tomseth and security officer Michael Howland, had gone earlier that morning to the For-

---

1. At that time, power in Iran had passed from the official, provisional government, to a collection of revolutionary institutions and vigilante groups that operated under ambiguous lines of authority to a Revolutionary Council and to senior clerics and which ignored and contradicted the prime minister and his officials.

eign Ministry and were now urging the officials of that hapless institution to react decisively to this latest challenge to their authority. By radio, we advised our three colleagues at the Foreign Ministry to stay away from the embassy for their own safety and to persuade those nominally in charge of the Iranian government to assume their responsibility for the safety of diplomatic personnel. We were also in telephone contact with Washington—where it was about 3:00 am on a Sunday. For our colleagues there, however, the usual ways of helping, such as direct high-level calls to Iranian officials, were not available. Any Iranian representative willing to take a call from Secretary of State Cyrus Vance or one of his deputies would have been in no position to act on our behalf. And those able to act were not taking calls from Americans.

We were in a fine kettle of Iranian fish. What passed for an Iranian government in those days—Prime Minister Mehdi Bazargan's provisional government—could not help us. By admitting the ailing, deposed Mohammad Reza Shah Pahlavi two weeks before (against the clear advice of our chief of mission), our Washington bosses had told us, in effect, that we were expendable. They had, in the eloquent words of a British diplomat writing seventy years earlier, "thrown a stone into the windows here and left [us] to face the policeman. . . . This was, I suppose, a sign that the Persian public opinion was not to be considered."[2]

If Persian public opinion was not consulted, then that public would express its opinion in a most uncivil way. President Carter had made his decision, and we at the embassy were left to face Iranians' inevitable, angry reaction. When the reaction came, there was little we could do in response. We were on our own; Washington was far away, and, having already done their damage, our leaders there could do nothing to calm the lawlessness and anarchy that ruled the Tehran streets. Whatever was going to be done that morning, we had to do it. At least such was our quick reading of conditions as the angry students battered their way into the compound and pounded at our doors.

No diplomatic mission can operate without protection from its host government. If that host government cannot provide security, then mission members have no business being in the host country. That morning, how-

---

2. Cecil Spring Rice (British Minister to Tehran) to Valentine Chirol (correspondent of *The Times*), September 1907. Cited in Kazemzadeh, *Britain and Russia in Persia*, 500. Spring Rice is referring to the announcement of the 1907 Anglo-Russian agreement that divided Iran into British and Russian spheres of influence and about which his own government had kept him in the dark.

ever, we were there, and we had to manage as best we could. Our priorities were two: keep everyone in the embassy safe, and delay the attackers as long as possible until cooler, more rational heads in Tehran had a chance to act. We also had to prevent our U.S. Marine security guards from shooting the attackers, a circumstance that would have led to a general bloodbath. The corpse of a dead demonstrator paraded through the streets of Tehran would have meant our facing tens of thousands of attackers instead of just the hundreds who had climbed over the compound walls. In the last analysis, none of us had any qualms about surrendering the unloved and unlovely embassy building if doing so was the price of avoiding a massacre.

With the nominal Iranian authorities in paralysis and no sign of help arriving from any other direction, I made one of the most foolish decisions of my Foreign Service career. I went out the barricaded steel door and met the attacking students on the second floor landing. The point, if there was one, was to calm the situation, ensure our safety, and see if we could talk them out of continuing their break-in. No one pushed me out the door. As one of the few American Persian-speakers at the embassy, I felt I had to make a try. It was a terrible idea, but nobody had a better one at the time.

I ended up on the landing facing a group of young people who were very excited and much disorganized. The situation was full of what Iranians call *sholugh*, a state in which everyone talks at once, no one listens to anyone else, and everyone gives orders, but no one takes them. I can still recall the students shouting at each other, and one of them in particular shouting at me and his friends in a thick Isfahani accent—an accent I had always associated (and still associate) with Iranian film comedians.

In my earlier experiences as a high school teacher and a university professor in Iran, I had found that I could sometimes defuse tense classroom situations and avoid confrontations by using humor, indirection, and carefully worded phrases that masked an unpleasant reality in euphemisms. As a proctor of an unruly group of university exam-takers, for example, I would tell the students, "Ladies and gentlemen. Please do not do anything that might lead to a misunderstanding on my part." The students understood perfectly my point—don't cheat on this exam (or don't let me catch you cheating)—but my avoiding any words of threat and not using the unpleasant and confrontational expression "cheat" gave the students the chance to demonstrate their magnanimity without appearing to yield to pressure.

Now I was playing in a high-stakes poker game with a pair of deuces in my hand. What had worked with unruly students ten years earlier just might work again. In any case, there were few alternatives. As far as we at the embassy knew, the authorities of the Iranian provisional government, despite their assurances, were not sending any rescue force to expel the attackers. Armed resistance from the handful of the embassy's Marine guards would have made the situation much worse. So I spoke to the attackers with the scolding attitude of a university professor—formal, distant, and measured. With a tone of deep personal disappointment, I asked them, "Do you understand how badly you are behaving? Does your government approve of what you are doing? Does the Revolutionary Council? What sort of behavior [from educated people] is this?" I then told them, "I would strongly advise you to get out of the embassy compound before you find yourselves in even deeper trouble."

In the meantime, my colleagues behind the door were being as helpful as they could. One called out, "We have just heard on the radio that Ayatollah Khomeini has ordered a unit of revolutionary guards to the embassy to clear out the attackers." Would that he had done so!

The agitated students were having none of it. These were not my rebellious university test-takers of ten years before. Not the fabrication about revolutionary guards, not my professorial arrogance, and certainly not my expressions of deep disappointment at their outrageous behavior made the slightest impression. They sensed they now held the upper hand and were not going to let their advantage slip away. The end was swift and obvious. After a few minutes of shouted exchanges, they tied me up, put a gun to my head, and threatened to shoot me and the captive embassy regional security officer if my colleagues did not open the barricaded door. A few minutes later (to my great relief), the door opened, our staff became prisoners, and fourteen months of captivity began.

## Doing It Better

I have often relived the events of that morning and my failure as a negotiator. I have asked myself, "What were the flaws in my negotiating technique? What other message or attitude might have persuaded the students to call off their attack? Should we have called their bluff at the steel door? Was there anything I could have done or said in that situation that would have changed the outcome?"

Years later, I joined a workshop in negotiation at Harvard Law School. The professor was Roger Fisher, master negotiator and coauthor of the classic *Getting to Yes*. Fisher and his colleagues introduced me to many useful ideas for successful negotiation. We discussed BATNAs (Best Alternative to a Negotiated Agreement), objective criteria, underlying interests, "yessable" propositions, preserving relationships, separating the person from the problem, and so on. The unanswered question for me, however, remained: what could or should I have done differently on November 4, 1979?

Professor Fisher's course never answered that question, but it did provide some assurance that the events of that day—and what followed—were of a nature to frustrate even someone using the best negotiating techniques. At one point during the class, Fisher pulled me aside to describe how he, during the long crisis, had spoken by phone to Ayatollah Mohammad Beheshti, one of the most influential leaders in Tehran after Ayatollah Khomeini himself. Fisher admitted that his conversations with Beheshti, although interesting, had had no visible effect on ending our captivity. I could take some comfort in the realization that even Harvard's international grand master of negotiations could not, at the end of the day, do any better than I had done outside the steel door.

Would anything have worked better on that day? Probably not. The situation had already gone too far—and deteriorated too much—to be saved by face-to-face discussions between members of an excited crowd and a frightened, unarmed American diplomat. As Fisher might have put it, the students attacking the embassy saw their BATNA as better than anything we could offer. Thus, they had no reason to reach any agreement.

Although November 4, 1979, was a loss, that day's disastrous end did not, in my view, change the reality that there are principles that can guide the American who finds himself in a negotiation—commercial, political, or other—with an Iranian counterpart. Our frustration on that Sunday morning did not mean that negotiation with Iranians is never possible. If anything, that particular failure was one of policy, not negotiation. A series of bad policy decisions—admitting the shah to the United States; leaving a large, unprotected diplomatic staff in Tehran; and failing to recognize the new and dangerous realities in post-revolutionary Iran added to the whole shameful history of American-Iranian relations over the previous twenty-five years— meant that my negotiation attempts were doomed before they started. On that day, we should not even have been at the bargaining table.

## What Has Worked? What Will Work?

With that inauspicious start to my negotiating career, I have set out in the chapters that follow to examine what has worked and what will work (and what has failed and will fail) in negotiating with Iranians. I have assumed my audience is an American one and have shaped comments and recommendations accordingly. Not all of my case studies describe direct Iranian-American negotiations, although in every case the United States was one of the players, if not always the most important one for Iranians. Yet the American negotiator, whether he represents a university, a private firm, or the U.S. government, can still draw useful lessons from knowing how Iranians negotiated with, for example, the Soviets in 1946–47 and the British in 1951.

Why should we think about negotiations at all when American-Iranian relations for decades have been mired in nastiness—in threats, posturing, and self-righteousness? What kinds of negotiations are possible when each side believes it is completely right and reasonable and the other is completely wrong and irrational? How can the two sides negotiate when each has become the other's worst nightmare? Despite all these negatives, however, I am not convinced that Americans and Iranians are condemned to be enemies for eternity. Each side realizes that the other is not going away soon and that its presence and policies affect conditions in Iraq, Afghanistan, the Persian Gulf, the Caucasus, Central Asia, and other areas that matter to both Tehran and Washington. Under the right conditions, with balanced judgment and sound negotiating strategy, we can still reach understandings that suit the interests of both sides. Most important, we do not have to be friends to do so. After all, if Americans and Iranians could never agree on anything, then today I and my embassy colleagues would probably still be captives in Tehran.

There is much history in this work. For Iranians, history—or at least some version of it—is crucial to shaping the present. For that reason, I have opened with an examination of Iran's historical and cultural constants. In that chapter, I have avoided using terms such as "Iranian character" or "the nature of Shiism" or other such generalizations that have led some analysts—in their search for clarification—into oversimplification, distortion, and unhelpful statements about Iranians' "irrationality," "xenophobia," or "Shiite martyr complex." Such characterizations do not help negotiators. On the contrary, if Americans meet Iranians with the assumption that the latter are irrational and xenophobic by nature, their encounters are almost certain to end in failure.

At the same time, history and culture matter a great deal to Iranians. History has given them a sense of grandeur and grievance—the view that their country, once a world superpower that received tribute from dozens of subject nations, has been the feeble plaything of powerful outside forces for at least the last three centuries. The effective American negotiator need not be a scholar of Iranian history, but he should be aware of how that history has influenced his Iranian counterparts' positions.

For example, how many of the American negotiators who dealt with the issue of a Status of Forces Agreement (SOFA) in Iraq—where Iran played a crucial role—were aware of the importance of this issue in recent Iranian history? How many American negotiators knew about capitulations and the events of 1964 in Iran—events that gave the outspoken cleric Ruhollah Khomeini credibility with the nationalist heirs of Mosaddegh? How many know about the infamous 1828 Treaty of Turkmanchai, which, in the wake of a disastrous Persian military defeat, first granted judicial immunity to foreigners in Iran? Yet, these events and others stretching even to pre-Islamic times—with all of their glory and humiliation—will affect how Iranians, carrying all the burdens of their long history, approach a negotiation and look at their counterparts.

The four historical case studies of negotiation successes and failures, presented in chapters 2 through 5, are the foundation of this work. The intention is not to write new histories of these events but to examine them for lessons to help tomorrow's negotiator. Chapter 6 collects and elaborates on the suggestions highlighted in the case studies. In each case, American negotiators will find lessons to be learned, both positive and negative; and in each case there are clear instances of good judgment, misjudgment, realism, self-deception, self-interest, and self-destruction. The four case studies are

- **The Azerbaijan crisis of 1945–47,** in which the Iranians—although divided among themselves and holding few cards in their hands—successfully balanced competing foreign and domestic interests and preserved their country's independence and territorial integrity against very long odds. With limited American support, Iranians were able to negotiate occupying Soviet troops out of Iran and restore their authority over the country's richest province.

- **The oil nationalization crisis of 1951–53,** in which both the British and Iranians so demonized each other that agreement became impossible. Washington attempted to mediate between its friends and originally had sympathy for the aspirations of the Iranian nationalists. Preoccupied by Cold War rivalry with the Soviet Union, however, the Americans eventually came to share the British view that Prime Minister Mosaddegh himself was the problem and had to go.

- **The American Embassy hostage crisis of 1979–81,** in which what began as a 1970s-style student demonstration and sit-in became—after a series of misjudgments on both sides—a major international crisis that brought down an American president and enabled extremists in Tehran to seize undisputed power and bring years of bloodshed and suffering on most Iranians.

- **The Lebanon hostage crisis of 1985–91,** in which both sides—encouraged by self-interested intermediaries—deluded themselves into unrealistic expectations. Both sides lost sight of underlying interests and focused entirely on immediate goals. When circumstances changed and credible mediators became involved, problems that had previously seemed unsolvable were eventually settled. This chapter is in two parts.

  1. The arms-for-hostages (Iran-Contra) bargaining of 1985–86 in which both sides seemed to compete in outsmarting themselves.

  2. UN mediation and freeing the Lebanon hostages, 1989–91, in which competent mediation and the fortuitous miscalculations of Saddam Hussein allowed the hostages to go free and Iran to claim it had achieved its long-term goal of a search for justice after the Iran-Iraq war.

These four cases provide instances of both success and failure in negotiations with Iranians and illustrate the role of the historical constants discussed in chapter 1. The Azerbaijan crisis, for example, shows how fragile are stability and unity in the multiethnic state that is Iran. Outside powers, ambitious domestic politicians, tribal and ethnic interests, and other centrifugal forces are always ready to pull apart this easily broken structure. The oil nationalization crisis, with its unfortunate ending in the CIA-engineered coup of August 1953, has reinforced an Iranian sense of historical grievance, betrayal, and victimization.[3] Carrying those historical memories, the Iranian side may approach a negotiation with its mind made up (based on recent and not-so-recent experience) that the American side is not interested in reaching agreement—that it is interested only in imposing its will on a humiliated Iran.

For those seeking the essence of the matter (what the Iranians call *lob-e-matlab*), chapter 6 presents fourteen suggestions drawn from the historical case studies in chapters 2 through 5. These suggestions—when combined

---

3. In his interview with National Public Radio broadcast September 23, 2008, President Ahmadinezhad cited this incident as an example of Iran's continuing grievances against the United States.

with large doses of patience and good fortune—can help American negotiators overcome the persistent stereotypes, rhetoric, mythology, and misconceptions that for thirty years have ensnared Iran and the United States in a tangle of mutual demonization, insults, and recriminations. At one time or another in the examples studied, negotiators applied (or failed to apply) these principles, and negotiations progressed or collapsed accordingly. When they did apply them and enjoyed some measure of good luck—as in the cases of Azerbaijan and the UN mediation to free the Lebanon hostages—the results were usually positive. When ignored or misapplied—as in the case of oil nationalization and the American Embassy hostage crisis, the results usually were to increase misunderstanding and bring the two sides to deadlock and renewed hostility.

The study's final chapter originated in an exchange with undergraduates about ten weeks into a political science course titled "The United States and Iran." As the students looked at Tehran and Washington's disastrous encounters of the last thirty years and at the two sides' seeming inability to identify and act on mutual interests, they concluded, "Given the realities in the region, our long mutual estrangement makes no sense." They asked, "Why should the situation be so? Why all this hostility? Why can neither side act rationally?"

Good questions. I had no ready answers, but I suspect that the reason lies less in reality than in distorted perceptions and in the distressing fact that each side has constructed a mythology and an image of absolute evil in the other. I asked my students how, based on what they had read and learned in the course, they believed Iranians and Americans view each other. Looking at Iran and Iranians as Americans, the students responded with a long list of negative labels, stereotypes, and distortions that were the product of a particular reading of recent history. Then, in a remarkable display of empathy, they did the same thing looking at America and Americans from the Iranian point of view, and produced an equally uncomplimentary list.[4]

This work attempts to go beyond these caricatures and their associated loaded questions, such as, "How can one ever negotiate with them?" and "How can one ever reach agreement with someone who has said or done that?" For behind those questions lies the destructive assumption the other side is infinitely arrogant, dissimulating, crafty, and unreliable. These unhelpful preconceptions about the other side's motives do provide a useful warning: negotiations between Americans and Iranians will not be easy.

---

4. See chapter 7, for a detailed discussion of these "myth-perceptions."

Negotiators on both sides will have to wrestle with ghosts from their past, and, particularly in the Iranian case, that past is very long, and the ghosts numerous and powerful. History reinforces the above point. In all four cases studied, the path of negotiation was time-consuming, complicated, full of misunderstandings, and littered with the wreckage of failure. That difficult history has created a central reality: in negotiating with the Islamic Republic, the traps are many, and it will be vital to learn from the past and get the process right.

## Getting It Right

I hope this book will prove helpful both to those American negotiators dealing with Iran and Iranians next week and to those doing so in five or ten years. I also hope that it does not understate the difficulty in overcoming thirty years of hostility and estrangement. The May and July 2007 Baghdad meetings between Ambassadors Ryan Crocker and Hassan Kazemi-Qomi marked the first official and public bilateral American-Iranian contacts since relations were formally broken during the U.S. Embassy hostage crisis in April 1980. The two parties could come to the table then because Iraq's prime minister was the host. Neither side had to invite the other and thus risk rejection, and neither side had to concede anything by accepting an invitation from a third party. By all accounts, the meetings consisted of little more than exchanges of complaints about the other's misdeeds in Iraq, and never dealt with broader issues between the two countries. Yet in the context of decades of insults and threats, even these limited exchanges were progress of a sort. Previous contacts, productive or not, had been indirect, clandestine, or conducted within some multilateral framework. Earlier attempts to establish official dialogue had foundered on pervading suspicions and on fear that domestic political enemies would call any such moves betrayal. At the same time, in both capitals the prevailing view was usually "now is not the time" and "if they want to talk, then they must be up to something."

Like adolescents dealing with a prom invitation (to use Barbara Slavin's apt metaphor), when one side came forward, the other pulled back. Both sides missed opportunities. Tehran—hobbled by internal political disputes—rejected Secretary of State Madeleine Albright's 1998 offer to discuss, without preconditions, a roadmap to better relations. The United States ignored a 2003 Iranian proposal—transmitted through the Swiss in Tehran—to open discussions on all outstanding issues, including a broader Middle East settlement. It is ironic that the United States ignored such an approach after it had long insisted, in the aftermath of the 1986 Iran-Contra fiasco, that it would talk to Iran only through the official channel of the Swiss protecting power. By all accounts, Washington's refusal to talk in 2003 came from the illusory euphoria following an easy military victory in Iraq and from the view, popular with some in Washington at the time, that (in the phony macho jargon of the time) real men go to Tehran [in tanks].[5]

In the years ahead, it is possible that Tehran and Washington both may regain an appetite for resolving problems through negotiations rather than through chest-thumping about armored fighting vehicles. If so, we should be under no illusions that progress will be swift. Talking to Iran will still be difficult and unpleasant. Yet the lessons of history in this book can help negotiators avoid some of the missteps that have doomed previous attempts to end the shouting, start conversations, and resolve problems. Many of these points will be obvious to those with experience in negotiation and to those who have dealt with the Middle East in general and Iran in particular.

In the case of Iran, however, there is another difficulty. In the decades since 1980, the American government has lost its cadre of Iran expertise. Through the 1980s and 1990s, it trained few Persian speakers, and those it did train had little opportunity to use the language in a Persian-speaking setting. Eventually those with both language and country experience have aged and retired, leaving a gap that, with the best will in the world, will take at least a decade to fill.[6]

Creating a qualified new cadre will take time. Training someone to a level of professional speaking and reading proficiency in Persian—a process that experts believe requires at least nine months of full-time study—is just the beginning. Understanding nuances, historical references, cultural and class views, and other subtleties will take much longer, ideally through immersion in an Iranian social context. Yet without at least some understanding of these facets of the Iranian outlook, the American negotiator's task will be much harder.[7]

On the other side, few Iranian counterparts are likely to have much understanding of the United States. Iran's cadre of American-educated technocrats has also aged, and a new generation of Iranians from different social

---

5. The text of the Iranian 2003 proposal is in the appendix.

6. In 2008, for example, Ambassador to Iraq Ryan Crocker was among the last active-duty American diplomats who had ever served in Iran.

7. To quote Bill (*The Eagle and the Lion*, 392), "Persian is a language of great depth and subtlety. Although outwardly grammatically simple, it requires years of study and speaking experience to master adequately."

backgrounds has come to occupy important posts. Even those Iranians who studied in the United States often did so when they were older (most were graduate students) and lived—like many American expatriates in Iran—in an environment unaffected by and remote from the main currents of local life. Although the Islamic Revolution and the subsequent turmoil brought hundreds of thousands of Iranians to the United States, there are fewer and fewer people within the Islamic Republic's elite who have had any direct contact with America and Americans.

Many in power in Iran today—even those with some first-hand experience of the West—have gained their positions by riding waves of anti-American sentiment. Many leaders of the Islamic Republic see the power of American popular culture—without reference to who directs American foreign policy—as a direct threat to the austere strictures of the dominant ideology and, as such, the most serious challenge to the current rulers' control of the state. Ayatollah Khomeini once said that he did not fear America's ships and armies; America's most terrifying weapon, he asserted, was its popular culture, with its power to mislead Iran's young people and to divert them from the militant path of religion and revolution. Iranians' views of the United States are likely to be highly distorted either by the Islamic Republic's official hate machine or by an idealized picture coming from some Iranians' dislike for their own government. According to this latter view, if this government says America is the root of all evil, then America must be the source of all that is beneficent.

Absorbing the lessons of history and following the fourteen suggestions in chapter 6 will help negotiators, but doing so will still not guarantee the success of a negotiation. Expertise and helpful hints by themselves will not always overcome the formidable barriers to that success. Suspicions, festering resentments, and perceived grievances run so deep on both sides that the most skilled and experienced negotiators may still fail—or at least not achieve what is hoped for. One or two negotiating sessions are not going to make people—even those with no personal memories of the events—forget the real or imagined humiliations of the past decades and centuries. Success will require both sides to keep their expectations realistic and measure progress in small and symbolic steps. The key to moving forward will not be forgetting history; it will be acknowledging the power of history while dealing at the same time with the problems of the present and future.

## Acknowledgments

I scarcely know where to begin in thanking so many good friends and colleagues who helped me with this study. Many persons generously gave their time for interviews. Those I can name include Gary Sick, Sir Richard and Lady Elizabeth Dalton, Richard Bulliet, Jahan Salehi, Sa'id Arjomand, Ervand Abrahamian, Warren Christopher, Trita Parsi, Archie Bolster, Charles Naas, Giandomenico Picco, Ellen Laipson, Hillary Mann Leverett, Ali Ansari, Jerry Greene, Malcolm Byrne, and William Miller. Others assisting were Shaul Bakhash, Steve Fairbanks, James Bill, Bruce Laingen, Afshin Molavi, Michael Metrinko, Barbara Slavin, and Mark Gasiorowski. Michael Rubin, Ellen Laipson, and Ahdieh Mohabat gave special help in commenting on the section "Improving the Chances of Success" in a 2008 presentation at the United States Institute of Peace. Special thanks go to Steve Riskin of the United States Institute of Peace and to Nigel Quinney, who was most helpful in editing the manuscript. I also benefited from the help of Shane Christiansen of the U.S. Mission to the United Nations and from the encouragement of colleagues, such as Kevin Woods and Mike Pease, at the Institute for Defense Analyses. Of course, all misstatements, distortions, stereotypes, and so on are my sole responsibility. I would also like to apologize in advance to my Iranian friends for any of the ways I may have misread or misinterpreted their glorious history and culture.

# 1

# Historical and Cultural Constants

*Sinks whoever raises the great stones;*
*I've raised these stones as long as I was able*
*I've loved these stones as long as I was able*
*these stones, my fate.*
*Wounded by my own soil*
*tortured by my own shirt*
*condemned by my own gods,*
*these stones.*

—George Seferis, "Mycenae," 1935

Iranian negotiators, consciously or not, will be deeply affected by their country's long history and its rich civilization. For their part, American negotiators need not be scholars of Iran or know all about, for example, the Sassanians, Samanids, and Safavids. They should, however, at least be aware of the past that has gone into forming the views and approaches of the Iranian side. The key requirement for American negotiators is less scholarship than awareness. Their central question will be: "Now I know something about Iran's history and culture, about Shia Islam, and about what distinguishes Iran and Iranians. So what? How will knowing those things explain how Iranians will act and react and help me negotiate better with them over frozen assets, Iraqi Shia militias, a suspicious nuclear program, Afghanistan, or anything else?"

"So what?" is a fair question. For the negotiator, the relationship between Iran's history, culture, and religion and how its representatives negotiate today will always be elusive and subtle. What Darius the Great or Mosaddegh did (or purportedly did) in the past will not necessarily reveal what an Iranian negotiator will do tomorrow. If the relationship between yesterday and today were that clear, we would not view the Iranians as we so often do—as complex, unpredictable, and almost impossible to understand. Experts enjoy dwelling on these complications and will begin discussions of contemporary Iran and its policies with adjectives like opaque and murky.

In reality, there will almost never be a eureka moment for the American negotiator—a moment when he recognizes a direct connection between Iran's history and an Iranian negotiator's current action. There will almost never be a moment when he can be sure the Iranian side acted as it did or took a certain negotiating position because of this feature of Shia Islam or that event in Iran's past. Human beings—and history itself—almost never operate in such an unambiguous cause-and-effect manner. Certainly, Iranians have rarely done so.

American negotiators will find that their Iranian counterparts are, like all of us, captives of their country's history and culture. In the case of Iranians, that history is long and often tragic, and the culture is rich, complex, and full of paradoxes. At one level, for example, Iranians see themselves as superior to neighboring Arabs, who, Iranians believe, lack the deep traditions and values of Iranian civilization. At another level, however, almost all Iranians, as Shia Muslims, revere certain individual Arabs as prophets, imams, saints, and models of bravery, wisdom, and self-sacrifice. To Shia Iranians, Imam Ali, the prophet Mohammad's son-in-law, is the perfect man, the ideal of chivalry and manly virtue, and Mohammad's grandson, Imam Hussein, known as the "master of martyrs" (*seyyid al-shohada*) is the embodiment of self-sacrifice, courage, and resistance to oppression against overwhelming odds.

Beyond the names and dates of their history is the particular way in which Iranians view and interpret their own past. For American negotiators, understanding that history and culture will not necessarily enable them to understand or predict their Iranian counterparts' every move and response at the bargaining table. What the Americans will need, however, is consciousness of that history and culture and their long-term influence. At a minimum, that consciousness will protect the Americans from being confused and surprised by seemingly incoherent and inexplicable Iranian negotiating actions. Such consciousness will help the Americans put their Iranian opposite numbers' actions in a comprehensible setting. In so doing, they can avoid the mental trap that in the past has caught many Westerners, who, unable to understand the background of their Iranian counterparts' actions, explained them by concluding that Iranians were by nature irrational, emotional, and unstable. Such labeling and mental shortcuts, however, guarantee the failure of negotiations by eliminating nuance, hard questions, and exploration of what may lie behind the apparently inexplicable actions of Iranians.

## Cultural Traditions:
## Is There an Iranian National Character?

What sort of people are the Iranians?[1] I approach the subject of national character with great hesitation. The tumultuous events of the last thirty years have produced scores of immediate, superficial judgments about something called Iranian culture and Iranian character. Television experts, for example, have explained to us in their thirty-second analyses that Iran's current political turmoil and its anti-American policies are the results of some national personality trait with roots in Shia Islam and Iranian history. They tell us, for example, that Iranians are xenophobic and inherently fanatic and have a penchant for martyrdom. In addition, they tell us that Iranians dislike all compromise, suffer from paranoia, and ignore objective truth.

The authors of such superficial psychoanalyses should know better. They have taken some characteristics of some Iranians in some circumstances and applied them to an entire people. Even worse, they have made these selected traits the explanation for contemporary political conditions.[2] Such analysts have forgotten that Iranians are, like everyone else, the victims of their long history, their unique geography, and other circumstances that have shaped their political and social systems.

The reality is that Iranians have almost never been able to choose their political system. Instead, they have tolerated and survived governments whose only functions were to collect taxes and take sons for the military. Sultans, shahs, warlords, invaders, foreign governments, and others have usually made Iranians' political choices for them. They have imposed regimes that featured large measures of arbitrary rule, brutality, personality cult, and fanaticism. As for the Iranians themselves, for individual and collective survival they have had to adapt—with more or less sincerity—as best they could to whatever system prevailed at the time, whether it was a Turkish sultanate, a Shia empire, a military dictatorship, or a visionary and strident Islamic republic. It was this very ability to adapt to new rulers, customs, and ideologies that allowed Iranians to preserve their identity as a distinct civilization for almost three millennia. Beginning in the seventh century CE, Iranians could embrace Islam, become the scholars and preachers

---

1. Some of the following discussion of Iranian national culture and traditions originally appeared in *Iran: At War with History*.

2. What would a similar approach tell us about the American character if we based our analysis on the behaviors of Richard Nixon and Henry Kissinger?

of their new religion, and yet remain Iranian with roots in their pre-Islamic past. More than eight centuries later, they could do the same thing with Shia Islam.

The sad reality is that throughout history many of Iran's rulers have been thugs, bigots, hypocrites, and fanatics. Those who claim, however, that Iran's long history of dictatorship and theocracy has sprung from some national personality shortcomings (as imperfectly understood by outsiders) have ignored all the richness, complexity, and contradictions of the human species. Depending on the predisposition of the observer, such facile judgments in the case of Iran have led inevitably to the exaggeration of some traits and to glib and uninformed discussions. Some observers, for example, tell us that current political conditions are to be explained by religiously sanctioned dissimulation (*taqiyeh*) and by the existence of a Shia martyr complex. Although these explanations may not be entirely wrong, they misinform more than they enlighten. They have, by their selectivity, distorted and oversimplified a complex reality. Such explanations will by necessity overemphasize some factors and ignore or undervalue others that may be equally important elements of the Iranians' cultural heritage.[3]

Nevertheless, Iranians do have distinct cultural traditions that are special if not unique among nations. But the relationship of these Iranian traditions to whatever political system prevails at a given time or to the choices leaders of a particular regime will make is by no means certain. In Iran, political systems change quickly; cultural traditions change slowly if at all. And the links between the two are never obvious. In the Iranian case, however, there are enduring traditions that make the Iranians who they are—traditions that have defied changes of ruler, dynasty, and religion.

## A Long History as a Multiethnic Empire

More than twenty-five centuries of continuous existence have given Iran a rich and complex historical inheritance. In the Middle East, only Egypt has a longer history as a unified nation, but Iran retains the stronger ties to its

---

3. In the current American debates over Iran policy, advocates with an ideological ax to grind often introduce themselves as scholarly analysts and will describe Iranian national culture in terms that fit their ideological bias. Thus, we are told in these debates that Iranians inhabit a spectrum of personalities from the unreasoning and uncompromising fanatic to the misunderstood, victimized seeker of national self-respect. Their precise location on the spectrum seems to depend on the preexisting opinion of the advocate or analyst.

imperial and pre-Islamic past. The ancient Hittites, Phrygians, Urartians, and so on have all long vanished from the stage of history, but the Iranian identity has remained intact in one form or another for more than 2,500 years. Although many ancient peoples have remained only as names in inscriptions and other sources, one can follow a direct line from the great Achaemenian Persian Empire (550–330 BCE) described by Herodotus and the writers of the Old Testament to the contemporary Islamic Republic. Much has changed, but much has remained the same.

Over those centuries, empires and their monuments have risen and fallen, cities have flourished and declined, languages have changed, frontiers have expanded and contracted, new religions have appeared, and constant invasions and migrations have changed the ethnic makeup of the people inhabiting the Iranian plateau, the center of the historical land of Iran (Iran-zamin). All of these changes left their mark on Iranian civilization and added to its richness. Throughout that long history, and despite all of those changes, there has remained a core Iranian identity that new invaders, kings, imams, and prophets were able to influence but never to eliminate.

The bases of that identity were many and changeable. Iranian-ness could come from several sources, and one could be Iranian, and share in that ancient identity, in many ways. Governments of Iran-zamin have had their state religions and official languages, but Iran has never demanded conformity in faith or culture as the price of being Iranian. The first great Iranian empire was known in the Old Testament books of Daniel and Esther as the empire of the Medes and the Persians—that is, an empire ruled by two dominant peoples. Their original unification in the sixth century BCE under Cyrus the Great—according to Herodotus, a Mede on his mother's side—created an empire that featured both powerful, immutable laws and acceptance of a wide range of religions and customs.

Under the Achaemenians, the religions of the Jews, Babylonians, Egyptians, and others flourished under royal protection. The enormous stone reliefs of the famous Achaemenian site at Persepolis vividly illustrate both the king's power and the empire's diversity. Those reliefs show deputations from the many peoples of the empire—Lydians, Scythians, Indians, Bactrians, and so on—who, accompanied by Median or Persian escorts, all pay their respects and present tribute to the great king.

Even Iran's Sassanian rulers (224–651 CE), not usually known for their religious tolerance, provided refuge to Nestorian Christians branded heretics after the Council of Ephesus in 431 CE and to Greek philosophers expelled from the Byzantine Empire after the Emperor Justinian forbade pagans from teaching and closed the academy of Athens in 529 CE.[4] These refugee philosophers not only preserved but also continued to study and teach Aristotle's works under Sassanian patronage after the Byzantine emperors had suppressed the teaching of pagan ideas and philosophical speculation, which, in the emperor's view, encouraged heretics and inflamed disputes among Christians. Six centuries later, that Iranian refuge for Aristotle's philosophy was to have momentous consequences for Western intellectual history. After the Islamic conquests of Iran in the seventh century, Aristotle's works, forgotten in the Greek-speaking Eastern Roman (Byzantine) Empire but preserved in the Sassanian Empire (probably in Syriac-language versions), were translated into Arabic, now Iran's new language of classical scholarship. Five centuries later, they were translated from Arabic into Latin, courtesy of Christian, Muslim, and Jewish translators working at Toledo and other centers of new learning in Western Europe.

Today what makes an Iranian an Iranian? What connects an individual living in Shiraz or Tabriz to that special history and culture that, centered on the Iranian plateau, spread its influence into Central Asia, the Caucasus, the Indian subcontinent, Mesopotamia, the Anatolian highlands, and the edges of the Arabian Peninsula? The Persian language is part of the connection, although less as a spoken medium than as the widespread language of poetry, diplomacy, government, scholarship, and polite society. Even in today's Iran, only about half the population speaks some dialect of Persian as a mother language. Another 25 to 30 percent speak at home some form of Turkish (mostly Azerbaijani), part of a language family grammatically unrelated to Persian.[5]

One does not have to be a Persian speaker to be Iranian. Half of the Iranian population—Azerbaijanis, Kurds, Baluch, Arabs, Turkmans, Gilakis, and so on—whose mother language is not Persian and who inhabit the periphery of the country are no less Iranian than their Persian-speaking compatriots of the heartland regions like Yazd, Fars, and Esfahan.[6] Even those who do not speak

---

4. The Sassanian Emperor Khosrow (Chosroes) I Anushiravan considered these philosophers useful political pawns, although he had no interest in their speculations. One clause of the perpetual peace signed between Persia and Byzantium in 532 allowed these teachers to return home and practice their religion in peace. As far as we know, however, their schools were not reopened.

5. See Atabaki, *Azerbaijan*, 12–26, for a discussion of the relationship between Azerbaijani and Iranian.

6. Although the evidence is uncertain, some scholars have noted an increase in the percentage of Iranians speaking Persian as a first language. According to Columbia University's Ethnic Map of Iran (www.columbia.edu@farsinet.com), between 1964 and

Persian at home treasure that language as the medium of Hafez's graceful lyrics and Rumi's mystical verses. The Iranian identity of both groups, Persian speakers and non-Persian speakers, is equally strong.

Islam, particularly Twelver Shia Islam, is today another element in the Iranian identity. Although Shia Islam exists far beyond Iran's borders—in the Azerbaijan Republic, Lebanon, Iraq, Pakistan, Bahrain, and the Arabian Peninsula—Iran is the only country to have made Shiism its state religion. The values and practices of that faith—the veneration of saints, the mourning ceremonies, and the pilgrimages—often combined with older, pre-Islamic traditions, color much of contemporary culture in Iran. Just as Persian dominates the linguistic map of Iran, Shia Islam occupies the central place among religions. Although ethnic Persians comprise only about half of Iran's current population, Shia Islam is the creed of about 90 percent of Iranians. The country's two major ethnic groups—Azerbaijanis and Persians—are overwhelmingly Shia, as are most Gilakis, Mazanderanis, and Arabs. Sunni Islam is almost entirely a religion of the periphery and remote refuge areas— Kurdistan, the Turkman steppes, Baluchistan, and the isolated southern valleys between the central plateau and the Persian Gulf.

Although most Iranians today profess Shia Islam, Iran's recognized religious minorities—Sunni Muslims, Christians, Zoroastrians, and Jews—also possess a strong sense of being Iranian. They may complain of religious discrimination, especially under the theocratic rules of the Islamic Republic, but, officially at least, they enjoy full rights as Iranian citizens. On a deeper level, all carry a strong Iranian identity despite their status as minorities. Iran's approximately 3 million Sunni Kurds, for example, claim to be descendents of the Medes, the original co-rulers of the first great Persian Empire. Iranian Zoroastrians, although now a small community of about 25,000, have preserved the religion of pre-Islamic Iran and the memory of Iran as a world empire before the Arab invasions of the seventh century CE. Iranian Jews, likewise now a small community of about 25,000, are closely tied to the Islamic mainstream of Iranian life. Most live in Persian-speaking areas among Shia Muslims, and, with the inherent conservatism of a dispersed minority, have preserved Iranian folkways and cultural traditions—in music, language, and food, for example—that the Muslim majority has long forgotten.[7]

---

2004, that percentage, as a result of education, media, and urbanization, has grown from 50 to 63 percent.

7. For a variety of reasons, many members of religious minorities have left Iran under the Islamic Republic, and observers fear that the country will lose its traditions of religious diversity.

## Fragile Stability and Simmering Anarchy

A clear lesson of Iranian history is that prosperity and stability never endure for long. Decline, chaos, turmoil, and anarchy (all roughly characterized as that great social evil *fetneh*) are always lurking in the wings. A strong central authority might exist for a period, when emperors, sultans, princes, and kings—both Islamic and pre-Islamic—ruled vast territories, controlled great wealth, commanded powerful armies, and built splendid cities and monuments. As mighty as these structures appeared, the latent forces of disorder, both internal and external, would eventually prevail, and the weakened country would suffer long intervals of destructive chaos and conflict. As a consequence, Iranians have seen their history swing repeatedly between extremes of dictatorship and anarchy, and they have had little success in establishing a political system that could check either of the two.[8]

The contemporary scholar Homa Katouzian expresses this reality as follows:

> It is characteristic of Iranian history that the fall—often even the mere death—of an absolute and arbitrary ruler has resulted in rebellion and chaos, and persisting chaos has ended up in the return of absolute and arbitrary government (*estebdad*). This pattern was also observed in the twentieth century, although in a modern form. Traditional Iranian revolts involved the active or passive support of all the social classes to bring down an "unjust" arbitrary ruler and replace him with a just one. Invariably, the result was chaos, until one of the contestants for power eliminated the rest and restored absolute and arbitrary government, much to the relief of the common people, who by then were desperately longing for basic peace and security.[9]

Even during periods of apparently strong central authority, the grandiose titles, the flattery, and the exaggerated pretensions of the rulers could not always hide the rot festering underneath—rot that became apparent as a ruler's enemies sensed weakness, his allies deserted him, and rebellion spread. A perceptive American diplomat, for example, reporting from Tehran in 1964 when the ruler Mohammad Reza Shah Pahlavi appeared to be in undisputed control of the country, noted the distaste of many within the Iranian elite for the shah and his system and the reality of weakness and cynicism that lay hidden behind the appearance of power.

---

8. For a beautifully drawn literary picture of this fragility, see Terrence O'Donnell's short story, "The Holy Men of Isfahan," in his collection, *Seven Shades of Memory*.

9. Homa Katouzian, "Mosaddeq's Government in Iranian History," in Gasiorowski and Byrne, *Mohammad Mosaddeq and the 1953 Coup in Iran*, 2.

> Since the opposition is weak, divided, and dispirited, the regime
> ought to be feeling happy and secure, particularly as it has important
> political assets to its favor. But one of the remarkable factors is that
> the regime has so few supporters. Evidence of this is to be found at
> every turn: prominent members of the [pro-government] New Iran
> Party who express the belief, quietly and privately, that their party is
> a sham and a fraud; ... hand-picked *Majlis* [parliament] members who
> deplore "American support" for a regime which they call a travesty of
> democracy; civil adjutants of the Shah who belong to his most devoted
> supporters, yet who express the belief that Iran will never be able to
> solve its problems as long as there is no freedom of expression, no
> delegation of authority, and so little selection of personnel for merit; ...
> military officers who tip off the National Front [opposition] regarding
> actions planned against its demonstrators; Foreign Ministry officials
> who privately advise against courses of action they are officially urging
> on the U.S. with respect to the treatment of opposition spokesmen in
> the United States.[10]

The writer emphasizes an essential paradox: none of these critics who
were, in effect, attacking the monarchy and biting the hand that fed them,
were members of the opposition. All were part of the establishment and, to
all appearances, loyal to the shah and beneficiaries of his rule. Despite their
privileges and surface loyalty, however, the writer noted that they "are suffering from a profound malaise, from lack of conviction in what they are doing,
from doubts about whether the [Pahlavi] regime deserves to endure."[11]

## Adopt, Adapt, Improve, and Survive

Geography, too, has made the Iranian plateau vulnerable to invasion.
Throughout history, determined conquerors, usually entering Iran from the
northeast or the west, have been able to subdue the country's population
centers and control its main roads with relative ease once they penetrated
the major mountain barriers to the central plateau. With Iran's geographic
vulnerability has come a cultural openness, a readiness to adopt enthusiastically foreign ways in religion, politics, art, and social practice. Twenty-five
centuries ago, for example, Herodotus described this characteristic of the

---

10. Ibid., 22. Originally from Herz, *A View from Tehran*. Many were aware of this reality
at the time, but few expressed it so clearly.

11. Ibid., 23. There were many reasons for this dissatisfaction, including revulsion at
the corruption of the shah's relatives and claims by descendents of the previous (Qajar)
rulers—many of whom held important posts under the Pahlavis—that one of their
number should be king. Whatever its origin, fifteen years later this indifference and dissatisfaction among the shah's would-be supporters was, during the uprisings of 1978–79,
to do more to undermine his regime than the outright hostility of his opponents on the
left and right. See Limbert, *Iran: At War with History*, 110.

ancient Persians, noting that pederasty was unknown among them until their contact with the Greeks—when they adopted this foreign custom with great enthusiasm.[12]

This adaptability and openness to the ways of outsiders has been a key to Iran's survival as a distinct nation for more than twenty-five centuries. Foreign conquerors and foreign ideologies could change but not destroy the Iranian identity. Instead, Iranians have accepted and then mastered foreign customs by reshaping them into a (refined) Iranian form and making them a part of an enriched Iranian culture. When the soldiers of the victorious Arab armies originally brought Islam to the Iranian plateau in the seventh century CE, the Iranians did not so much surrender to the new religion as gradually embrace it, embellish it, and become its enthusiastic adherents, scholars, and missionaries. Iranian Muslims applied their existing skills to the new religion and its language and soon became masters of Arabic poetry and grammar, Islamic history, natural science, mathematics, mysticism, and religious scholarship. The founder of Arabic grammar, Sibuyeh the Grammarian, was a native of eighth-century Shiraz, whose grave there five centuries later was a pilgrimage site for those students wishing to master the complexities of Arabic conjugations and declensions. In the twentieth century, the site (by then known locally as Sang-e-Siyah, the black stone) had lost its connection to Sibuyeh and Arabic grammar but still drew visitors seeking a cure for children with whooping cough.

Even Twelver Shia Islam, today considered central to the Iranian national identity, was originally a foreign ideology. The Arab soldiers and colonizers from southern Iraq first brought Shiism to Iran in the earliest centuries of Islam. The original centers of Shiism in Iran were Arab military colonies such as Qom and refuge areas such as Mazanderan. In 1500 CE, 850 years after the Arab conquests, a Turkish-speaking dynasty (the Safavids) based in Azerbaijan and supported by Turkman tribesmen from Anatolia, imposed Shiism as the state religion of what had been a majority Sunni country. Yet despite their foreign origins, both Islam in general and Shia Islam in particular have today become fundamental elements of the Iranian national identity.

Iranians probably owe their survival as a people to their having adopted two foreign innovations: the Islamic religion, which linked Iranians to a worldwide community, and the Arabic script, which became the medium for the new Persian language in the tenth century CE. That new written language broke the narrow limits of the arcane pre-Islamic Middle Persian script

---

12. Herodotus, *The Histories*, I.135.

to become a rich world language of scholarship, literature, and diplomacy. From the Arabs, Iranians took religion, script, and much vocabulary, and in return gave the new Islamic world their great creativity in politics and in the arts and sciences. All sides benefited from the exchange. Iranians shared their knowledge of art, architecture, music, natural science, and administration with ruling Arabs and (later) Turks, whose native traditions in these areas were relatively weak.

As Iranians adopted and refined the ways of other peoples, they also absorbed that of their conquerors, particularly their Turkish rulers—who dominated Iran from the eleventh century until the twentieth—into an enriched Iranian-Islamic civilization. What we today call Islamic in art, architecture, and music derives in large part from Muslim Iranians' applying their considerable talents in those areas to create a fertile, universal civilization. Muslim scholars, traders, artists, and poets—many of whom were Iranians—then transmitted this civilization far beyond the boundaries of the Arabic- or Persian-speaking world.

In more recent times, Iranians have taken enthusiastically to two other foreign imports—the art cinema and the Internet. Borrowing the medium from abroad, they have fashioned original works in a distinctive Persian style characterized by great imagination and creativity. Their output has often outdone the original, Western models. Persian is now reportedly the world's fourth most-utilized language for Internet bloggers. In the world of art cinema, Iranian filmmakers have won wide international acclaim for such thoughtful, original, and provocative works as *Under the Olive Trees*, *Kandahar*, *Border Café*, and *President Mir Qanbar*—all produced with very modest technical means, limited budgets, and within the severe restrictions on content imposed by the authorities of the Islamic Republic.

## The Centrality of Religion: Three Watershed Events

Religion has always been at the heart of Iranian society and politics. The Achaemenian kings associated themselves with the Iranian god Ahura Mazda and with the gods of their many subject peoples. In the third century CE, the Sassanians established Zoroastrianism as their state religion, and the Safavids (1502–1736 CE) did the same with Twelver Shia Islam at the beginning of their reign. The Pahlavi shahs (1925–79), imitating Ataturk's anticlerical measures in neighboring Turkey, attempted to separate religion and politics, but their efforts met with little success beyond the top levels of society. In some ways, these efforts backfired when religion and religiosity became, even among secular-minded Iranians, symbols of opposition to the excesses of Pahlavi rule. The current Islamic Republic has drawn considerable strength from its leaders' effective use of the religious vocabulary and symbols familiar to most Iranians, who often resented the Pahlavis' attempts to limit the public role of religion and transform Iranians willy-nilly into citizens of a secular state.

Even casual visitors to Iran will notice the pervasive influence of religion in daily life. Religion—and not only Shia Islam—shapes even intimate details, such as speech patterns, personal relations, and family life. Pictures of Imam Ali and other saints are everywhere. Communal prayer has an obvious social side, and pilgrimages to the tombs of holy men and women and visits to the graves of deceased relatives are popular activities. The major Shia shrines at Mashhad, Qom, Shiraz, and Rey (a few miles south of Tehran) are also tourist centers, where pilgrims can shop, sightsee, trade, and meet visitors from other parts of Iran and the Shia world. Pilgrims can enjoy the sensuous spectacles of monumental buildings, sermons, Quran recitations, and special foods at these major shrines. Many Iranian villages have a local saint's tomb (*imamzadeh*), which draws visitors from nearby towns for an outing in the country.[13]

Two of the three central events of Iranian Islam revolve around the internecine conflicts during the decades following the death of the prophet Mohammad (632 CE). Although some Muslims supported the claims of Ali b. Abu Talib, the prophet's son-in-law and first cousin, most Muslims at that time (including Ali himself) accepted the election of the Prophet's friend, companion, and father-in-law Abu Bakr as caliph (successor). The supporters of Ali's claims became known as the Shiat Ali (Party of Ali), and, eventually, the Shia. Following the deaths of the first three caliphs (whom the Shia all see as usurpers), Ali himself became caliph in 656 CE but was murdered five years later. Although the caliphate fell into the hands of Ali's Omayyad rivals, the site of his tomb in the southern Iraqi town of Najaf eventually became a center of both pilgrimage and scholarship for the Shia world. Every year on the twenty-first of Ramadhan, the world's Shia mourn the anniversary of Ali's death. With Ali gone, the Shia continued to support the cause of the Prophet's family, and developed the belief that Ali and his male descendants

---

13. Such practices are almost unknown among the most conservative Sunnis, who consider tomb visits a form of idolatry and revering the dead.

(through the Prophet's daughter Fatemeh) were infallible *imams* (leaders) in whom, by reason of their heritage and virtue, all temporal power resided.[14]

The second seminal event for Iranians was the martyrdom of Ali's son Hussein, who led a failed uprising against the Damascus-based Omayyad caliph, Yazid, in 680 CE. The caliph's forces slaughtered Hussein—deserted by all but a few of his original supporters—and most of his companions at Karbala, southwest of present-day Baghdad. A major shrine and a center of Shia pilgrimage arose at the site. The anniversary of Hussein's martyrdom, known as Ashura (i.e., the tenth day of the Arabic month of Muharram), is the deepest mourning day in the Shia calendar and is marked by processions, passion plays, and recitations of the tragic events of Karbala and the sufferings of Hussein, his family, and companions.

The third event is the occultation, or disappearance, of the twelfth in the line of imams from the family of Ali in the ninth century CE. In Shia tradition, the twelfth imam, Mohammad al-Mahdi (the rightly guided one) did not die but went into hiding to return and establish universal justice and restore the usurped rights of the house of the prophet. As the still-living imam, the Mahdi continues to be the legitimate holder of all temporal power, and those who rule as kings, presidents, and sultans can do so only in his name and as his trustee. His titles—the Hidden Imam, Lord of the Age, and so on—reflect his power and status, and his birthday—15 Shaban on the Islamic lunar calendar—is a major day of celebration for Shia Muslims.[15]

These three events in the first three hundred years of Islam have done much to shape, consciously or not, Iranians' prevailing views of history, society, culture, and politics to the present day. These events have also raised issues of the relationship between what is strictly Iranian and what is Islamic and the relationship between religion and the state—questions that continue to bedevil Shia scholars and provoke vigorous debate. For example, if the Hidden Imam holds all legitimate authority on earth, then what is the legal

---

14. The Sunni community hold Ali in great respect as one of the first to accept Mohammad's message, as a brave and chivalrous defender of Islam, as a just and wise ruler, and as the fourth and last of the so-called rightly guided caliphs. The Sunnis, however, do not accept the Shia view that the first three caliphs usurped Ali's rightful position as successor, nor do they accept the Shia view of imamate residing in the family of the prophet.

15. The importance of the twelfth imam provides the distinguishing name of "Twelver" for the predominant group within Shia Islam. There exist smaller Shia communities who follow different lines of leadership, notably the Ismailis ("Seveners") of East Africa and the Indian subcontinent, and the Zaidis ("Fivers") of Yemen. It is worth noting that Iranian Shia pay little attention to the birthday of the prophet Mohammad, a major festival in most of the Sunni world.

status of temporal rulers? Is all their authority illegitimate or, at best, conditional? Who is authorized to speak, rule, and make interpretations of law in the name of the Mahdi? For a devout Shia Muslim, what is the status of manmade laws and republican-style institutions such as parliaments and ministries? Is democracy a legitimate form of government when all power resides in one (absent) figure? And how can religion and politics be separate when the imam of the Shia is the ultimate source of all authority?

Aspects of all these events—martyrdom, betrayal, self-sacrifice, injustice, return of an absent savior, chivalry, faith, loyalty, and devotion to the Prophet's family—are woven into the everyday fabric and discourse of Iranian life.[16] During the uprisings of 1978–79 and in the tumultuous years that followed, the leaders of the Islamic Republic, from Ayatollah Khomeini down to the local Friday prayer leader, were masters at converting these and other familiar events from Islamic history into powerful symbols of a political ideology. Thus Saddam Hussein, for example, became the hated Yazid; Mohammad Reza Shah became the *taghut*, a modern-day idolatrous pharaoh who rejected God's commands; and members of the leftist opposition, the Mojahedin-e Khalq organization, were renamed and denounced as *Monafeqin*, the hypocrites of seventh-century Medina who pretended to accept Islam and support the Prophet while working secretly to undermine his mission.

The events of early Islam—particularly the character and deeds of Ali— have also blended into pre-Islamic Iranian folklore to create a heroic persona who combines his Islamic piety and wisdom with the superhuman strength and chivalry of Rostam, the Hercules of the Iranian national epic, the *Shahnameh*. Thus, we find throughout Iran fifty-foot-long depressions that the local people call *qadam-gah*, the place of Ali's footprints. Many monuments and natural wonders, large and small, throughout the Iranian plateau are connected with Ali, who—if we believe the literalist, killjoy historians— never visited that part of the Islamic world.

## The Appeal of the Unorthodox

If religion is humankind's search for how best to live in harmony with divine commands, then Iranians have pursued that search both with great enthusiasm and in unexpected directions. Throughout history, Iran has been a fertile

---

16. There is much familiar to non-Shia Muslims in these events. There is a strong Mahdist tradition in Sunni Islam, for example, and the idea that Imam Hussein willingly sacrificed himself should be very recognizable to Christians.

land for unorthodox ideas, and Iranians seem as prolific in creating and refining religions—and variations thereof—as they are in creating beautiful objects from cloth, metal, clay, and wood. For if Iran is a land of faith, it is also a land of heresy and heterodoxy, where the people, unsatisfied by the straightforward answers of the orthodox, have often rejected conventional wisdom in a search for a more subtle, complicated, and ambiguous divine truth.

The list of Iranian-based heresies is a long one. Manichaeism—whose teachings treated the physical world as a manifestation of evil—arose in Persian-ruled Mesopotamia in the third century CE and spread widely through Christian Europe and North Africa, counting even the young Saint Augustine as an adherent in the fifth century CE. Catholic rulers and the Holy Inquisition suppressed the Manichean Cathars in southern France only after difficult and brutal campaigns in the thirteenth and fourteenth centuries. Mazdakism, which appeared in Iran in the late fifth century CE, advocated radical social reform (including communal possession of property) and curbing the power and wealth of the Zoroastrian clergy. The heresy flourished for a time under Sassanian imperial patronage until its bloody suppression in 524 CE.

After the coming of Islam in the seventh century, Iranians remained attached to the unorthodox. Violent schismatic movements, collectively known in hostile Islamic sources as *bâtiniyya* (esotericism), mounted serious threats to central authority of caliphs and sultans. Among the most important of these movements were the ninth-century Khorrām-Dīnān of Azerbaijan and the eleventh to thirteenth century Ismaili Assassins of Alamut (a mountain fortress northwest of present-day Tehran). Today's Iranian state religion of Shia Islam itself originated as a schism within the community of Muslims and emerged much later as the predominant Iranian belief, beginning in the sixteenth century. Many conservative Sunnis still consider Shias as heretics and feel particularly offended by the Shias' rejecting the first three orthodox caliphs. Although neither its adherents nor its opponents would agree, the Baha'i faith, which appeared in Iran in the mid-nineteenth century, is perhaps only the most recent manifestation in a series of Iranian heresies dating to pre-Islamic times.

## Love the Religion, Hate the Clergy

As much as most Iranians are devoted to their Shia Islam and its saints, their relationship with its clerics, preachers, and scholars is often difficult and full of contradictory feelings. A deep religiosity permeates the Iranian national spirit, but there is also a parallel strain of anticlericalism that draws strength from free-thinking and artistic currents within Iranian culture—currents at odds with the strict rules and legalisms that the clergy promulgate. As for individual clerics, they provoke a range of public reaction from extreme veneration to derision. At one extreme was Imam Khomeini, who earned great respect for individual piety, honesty, and learning. At the other extreme, Iranians fear the power of clerics and ridicule them for greed, hypocrisy, ignorance, and political ambition under a mask of piety. Khomeini himself drew his public admiration as much from his modest lifestyle and his personal and political incorruptibility (in a society that believed most political leaders were prepared to sell out the nation's interests to the highest foreign bidder) as from his religious credentials.

The Iranian cleric has a difficult mission. He must reconcile two traditions that, at first glance, have little in common. He must tell his listeners what they do not wish to hear: that they should be thinking less of the pleasures (*eshrat*) of this world—music, poetry, wine, and so on—and more of their eventual fate (*aqebat*) in the next. In the society, there is continuing tension between the austerity demanded by the strict rules of religion—which frowns on music, images, and mysticism—and the realities of an Iranian cultural tradition that elevates all three. That tradition has created some of the world's greatest lyric and mystic poetry celebrating all those pleasures that religion forbids.[17] This conflict periodically comes to a head when the deepest mourning period of Shia Islam—the lunar month of Moharram—coincides with the national festival of Nowruz, the ancient holiday marking the beginning of spring and the first day of the Iranian solar year. Because the lunar date rotates through the solar calendar, the two occasions will sometimes coincide. Yet, what for some cultures might be an irreconcilable collision of traditions is, for most Iranians, an opportunity to show themselves to be loyal to both sides of their identities and to be both good Shia Muslims and good Iranians. Somehow, Iranians are able to mark both occasions with equal fervor and preserve their multiple identities as both pious Muslims, paying due respect to the martyred Shia saints, and worthy heirs to the rich, imperial culture of pre-Islamic Iran.

---

17. Writing in the fourteenth century CE, Iran's greatest lyric poet—Hafez of Shiraz—made much of the opposition between the dry piety (*zohd*) of the ascetic and the questioning spirit (*rendi*) of the free-thinking hedonist.

## The Ozymandias Factor: Past Glory, Recent Humiliation

The Iranian plateau is covered with monuments that inspire both pride and despair. They bear witness to Iranians' past glories and achievements. At the same time, they serve as daily reminders of how far Iranians have fallen from the heights of their ancestors' triumphs. At the ruins of Persepolis, Iranians can see how their pre-Islamic kings ruled a world empire and received tribute from Egyptians, Scythians, Cappadocians, Ionians, and many others. Elsewhere, they can see rock carvings showing more evidence of ancient glory, including of their third-century CE Sassanian King Shahpour capturing and humiliating the Roman emperor Valerian.

Historians and archaeologists may link these monuments to such pre-Islamic kings as Cyrus, Darius, and Xerxes; to such ancient dynasties as the Achaemenians and Parthians; and to such vanished peoples as the Elamites, Medes, and Scythians. But the Iranian people, who have forgotten most of those ancient names, instead connect these magnificent ruins to Islamic prophets (particularly to Solomon) and to Jamshid and Rostam, heroes of pre-Islamic Iranian mythology.[18] Only those few Iranian specialists who have studied archaeology and foreign literary sources know the real identity of these remains. Whatever the true history of the monuments at Persepolis (popularly known as Jamshid's throne), Pasargadae (called the mosque of Solomon's mother), Naqsh-e-Rostam, these sites—with their huge reliefs, mythical beasts, and unreadable inscriptions—are clear evidence to Iranians that their nation was once a world power, in which mighty kings ruled a vast empire.

Iran is a world power no more. The contrast between these ruined testimonials—whoever built them—to Iran's past glories and the uninspiring and depressing last few centuries of the country's history is extreme. However one describes Iran's history since the eighteenth century CE, the country has certainly not been a world power. During that time it has preserved its few shreds of national independence only by playing powerful foreigners off against each other and by yielding to superior force. For the last three hundred years, Iran has been a pawn in the games of others who have ignored Iran's sovereignty; frustrated its desires to take control of its own affairs; and

---

18. The Iranian Jews have done the same. Scholars say that the tomb of Queen Esther at Hamadan is in reality the tomb of a Jewish wife of a Sassanian monarch, who lived centuries later than the famous Old Testament queen.

bought, betrayed, and subverted Iranian politicians, who were often only too ready to serve foreign masters.

Iran's list of historical humiliations is a long one. In recent times, outside powers usually preferred to maintain the façade of Iranian independence and dominate the country indirectly through local agents, who, either for personal belief or profit, were willing to do the foreigners' bidding. At times, however, even that tattered mask of restraint would slip away, and the British, Russians, or Americans would intervene directly, as though needing to debase Iranians even further by reminding them publicly of who is master and who is servant.

In the early nineteenth century, Iran suffered serious military defeats at Russian hands, and in the treaties that followed had to pay heavy indemnities and sign away claims to rich territories in the Caucasus and to important political and economic rights, including navigation on the Caspian Sea. It also had to grant the hated capitulations, whereby foreign subjects and those Iranians who could claim foreign state protection were immune from the jurisdiction of Iranian courts. To raise money, the perpetually bankrupt Qajar rulers (1779–1925) would sell lucrative concessions such as the customs, a tobacco monopoly, and oil resources to foreign adventurers willing to make quick cash payments for these lucrative economic privileges.

In 1911, Russian troops intervened directly to suppress Iran's fledgling constitutional movement. During the First World War, Turkish, Russian, and British forces ignored Iran's declaration of neutrality and made the country a battleground for themselves and their surrogates. Only the Bolshevik Revolution of 1917, the subsequent withdrawal of Russian troops, and the collapse of Ottoman armies in late 1918 gave a feeble Iran some respite from these foreign incursions. In 1941, however, British and Russian armies invaded Iran and deposed Reza Shah to secure a supply route (the bridge of victory) to a Soviet Union fighting for its life against Nazi Germany.

The humiliations did not end after foreign forces evacuated Iran at the end of World War II. In 1953, the British and American intelligence services helped pro-monarchy forces stage a coup to overthrow the nationalist prime minister, Mohammad Mosaddegh. To rub salt into Iranian wounds, CIA operative Kermit Roosevelt, the self-described American architect of the 1953 events, later reportedly bragged about how easy it all was. In 1963–64 the United States forced a shah and his reluctant parliament to accept changes to the existing Status of Forces Agreement (SOFA) that gave resident American military advisers and members of their families immunity from Iranian legal jurisdiction. The changes—which Washington claimed were mere technical adjustments—infuriated Iranians, who saw the new agreement as another humiliation and capitulation forced from a defeated Iran more than a century earlier.[19] Iranians—encouraged by Ayatollah Khomeini's outspoken denunciations—saw the agreement as further evidence of their country's degradation and of the shah's surrendering Iran's pride and sovereignty at the commands of foreigners.

With the publication of works such as former court minister Asadollah Alam's memoir, *The Shah and I*, outsiders came to understand the depths of Mohammad Reza Shah's weakness behind the façade of royal power. Alam's account recalls how the shah, while delivering sermons to the West on the folly of its ways, was desperately insecure. He saw every criticism in the foreign press as a signal that he had somehow displeased Washington or London and as a warning that they could always withdraw their all-important support. After all, those who had put the shah in power could always remove him. The British and Americans had saved the shah's throne in 1953; his staying in power, he believed, depended on his continuing to please his fickle Western patrons.

Alam recounts a strange story that reveals the depths of the shah's lack of self-confidence. According to Alam, that insecurity was so profound that the shah felt obliged to contribute—when American Ambassador Joseph Farland made the request—to President Nixon's 1972 reelection campaign. Although Alam is not explicit about the ambassador's appeal, he strongly implies that Farland was collecting campaign cash for Nixon's notorious CREEP (Committee to Reelect the President). Alam wrote, "Turning to the practicalities of the [American] election, the ambassador put a request to me that even fifty years from now I could not divulge for fear that it would irreparably damage relations between our two countries."[20] Although few Iranians would have known about the ambassador's request, the shah's apparent actions in this case were entirely consistent with their opinion of him.

---

19. According to an American diplomat who served in Tehran at the time of the SOFA controversy, the Departments of State and Defense were pressuring the Iranians in response to lobbying by parents of American servicemen, who were concerned their offspring would be victimized by Iran's primitive justice system. There was apparently no one among the embassy's senior staff who advised against pushing the agreement, and the embassy found itself caught unaware in the resulting firestorm. Interview with Archie Bolster (former political officer, U.S. Embassy Tehran), November 11, 2008, Arlington, Virginia.

20. See Alam, *The Shah and I*, 233. Ambassador Farland died in 2007 without ever revealing exactly what had happened in that July 1972 meeting.

# 2

# The Azerbaijan Crisis of 1945–47

*The Soviets had come up empty handed in Iran. In the words of one
observer, "They were in fact the victims of one of the biggest pieces of
double-dealing in Persian history."*
                                        —James Bill, *The Eagle and the Lion*

istorical weakness has led Iranians to view negotiations as much more than a means of communication and reaching agreement. Instead, negotiations have become Iranians' instrument of survival, often against much stronger adversaries with ambitions against Iranian territory, independence, and resources. From the eighteenth century through the Azerbaijan crisis of 1945–47, however, Iranians had great difficulty preserving their independence, whether by negotiations or other means. During that long and difficult period, foreign armies marched through Iran with impunity, foreign countries took pieces of Iranian territory, foreign politicians issued orders to titular shahs about what they could and could not do in whatever land remained under their nominal sovereignty, and foreign leaders squabbled and reached agreements among themselves over Iran's destiny. In the first half of the twentieth century, Iranians attempted to assert themselves, first in the constitutional movement of 1906–11 and then through the statist, modernizing reforms of Reza Shah Pahlavi (1925–41). In both cases, these efforts foundered on internal divisions, political failures, and powerful foreign forces (particularly British and Russian) that ignored Iranian sovereignty in pursuit of their own interests.

In such a setting, Iran could not hope to preserve itself by directly confronting stronger outside powers. Throughout the nineteenth and early twentieth centuries, a bankrupt Iran preserved a few shreds of independence thanks only to great power rivalry and the fact that neither the British nor the Russians could accept the other's taking undisputed control of Iran. In World War I, Iran, officially neutral, was occupied by Turkish, Russian, and British armies that fought on Iranian territory and organized local militias as though the Iranian state did not exist. Under the Pahlavi shahs, despite the reforms and economic development, Iranian independence remained precarious and depended on the country's skill at negotiating its way through political minefields. Just how shaky Iran's independence was—and just how much Iranians depended on their negotiation skills for continued existence as a country—were both vividly demonstrated during the 1940s by the Allied occupation during World War II and by the dramatic aftermath in which Iran survived a serious and direct threat to its existence.

## The Great Game Resumes

At the end of the Second World War, Iran found itself a focus of world attention. It became the center of the new Cold War between the United States and the Soviet Union and the subject of three of the first five resolutions of the newly created United Nations Security Council. The 1945–47 conflict to settle the fate of Iran's Turkic-speaking northwestern region of Azerbaijan and, in a larger sense, to determine if Iran would survive as a unified and independent country became a major international crisis. In one way, Iranians in these events found themselves on familiar territory. Once again Iran was the object of others' great game as larger powers competed for influence, resources, and territory at Iranian expense. In other ways, however, there were elements in the crisis that were new in the Iranian experience. The United States, which had previously been a minor player on the Iranian political stage, now assumed a major role for the first time. With some skilful diplomacy, good luck, and timely outside support, the Iranians themselves were able to take a hand in determining their country's fate and preserving its boundaries and independence—something they had not been able to do for a very long time.

The Soviet Union and Great Britain had occupied Iran in August 1941 and converted the country into a "bridge of victory," an overland supply route to a Soviet Union fighting for its life against Nazi Germany. At the same time, the occupying Allies deposed and exiled Reza Shah Pahlavi for his alleged pro-German sympathies. In a tripartite (UK-USSR-Iran) treaty of January 1942, the occupying powers undertook to guarantee Iran's independence and territorial integrity and promised to withdraw their forces from Iran within six months of the end of the war (however that end might be defined). After the United States entered the war in December 1941, it joined the Allies in logistics operations in Iran. American units began arriving in late 1942, and eventually 30,000 U.S. troops took part in the occupation.

For Iranians, the pattern appeared familiar. The wartime occupation allowed the Soviets to reestablish traditional Russian dominance of northern Iran and the British to do the same in the south, a region that included the Khuzistan oil fields and the large refinery at Abadan. Thirty-five years earlier, Great Britain and Czarist Russia had formally codified a similar division in the 1907 Anglo-Russian treaty, which divided Iran (which the international community then knew as Persia) into Russian and British spheres of influence and a neutral zone, while disingenuously guaranteeing the country's independence and territorial integrity.[1] Although Germany was the common enemy in both the 1907 and 1941 arrangements, the major difference was that in 1907 oil was not a factor for the British—Iran's rich southwestern oil fields were still undiscovered and lay in the neutral zone between the two spheres. In 1907, the British were primarily interested in ending their rivalry with Czarist Russia over Persia and in creating a buffer between Russian possessions in central Asia and India, the jewel in the crown of the British Empire.

The Allies' occupation both ended Reza Shah's rigid central control and strengthened those centrifugal forces that, throughout history, have always threatened to break apart Iran's unity as a state. The breakdown of Iranian central authority encouraged both tribal independence and, in the northwest, important regional movements for autonomy. In both Kurdistan and Azerbaijan, local movements for separation based on ethnic, cultural, and economic grievances gathered strength in the absence of Tehran's control, and, particularly in the Azerbaijan case, enjoyed protection from the occupying Soviet forces.

## It's All About Oil

During the war, both American and Soviet representatives pressed the Iranian government with requests for oil concessions. In the American case, two companies (Standard Vacuum and Sinclair) presented competing offers, apparently without coordination with the American mission in Tehran. An

---

1. The treaty became a dead letter after the collapse of Czarist Russia and after the Soviet Union renounced Czarist privileges in Iran in the Iranian-Soviet treaty of 1921. That treaty (in the famous Article 6) did, however, give the Soviet Union the all-important right to intervene in Iran to prevent aggression against the USSR by a third party.

irritated American financial adviser, Arthur Millspaugh, wrote, "Oil occupied a prominent place among the nationalist objectives of the United States in the Middle East, but in the Persia of 1944, this feature of our program proved more inflammatory than lubricating."[2]

The Soviet quest for oil concessions in northern Iran was more ominous and came straight from the government in Moscow. In the summer of 1944, a Soviet delegation led by Assistant Commissar for Foreign Affairs Sergei Kavtaradze arrived in Iran, visited potential northern oil sites, and held meetings with Prime Minister Mohammad Sa'ed. The USSR was seeking exploration rights not only in the provinces of East and West Azerbaijan, but also in Gilan, Mazanderan, and parts of Semnan (particularly in the subdistrict of Khurian).[3]

When Sa'ed attempted to put off Kavtaradze's demands for Tehran's immediate agreement to an oil concession, the Soviet visitor, at a Tehran press conference, lashed out as follows:

> … Since the Iranian government has adopted an unsympathetic and unfriendly attitude toward the government of the Soviet Union, it has made the future cooperation between Soviet representatives, and the administration of Sa'ed, impossible. . . . The Soviet cabinet is expecting that the Soviet proposal be accepted and the Iranian government without any further delay appoint its representatives for signing the agreement.[4]

The Soviets attempted to break the stalemate by organizing demonstrations of their Iranian supporters against Sa'ed and his government. In November 1944, Sa'ed's government resigned, but the Iranian parliament (Majles) intervened a few weeks later by approving a law forbidding Iranian government officials from discussing or signing a petroleum concession with any foreign representative as long as foreign troops remained on Iranian soil. Furthermore, according to the new law, any foreign oil concession now required approval by an Iranian parliament elected after the agreement was signed. Nor could the Iranians hold elections for that parliament while foreign troops remained on Iran territory. The moving spirits behind this law were the Majles member, veteran politician, and future Prime Minister Mohammad Mosaddegh and a group of his political allies.

---

2. Arthur Millspaugh, *Americans in Persia* (Brookings, 1946), 233.

3. Tale and Tale, *Iran in the Claws of the Bear*, 13. The authors believe that large-scale demands (or reports of demands) for oil concessions by the British and Americans led the Soviets to escalate their demands.

4. Mohammad Sa'ed, *Kavtaradze in Iran*, 22–27, cited by Tale and Tale, *Claws of the Bear*, 14.

## The Azerbaijanis Move to Separation

At the Potsdam summit meeting in August 1945 the leaders of the victorious Allies declared that their forces would withdraw immediately from Tehran and in stages from the rest of the country, thus reaffirming the original tripartite agreement of 1942 requiring that all Allied forces leave Iran within six months of the end of the war. The Allies, apparently at Soviet insistence, now agreed that the war's end would be the date of Japan's surrender (which would come in September 1945).[5]

In Iranian Azerbaijan, however, events were moving in a different direction. Frustrated in the 1944 oil concession negotiations, the Soviets began providing direct support to the Azerbaijani separatists. On September 3, 1945, the day after Japan's surrender, a group of local separatists announced the formation of the Democratic Party of Azerbaijan (DPA). In Tabriz, the Azerbaijani capital, the Iranian Communist Party (the Tudeh) closed its provincial chapter and ordered its members to join the new DPA.[6] By the end of December, the separatists, with Soviet help, had overrun Iranian government barracks in the region and were in control of most towns in both East and West Azerbaijan provinces, with the important exception of the Kurdish centers in the latter. At the same time, the Soviet occupying forces blocked Tehran's efforts to dispatch military units to restore central government control over the region.

## A Weak Negotiating Position

In late 1945, Tehran faced a grim situation. It was losing control over one of the country's richest and most important regions and seemed to have few options. Soviet forces had stopped the movement of Iranian army units at Qazvin, only 75 miles west of Tehran, and prevented them from advancing into the rebellious northwest. The intentions of the Americans and British were unclear: the former were withdrawing their troops from Iran quickly, and the latter announced their intention to do so by March 1946. At the same time, the Iranians faced demands from the Soviets that would have, in effect,

---

5. Perhaps the Soviets were counting on another two or three years before Japan surrendered—time enough to ensure their agents were well-installed in Iranian Azerbaijan.

6. Tale and Tale, *Claws of the Bear*, 19. The authors provide (162–64) a translation of detailed instructions, dated July 6, 1945, from the Moscow politburo to the first secretary of the Soviet Azerbaijan Communist party titled "Measures to Organize a Separatist Movement in Southern Azarbaijan and Other Provinces in Northern Iran."

reestablished the hated Czarist privileges that Russia imposed on Iran in treaties after her military victories in the early nineteenth century. According to American diplomatic sources, the primary Soviet demands, which would have struck serious blows to Iranian sovereignty, were as follows:

- oil concessions for northern Iran;
- air transport rights between the USSR and Iran and for domestic routes between northern Iranian cities;
- (unspecified) privileges at the Iranian port of Bandar Pahlavi (today's Anzali) on the Caspian Sea; and
- agreement on maintenance of the Astara-Rasht-Qazvin highway, one of the main land routes from Tehran to the Soviet border.[7]

In late 1945, it was by no means clear to Tehran how much support it could count on from Washington or London to resist these Soviet demands and reestablish central government authority in the Northwest. It appears that the Soviets and their DPA protégés intended to establish facts on the ground in Azerbaijan before the British and Americans could raise the issue at the Moscow Allied foreign ministers meeting, which began on December 16.

Because the Iranian government was both internally divided and too weak to expel the Soviet occupiers by force, it had to enter a difficult and protracted series of negotiations to achieve the following:

- departure of Soviet forces from northern Iran;
- reestablishing Tehran's authority over the breakaway regions of Azerbaijan and Kurdistan;[8]
- gaining the support of the United States, Britain, and the newly formed United Nations for Iran's side in the dispute; and

---

7. U.S. ambassador's telegram to the Department of State, November 26, 1945. Cited by Tale and Tale, *Claws of the Bear*, 21–22. These demands were never explicitly linked to a Soviet withdrawal from Iranian Azerbaijan or to an end of Soviet support for the separatists there.

8. Although not a part of this case study, in 1945–46 a group of Kurdish nationalists had profited by the breakdown of the central government's authority in neighboring Azerbaijan to form an autonomous republic in an area of West Azerbaijan province outside British or Russian occupation. In early 1946, the leaders of the Democratic Republic of Kurdistan established their republic with its capital at Mahabad and its president, Qazi Mohammad, a respected religious leader of the town. Although the two republics were separate entities, the survival of both depended on Tehran's inability to assert its authority. For more on the Kurdish movement, see Eagleton, *The Kurdish Republic of 1946*.

- limiting Soviet economic and political influence over Iran—whether in the form of an oil concession or by agreement to the other Soviet demands listed above.

## Divided We Stand

The above maneuvering came in the midst of many-sided political battles in Tehran. The 1941 Anglo-Russian occupation had ended Reza Shah's dictatorship and had inaugurated a period of lively political activity in which his son, the young Mohammad Reza Shah, was just one player among many—and not necessarily the most important. The war and postwar years in Iran were years of vigorous debate and competition among several factions and parties led by strong-willed and ambitious politicians. The British and the Soviets also had their traditional Iranian friends, and still other aspiring politicians competed for support from the United States, the newest arrival on the Iranian domestic political scene.

Veteran, aristocratic politicians of the late Qajar period, whose voices the authoritarian Reza Shah had silenced after 1925, returned to the political arena. Ahmad Qavam, who had led three pre-Pahlavi cabinets under his aristocratic title Qavam al-Saltaneh, served as prime minister in 1942–43 and in 1946–47. Mohammad Mosaddegh, who as Mosaddegh al-Saltaneh had been minister of justice, finance, and foreign affairs under the last Qajar shah, won election to the Fourteenth Majles in 1943 and, in 1944, sponsored the bill (noted above) that forbade the Iranian government from discussing or signing oil concessions while foreign troops remained on Iranian soil.[9] Seyyed Zia al-Din Tabataba'i, a journalist who had collaborated with Reza Shah (then the Persian Cossack Brigade officer Reza Khan) in the coup d'etat of 1921, returned from exile in 1943, organized the National Will (Eradeh-ye-Melli) party, served in parliament, and became known as a loyal servant of the British and their interests.[10]

## A Question of Motive

How did the Iranians eventually succeed in getting the Soviets to leave and abandon their protégés in Tabriz? Crucial to their success in 1945–47 was

---

9. Among Reza Shah's important reforms was abolishing the old aristocratic titles and forcing all Iranians to adopt family names.

10. On Seyyed Zia al-Din's role, see Cottam, *Iran and the United States*, 72.

their accurate identification of Soviet (and other foreign powers') motives and underlying interests (always a prerequisite to successful negotiation). Although some Iranian politicians and parties advanced their fortunes by serving the interests of Britain, the Soviet Union, or the United States, most recognized that preserving a weak Iran's independence required balancing powerful outside powers against each other—a doctrine that came to be known as positive equilibrium. Doing so also meant that the successful Iranian politician had to act carefully to avoid aligning himself too closely with any major foreign power while remaining acceptable to all of them.

In 1945–46, the Soviet Union appeared to have three objectives in Iran:

- obtaining an oil concession (and other commercial advantages) in the north of the country in a manner that would balance the British position in the south

- advancing the fortunes of the Tudeh party in the Iranian central government; and

- nourishing and protecting the separatist movement in Iranian Azerbaijan so that the Soviet Union would face a friendly neighbor on its southern border.

As for the first objective, we have already noted how the Soviets had brought heavy-handed pressure for a concession on the Iranian government during the war and how the Iranians responded with Mosaddegh's oil concession law.

As for the British and Americans, the objectives were less clear. For the Americans, the first interest appeared to be withdrawing their forces from Iran and returning to their traditional role of minor player in Iranian affairs. The Americans, of course, did not want to see an indefinite Soviet presence in Iran or a Soviet puppet state in Azerbaijan, but it was by no means certain how far Washington was prepared to go in pursuit of its goals.

As for Britain, it had no illusions it could do anything about the continuing Soviet presence in the north. London's main concern seemed to be maintaining its preeminent position in the southern Iranian oil industry. With her oil interests in mind, Britain delayed withdrawing her forces until Soviet intentions became clear. In the spring of 1945, the Iranian ambassador in Moscow Mozaffar Firuz told UK foreign secretary Ernest Bevin, "If the world's big powers consider Iran Asia's Switzerland and, according to special treaty, guarantee her independence and refrain from interfering in her internal affairs, it would be good for world peace." Firuz records Bevin's response, with its blunt admission of the preeminent place of Iranian oil, as follows: "Bevin said it was a good idea, but Switzerland has no oil, and in the case of Iran, the problem is oil. He implied if the oil could reach to everyone and be divided in accordance with an agreed plan, it would be excellent."[11]

## Enter Qavam

When Ahmad Qavam became prime minister of Iran in January 1946, he faced a bleak situation. Separatist movements were in control of Azerbaijan and Kurdistan, and Soviet troops were making no move to leave Iranian territory while blocking efforts by the Iranian army to assert central authority in the breakaway regions. As for Qavam himself, he came from one of Iran's most powerful aristocratic families with strong roots in the Qajar dynasty (1779–1925). In the course of the nineteenth and twentieth centuries, eight members of his extended family, including his cousin Mohammad Mosaddegh, served as prime ministers of Qajar and Pahlavi rulers. Exiled and kept out of politics by Reza Shah, Qavam, along with other veterans of earlier political struggles, returned to the political stage following Reza Shah's departure in 1941.[12]

Qavam's precise role in the events that followed is still a matter of debate, and historians continue to differ about how much credit he deserves for the Soviets' eventual diplomatic defeat. Some historians consider him an astute and skillful politician who managed to earn and keep the trust of the Soviets while outmaneuvering them at every turn.[13] In this version of events, Qavam cleverly used the Soviets' desire for an Iranian oil concession to persuade them to withdraw their forces from Iran in 1946. He then used that same Soviet desire for oil to allow the Iranian government both to crack down on its domestic Communist party (the Tudeh) and to reoccupy Azerbaijan, whose separatist government the Soviets had originally sponsored. The historian Ervand Abrahamian, however, believes that the "enigmatic" Qavam benefited more from good fortune than from any far-sighted planning on his part. About Qavam, Abrahamian writes:

> The public image he sought to project was that of a decisive leader in full command of the situation, but all the while he was under constant challenge from both the right—the shah, the army, and the tribal

---

11. Firuz to Foreign Ministry, April 1945. Cited in Tale and Tale, *Claws of the Bear*, 17.

12. Bill, *The Eagle and the Lion*, 37.

13. See, for example, Bill, *The Eagle and the Lion*, 33ff; Cottam, *Iran and the United States*, 69ff; and Ansari, *Confronting Iran*, 25.

chiefs—and the left—the Tudeh, the Democratic Party of Azarbaijan, and the Democratic Party of Kurdistan. He portrayed himself as a world statesman fully the match of Stalin, Churchill, and Truman, even though in reality he represented a weak and underdeveloped country whose very existence could be erased overnight by any one of the Great Powers. He sought to assure his followers that he pursued a secret blueprint for national survival; but he was rarely in command of events, being left to muddle through one crisis after another by improvising from day to day, juggling political pieces, and exploiting rather than creating opportunities.[14]

Whatever the reality, what is certain is that Qavam was playing a very weak hand. Whether or not he played it with skill, the outcome was to free Iran of Soviet troops, restore central government control over Azerbaijan and Kurdistan, and frustrate a Soviet attempt to obtain an oil concession and a privileged position in northern Iran. Another outcome was that the United States became, perhaps for the first time, deeply involved in Iran's internal affairs. As the historian Richard Cottam writes, "… day by day the matters taken up by the [American] ambassadors with Iranian officials moved more deeply into matters of domestic policy concerns."[15]

When Qavam became prime minister in January 1946, he did so despite the opposition of the shah, who, like his father, harbored a profound distrust for the members of the old Qajar aristocracy. Qavam was known to enjoy the support of the Soviets, who believed he would look favorably on their demands in Iran. He never disabused the Soviets of that idea and maintained his relationship with them even as, according to some, he was double-dealing them out of their objectives by dangling the promise of a northern oil concession (which they never obtained).

In early 1946, the United States would not provide Iran with the all-important leverage of a threat of force against the continued Soviet presence and instead supported Iran's case in the United Nations Security Council. (See UN Security Council Resolution 2, of January 30, 1946.) Qavam, for his part, wasted no time in pursuing his objectives. Two days after becoming prime minister, he sent a note to Stalin reassuring the Soviet leader of his (and the Iranian people's) friendship and requesting direct bilateral negotiations.

---

14. Abrahamian, *Iran between Two Revolutions*, 225.

15. Cottam, *Iran and the United States*, 84. According to Habib Ladjevardi ("The Origins of U.S. Support for an Autocratic Iran"), the United States' decision to side with the shah against Prime Minister Qavam in 1947 established the precedent for its eventual actions against Mosaddegh in 1953.

Stalin's response was friendly, and in mid-February the prime minister led an Iranian delegation to Moscow.[16]

Qavam had originally planned to remain in Moscow only a few days, and, after meeting with Stalin and Foreign Minister Molotov, return to Tehran and leave the detailed negotiating to the rest of his delegation. He ended up staying longer, however, until March 7, once he realized that the Soviets were insisting on their right to keep forces on Iranian territory. For Qavam, there were two central and interlocking issues: ensuring the withdrawal of Soviet forces and preventing the dissolution of Iran by the loss of its important northwestern provinces. These issues became his mission's overriding objectives, to which other aims could be subordinated. In his first meeting with Stalin, on February 21, 1946, Qavam, according to his later report to the Iranian parliament, kept these two related issues at the center of discussions. He also referred to withdrawal as a matter of equity, explicitly avoiding the legalisms of the 1921 Soviet-Iranian friendship treaty.[17] According to Qavam's report, he told Stalin,

> I am not here to discuss legal matters or refer to certain treaties, although they have their own place. But I am here with honest and friendly intentions to ask you to act with a strong will in taking the initiative in [establishing] friendly relations and removing the problems between Iran and the Soviet Union, which is the immediate withdrawal of Soviet forces from Iran, and to give us moral support in the case of Azerbaijan, which in its present situation is contrary to the laws and sovereignty of Iran.[18]

The Moscow discussions were difficult. Playing his few cards as well as he could, Qavam continued to insist that the Soviets set a firm date for total withdrawal and recognize Tehran's control over its breakaway provinces. The Soviets, returning to Article 6 of the 1921 treaty and to (unspecified) evidence of Iranian hostility, avoided committing themselves and responded by noting how Iranian delegates to the 1919 Versailles peace conference had advanced hostile claims to Russian territory in the Caucasus and central Asia. On the issue of Iranian Azerbaijan, the Soviets pressed their claim to be the ones deciding the fate of that region and went so far as to offer the Iranians a list of suggestions for dealing with the separatists. Their suggestions included forming autonomous provincial and district councils, giving official status to the Azari language, earmarking 70 percent of the region's

---

16. Tale and Tale, *Claws of the Bear*, 84–85, gives the text of Qavam's message to Stalin.

17. See chapter 6 for a discussion of legalisms and justice in Iranian negotiations.

18. Cited by Tale and Tale, *Claws of the Bear*, 87.

taxes for local expenditure, and increasing the region's representation in the national Iranian parliament.[19]

## An Agreement Signed: The Soviets Leave

When Qavam and his delegation returned to Tehran, they returned without an agreement on Azerbaijan and Soviet withdrawal but with the understanding—as Qavam told American ambassador Wallace Murray—that what the Soviets were really after in Iran was an oil concession.[20] Apparently Qavam decided that he could use northern Iranian oil as bait, or at least as the lever to soften Moscow's positions on troop withdrawal and the Azerbaijan separatists.

In the meantime, Hussein Ala, Iran's ambassador to the United Nations, had, with the support of American Secretary of State James Byrnes (and despite the cautions of Ambassador George Allen, Murray's successor in Tehran), submitted the Azerbaijan case to the Security Council. According to Cottam, Ala was pursuing a policy favored not by Prime Minister Qavam but by the shah—to involve the Americans directly in the Iranian-Soviet dispute and to limit Qavam's independence of action with Moscow. The shah, in Cottam's opinion, was seeking to paint this dispute in Cold War terms as a direct Soviet challenge to which the United States would be obligated to respond.[21]

During the Moscow meetings, the Soviets had agreed to send a new ambassador to Tehran (Ivan Vasilivich Sadchikov), and Qavam continued negotiations after his return to Tehran. On April 4 the two sides announced that they had reached a three-point agreement:

- The Soviets would withdraw all their forces from Iran by the middle of May 1946.

- The Iranian central government would reach a peaceful solution to its differences with the Azerbaijani separatists.

- Qavam would submit to the next (Fifteenth) Majles a proposal for formation of a joint Soviet-Iranian oil company, 51 percent Soviet owned.

---

19. Iranian Foreign Ministry Archives, February 25, 1946, cited by Tale and Tale, *Claws of the Bear*, 93.

20. Cottam, *Iran and the United States*, 70.

21. Ibid., 72–74.

Although it was not spelled out in the public announcement, Qavam also agreed to withdraw Iran's complaint against the Soviet Union that it had made to the United Nations Security Council.

The historian Abrahamian, although no great admirer of Qavam (see above), gives the Iranian prime minister credit for negotiating the Soviets out of Iran by identifying Moscow's underlying interests and by not giving up after he had apparently reached a deadlock in the February–March Moscow meetings. Abrahamian describes the agreement as follows:

> Qavam's achievement was considerable. It permitted the Russians to leave without losing face. It had been reached without open intervention from the West. It counterbalanced a Soviet concession in the north against the British company [the Anglo-Iranian Oil Company] in the south. And it implicitly tied what Qavam wanted, the Soviet withdrawal, with what the Soviets seemed to want most, the oil agreement. For without troop withdrawal, there could be no elections; without elections, no Majles; and without Majles, no oil agreement. As the last Soviet contingents left in early May, the shah felt obliged to confer on Qavam the title of *Jenab-e-Ashraf* (Noble Excellency).[22]

## A Balancing Act

Although the agreement was signed and the Red Army was leaving Iran, Qavam knew that he had no power of his own to enforce its provisions, and remained dependent on the Soviets' good faith (and their desire for Iranian oil) to ensure their compliance. Once the Soviets were out of Iran, the Iranians had to keep them out. It was vital, therefore, that Qavam—who had made the deal—appear to be acting in accordance with its terms and to avoid being seen as hostile to the USSR to keep the trust of the Soviets. To strengthen his position vis-à-vis the shah, he also needed to retain the trust of the Americans, who might bring down his whole house of cards if they sided with the shah against him (as they eventually were to do in late 1947).

Qavam continued to walk a very fine line amidst competing forces. Even before the Soviet-Iranian agreement was announced, he offered the Americans an oil concession in southeastern Iran (Baluchistan), an area long desired by British oil companies.[23] The same day the Iranian-Soviet accord was announced, the UN Security Council approved Resolution 3, noting that the USSR had agreed to complete withdrawing its forces from Iran by May 6,

---

22. Abrahamian, *Iran between Two Revolutions*, 228.

23. U.S. Ambassador to the State Department, March 22, 1946, *Foreign Relations of the United States*, VII, 369–73. Cited by Abrahamian, *Iran between Two Revolutions*, 228–29.

1946, and deferring any action on the Iranian case until that date (to keep the threat of UN action over the heads of the Soviets).

A week later, on April 11, Soviet ambassador Sadchikov visited Qavam and pressed him to withdraw the Iranian complaint to the council. According to Qavam's account to the American chargé d'affaires, the Soviet representative told the prime minister, "After the signature of agreements on April 4, there was no reason for keeping the matter before the Security Council. [The] Iranian attitude indicated lack of confidence in Soviet word and would strain relations between the two governments."[24] Acceding to Soviet Ambassador Sadchikov's request, four days later Qavam instructed Iran's UN Ambassador Ala to withdraw Iran's Azerbaijan case from the Security Council. Ala's primary loyalty, however, was not to Qavam but to the shah. The Americans, for their part, insisted on pursuing the Azerbaijan matter, apparently hoping to embarrass the Soviet Union even after it had reached its agreement with Qavam. Caught between American and Soviet pressures on this issue (and not wishing to offend either side), Qavam instructed Ala to withdraw the Iranian complaint and then agreed that it could remain quietly on the agenda until May 6, 1946.[25]

On June 13, 1946, in accordance with his agreement with the Soviets, Qavam reached an autonomy arrangement with the Azerbaijani separatists after negotiations between Mozaffar Firuz and DPA chief Jafar Pishavari, mediated by the Soviet ambassador. While the Azerbaijanis recognized Iranian sovereignty over their region, Qavam made concessions to the Tabriz authorities on regional economic, cultural, and security autonomy. The agreement, however, deferred decisions on the two most sensitive issues: the claims of pro-Tehran Azerbaijani landlords, whose lands the DPA had confiscated, and military issues, such as the role of the central Iranian army in Azerbaijan and the status of Iranian military officers who had joined the separatists.

According to the historian Atabaki, the agreement heavily favored the Iranian central government. On the two important points noted above, the Azerbaijanis had to settle for vague promises from Qavam and the Tabriz government had to "resign itself to being a provincial administration under the central government."[26] In announcing the agreement, Pishavari took a defensive tone against those opponents who were claiming Qavam had

---

24. U.S. Embassy report, April 11, 1946, cited by Tale and Tale, *Claws of the Bear*, 133.

25. Cottam, *Iran and the United States*, 71.

26. Atabaki, *Azerbaijan*, 159.

tricked him and insisted that the agreement was fair. Qavam, however, did not hesitate to claim a victory. Atabaki writes,

> In contrast to his Azerbaijani counterparts, Qavam had every reason to consider the signing of the Azerbaijan agreement as a victory for the central government. In an address broadcast by Tehran Radio, he described the Azerbaijani dispute as the "most serious problem" he had to contend with "since coming to power" and thus characterized the agreement reached with the Azerbaijani Democrats as a "step in the direction of liberty and Iranian national unity."[27]

Qavam knew he had to be seen as carrying out his side of the agreement with the Soviets. Both to keep Moscow's confidence and to strike at the prerogatives of the shah and his Anglophile allies, in August 1946 Qavam formed a leftist coalition government including the Tudeh, the Democrat Party (Qavam's own organization), and the Iran Party (a grouping of non-Marxist, nationalist intellectuals including Mehdi Bazargan and Allahyar Saleh). In his new government, Qavam gave three ministries (health, education, and trade and industry) to the Tudeh and also offered a minister without portfolio position to the Democratic Party of Azerbaijan.[28]

## The Unravelling

In the turmoil of Iranian politics in 1946 and under multiple competing pressures from within and without, these arrangements could not endure for long. The prime minister's coalition with the Tudeh was the first to go. In October, Qavam faced attacks from the right, including violent opposition from the southern Qashqa'i tribes, whose leader, Naser Khan Qashqa'i, denounced the Tudeh role in the government and claimed that atheism and communism were threatening the nation and religion. Pro-shah army commanders and British officials unhappy with Qavam's friendly relations with the Soviets reportedly encouraged the Qashqa'is and joined in the onslaught. Even American support became uncertain, and in response to the unrest, U.S. ambassador Allen urged Qavam, among other things, to dismiss Deputy Prime Minister Mozaffar Firuz and the three Tudeh ministers and to tone down "his warm expressions of friendship toward the Soviet Union."[29]

---

27. Cited Atabaki, *Azerbaijan*, 159.

28. Abrahamian, *Iran between Two Revolutions*, 234. Many Iran party figures became key allies of Mosaddegh in the National Front. In the sixties, the principal pro-shah party was the New Iran (Iran-e-Novin) Party, an attempt to associate the monarchy with the earlier nationalist movement.

29. Cited by Abrahamian, *Iran between Two Revolutions*, 237. Muzaffar Firuz, another

In October 1946, in response to these attacks, Qavam changed direction. He dismissed the three Tudeh ministers and formed an alliance with the Qashqa'is. He formed a new cabinet from members of his own (Democrat) party and excluded representatives of the Iran Party. At the same time, provincial authorities in Khuzistan, Esfahan, and elsewhere moved to close down local Tudeh operations. This new turn to the right greatly displeased the shah, who now saw himself facing an unfriendly alliance of Qavam (whom he had always disliked and distrusted) and the Qashqa'is, whom he suspected of building an independent tribal power base in southern Iran. In response, the shah approached the American ambassador asking for American support in removing Qavam from power.[30]

Next to go were Qavam's arrangements with Azerbaijan separatists, who were unable to maintain themselves in the absence of Soviet troops. On December 10, 1946, the Iranian army reoccupied Azerbaijan, where the DPA had already lost control of the situation. When the Iranian army reached Tabriz, pro-Tehran groups already ruled the city. Most of the armed separatists either surrendered without a fight or fled to the Soviet Union. The Mahabad autonomous Kurdish regime, without its Azerbaijani buffer, also fell quickly to government forces. Its civilian leaders were executed, and its armed forces fled north into Soviet territory.

## The Soviets Stay Out

Why did the Soviets swallow these two humiliations? Why did the Soviets not intervene to help either the Tudeh or the Azerbaijanis? In the case of the crackdown on the Tudeh, we hear almost nothing about Soviet objections. For Moscow, the loss of some Iranian communists was apparently a small price to pay for the larger prize of the oil concession. The case of Azerbaijan, however, was more serious. Soviet ambassador Sadchikov had warned Qavam in late November 1946 that "the dispatch of armed forces from Teh-

---

descendent of Qajar nobility, had been Iran's ambassador to Moscow and was a close adviser of Qavam and a key figure in his Democrat Party. Reza Shah had murdered Firuz's father, and the son advocated a strong stand against the monarchy. It is worth noting that two months before, Allen had not been alarmed about Tudeh representation in Qavam's government and had informed Washington, "I feel confident changes of ministers resulted from Qavam's belief [that] he can handle [the] Tudeh better inside the government that out and from his effort to absorb [the] Tudeh organization into his political party" (Ladjevardi, "The Origins of U.S. Support", 231).

30. Allen to Washington, October 14, 1946. Cited by Ladjevardi, "Origins of U.S. Support," 232.

ran either to the interior of Azerbaijan or the Soviet frontiers might create problems."[31] Qavam's response, according to one historian of the period, was to reassure the Soviet envoy of his "friendship" and "good intentions" to the Soviet Union and to point out that his only goal was to ensure that conditions in Azerbaijan permitted elections (presumably for the Fifteenth Majles) to be held.[32]

Qavam's point about Majles elections was critical. He was gambling that the Soviets' principal aim in Iran was the oil agreement, for which they would be willing to sacrifice even their Azerbaijani protégés. As noted before, final approval of the oil deal ultimately depended on the Soviets staying out of Iran. It required approval from the (still unelected) Fifteenth Majles, and the Iranians could delay holding elections for that Majles on the grounds that some of their territory was not under government control. Furthermore, Iranian law forbade holding any Majles election while foreign troops remained on Iranian territory. Ambassador Sadchikov would almost certainly have understood Qavam's point perfectly: "If you want the oil agreement, stay out of Iran and let us deal with the situation in Azerbaijan."

Neither the prime minister nor the shah was willing to give the other any credit for the reoccupation of Azerbaijan. According to Abrahamian, Qavam had been reluctant to act against the breakaway region because he worried about Soviet reactions and feared that an Azerbaijan under Tehran's military control would send promonarchy deputies to the future Majles. That reluctance, however, did not prevent Qavam from maintaining that it was his standing with Moscow that persuaded the Soviets not to intervene.[33]

The shah also claimed the credit, saying that he had persuaded the Americans to back the Iranian action with a firm stand against the Soviets. The Soviet nonresponse, however, also puzzled the Americans, who in reality were in no position to react with force if the Soviets had sent their troops back into Iran. Historians have found no evidence of any American ultimatum to Stalin on the subject. Ambassador Allen admitted he could not explain Soviet inaction. In his analysis for Washington, he gave little importance to American firmness.

> It is suggested that the Soviet failure to send combat units to support
> Azerbaijan may have resulted from the fact that the Azerbaijan regime

---

31. Iranian Foreign Ministry to its Washington Embassy, cited by Tale and Tale, *Claws of the Bear*, 142.

32. Khanbaba Bayani, *Ghaele Azarbaijan* (The Azarbaijan Uprising) (Tehran, 1996), 612. Cited by Tale and Tale, *Claws of the Bear*, 143.

33. Abrahamian, *Iran between Two Revolutions*, 238, 240.

collapsed too fast, from internal considerations in USSR, from broader
questions of foreign policy connected with Europe, from fear of SC
[United Nations Security Council] and world opinion censure, or
combination of all of them.[34]

Whatever the real reasons for Moscow's inaction, one thing is certain: the
Soviets realized that the Azerbaijani separatists could not survive without
long-term Soviet military support, and Moscow made it clear to the Iranian
Azerbaijanis that they could expect no such support. When the end came in
December 1946, the Soviets advised their protégés that they were better off
running than fighting Tehran in a lost cause. According to one witness (the
deputy premier of the autonomous Tabriz regime), the Soviet Azerbaijani
security chief told DPA leader Ja'far Pishavari, "The one who brought you
in now tells you go."[35]

## Journey's End: The Oil Agreement Fails and Qavam Falls

The Fourteenth Majles had ended its term in March 1946, two months after
Qavam became prime minister and shortly before the April 4 signing of the
Iranian-Soviet agreement. Although Qavam had agreed to submit that agreement to the new (Fifteenth) Majles for ratification within seven months of its
signing, he was in no hurry to organize elections for the new parliament.
Elections did not begin until December 1946 (eight months after the signing
of the agreement), continued over several months, and the new Majles did
not convene and begin its work until June 1947. Although Qavam's Democrat
Party held a nominal majority over rival pro-monarchy and pro-British
factions, his majority proved to be short-lived. In his desire to consolidate
power, the prime minister had constructed a party out of individuals and
factions that he could not hold together. As the pro-British paper *Qiyam-e-Iran*
put it,

> The Democrat party includes wolves as well as sheep: millionaires,
> industrialists, and powerful merchants who coerce and terrorize the
> masses; as well as workers and peasants who are bribed and herded
> into the voting polls. The party press claims that Aziz Nikpay [a wealthy
> industrialist] is a "workers representative"; in fact, he is a "robber
> baron" who exploits his workers. What is more, Herati, the millionaire

---

34. U.S. Foreign Relations, 1946, cited by Cottam, *Iran and the United States*, 77.

35. Nosratollah Jahanshahlou Afshar, *Sargozasht-e-Maa va Biganegan* (The History of Us
and the Foreigners), Ketab Co., 2004, 358. Cited by Tale and Tale, *Claws of the Bear*, 186.

> industrialist from Yazd, has the audacity to argue that he will protect
> workers better if he travels to the majles in a Cadillac.[36]

Under the pressure of its own internal contradictions, and under pressure of attacks from rival factions, Qavam's party in the Majles broke apart. When the prime minister, after much delay and under pressure from the Soviet ambassador, finally submitted the oil agreement to the Majles in October 1947, he distanced himself from the agreement, thus avoiding making the vote on the deal a vote of confidence in his government. When the bill came before the parliament, party discipline had collapsed, and most of the Democrats joined the opposition. On October 23, 1947, the Majles deputies rejected the agreement by a margin of 102 to 2.

In the process of killing the agreement, the parliament actually did two things. In the short term, rather than vote directly for or against the agreement, it approved a separate bill that declared the original Iranian-Soviet arrangement null and void because it violated the 1944 law prohibiting Iranian officials from signing or discussing oil concessions while foreign troops occupied Iranian territory. Although Qavam claimed that what he had signed with Sadchikov in April 1945 was technically not a concession but an agreement to form a joint Soviet-Iranian company, his reasoning convinced no one. In a move with longer-term implications, when the members of parliament approved this bill, they included a provision that called for reexamining all existing Iranian resource arrangements, including, implicitly, the 1933 agreement with the Anglo-Iranian Oil Company (AIOC). According to Tale and Tale, that provision of the bill would later have momentous consequences in the form of the oil nationalization crisis of 1951–53. They write, "… with the rejection of the formation of the Iran-USSR oil company by the Majlis, the groundwork was set for reclaiming national rights from the British oil company operating in southern Iran."[37]

The Iranian government officially informed the Soviet Embassy of the Majles action on November 5, 1947. The Soviets were very unhappy but could do little but make a strong protest. Two weeks later, Ambassador Sadchikov sent a letter to Qavam informing him of Moscow's official response. Specifically, the Soviets expressed their unhappiness at both the Iranians' delay in submitting the agreement for ratification (the original agreement had stipulated they would do so within seven months—that is, by November 1946) and at the rejection itself. The note concluded,

---

36. Cited by Abrahamian, *Iran between Two Revolutions*, 243.
37. Tale and Tale, *Claws of the Bear*, 151.

> Therefore, Iran has clearly defaulted on what it had agreed to undertake. The Soviet government cannot fail to comment that it finds itself gravely discriminated against, since the decision by the Majlis to reject the formation of the joint Iranian-USSR oil company for the oil in the northern part of Iran is in direct contrast to the oil concession for the Iran-Britain company [Anglo-Iranian Oil Company] in the south that still remains in effect.
>
> Taking into consideration all of the above points, the government of the Soviet Union strongly protests against the hostile action of the Iranian government, which is contrary to the normal relations between two countries and places the responsibility for the consequences of these actions on her shoulders. We renew our respects.[38]

It is worth noting that more than a year before the Majles rejected the oil agreement, the Soviets realized that the Iranians may have duped them and the agreement could be in trouble. On September 30, 1946, Stalin wrote an angry message to the members of the Politburo, noting the Soviet Foreign Ministry's mistake in allowing a loophole for the Iranians. Although the April 1946 agreement provided for Majles ratification within seven months, five months later no Iranian Majles existed, and the Iranian government had not scheduled elections for a new one. As such, the agreement's ratification appeared to remain in limbo. Responding to Stalin's criticism, the Politburo sent a note to the Iranian government and reprimanded Ambassador Sadchikov for failing to secure Majles approval.[39]

Qavam himself survived the rejection of the oil agreement, but he found himself severely weakened and remained in office for only a few more weeks. He attempted to rally support by raising anti-British causes: renegotiating the 1933 oil agreement with AIOC and reviving Iran's claim to Bahrain. Qavam also insisted that Iran would maintain its good relations with the Soviet Union in pursuing its policy of positive equilibrium. The prime minister, however, now faced defections within his own party and the combined opposition of the shah, the British, and even the Americans. Although the record is not completely clear, Ambassador Allen had apparently come down on the shah's side as early as October 1946.

A year later, after the oil deal's rejection, the shah felt he had obtained both British and American support to move against Qavam, who had outlived

---

38. Cited by Tale and Tale, *Claws of the Bear*, 149–50.

39. Vladimir O. Pechatnov and Vladslav M. Zubok (translator). "Foreign Policy Correspondence between Stalin and Molotov and Other Politburo Members, September 1945–December 1946." Woodrow Wilson Center, Cold War International History Project, Working Paper No. 26, September 1999, 20 (www.wilsoncenter.org/topics/pubs/ACFB29. PDF).

his usefulness and, if he stayed in office, would remain a serious rival to the monarch. In early December, Qavam's cabinet quit, and a few days later the prime minister lost a vote of confidence and resigned. He then left for Paris for medical treatment, and the shah even stripped him of his Jenab-e-Ashraf title. Commenting on Qavam's fall (and the shah's rise), the British ambassador wrote,

> The fall of Qavam seems likely to mark the end of a phase in the development of Persian politics. Earlier in the year there had already been signs of increased political activity by the court. The shah had felt, since December 1946 (when the central government took control of Azerbaijan), that too much credit had been given Qavam and insufficient to himself.[40]

## Conclusion: Making the Most of a Little

Historians still debate the events of 1945–47. They pose the questions: Why did the Soviets agree to leave Iran? Why did they not react more strongly when the Iranians overthrew the Azerbaijan separatist regime and when the parliament later rejected the 1946 oil agreement? Who deserves the credit for the Soviet withdrawal? How important was the American role in those events? Was Prime Minister Qavam a subtle and skilled diplomat who outwitted the Soviets while convincing them he was their friend? Or was he an autocratic, ambitious politician who improvised from one crisis to the next until his entire political house of cards collapsed in late 1947?

Whatever the answers to the above questions, three facts are undeniable: the Soviets withdrew their troops from Iran; the Iranians regained control over the rebellious regions in the northwest; and Tehran avoided granting important economic privileges to Moscow. Even if we do not understand all of the details, the events illustrate important points and lessons about Iranian negotiating.

- **In the balance between legalism and nonlegalism, the latter prevailed.** The Iranians avoided legal arguments about the exact meaning of Article VI of the 1921 Soviet-Iranian friendship treaty (see Qavam's comment to Stalin above). At the same time, Qavam was able to use the December 1944 Iranian oil law, which specified conditions for Majles elections

---

40. Cited by Ladjevardi, "Origins of U.S. Support," 234. Ladjevardi maintains that the American decision to support the shah against Qavam guaranteed the establishment of royal dictatorship in Iran, and, as such, was the direct predecessor of the decision to support the monarch against Mosaddegh in 1953.

and for oil concessions and their ratification, as leverage against his Soviet interlocutors. During the original Moscow negotiations (February–March 1946) the Soviets sought to break the deadlock by shifting the discussions from the hated term "concession" to forming a joint oil company. In October 1947, however, the Iranian Majles, when rejecting Qavam's agreement, ignored this legal distinction, which both Qavam and the Soviets apparently had thought important.

- **What appeared to be Iranian cunning may have been just improvisation.** The conventional wisdom, as cited in the quotation from James Bill at the beginning of this chapter, is that a crafty and duplicitous Qavam, using Moscow's desire for an oil concession, executed a subtle plan that persuaded the Soviets to withdraw their forces from Iran, excluded the Tudeh party from the government, and restored Tehran's authority in the breakaway northwestern provinces. He did all of those things while pretending to be a sincere friend of the Soviet Union and by using the bait of an oil agreement that he knew the Iranian parliament would never approve. In this version of history, Qavam even staged the Qashqa'i uprisings of October 1946 as a pretext to expel the Tudeh ministers from the government.

  Although Qavam certainly deserves considerable credit for the outcome, the evidence suggests he was not operating according to any long-range or coherent plan. In reality, he constructed an intricate house of cards, placed high-stakes gambles, and coped short term with a very fluid political situation. The evidence also suggests that, although by background and disposition a member of Iran's wealthy elite with no interest in leftist ideology, he saw benefit for Iran (and himself) in balancing traditional British influence with better relations with the USSR.

- **Despite factional strife, Iranians were united on fundamental questions of national unity.** The years of the Azerbaijan crisis were ones of disorder and conflict on the internal Iranian political scene. There was a many-sided conflict among the shah, the military, the prime minister, tribal and regional interests, and foreign powers, notably the Soviets, Americans, and British. Despite these conflicts, there was a degree of accord that helped Tehran achieve successes in restoring central government control to the Northwest. Almost all Iranians (except the DPA and its supporters) agreed on two basic points: withdrawing foreign forces and restoring Iranian sovereignty in Azerbaijan and Kurdistan. Even the Iranian Tudeh party—considered subservient to Moscow—was uncomfortable with the Azerbaijani separatists, despite their common links to the Soviets. This unity, although very important, was still limited. Once the Iranians had achieved those two aims, the parties could resume politics as usual and continue their internecine battles.

- **Iranian negotiators had to make the most of a weak hand.** In 1945–46 the Iranians knew that their position was very weak. The central government had lost control of Azerbaijan and Kurdistan, the Soviet forces were protecting the Azerbaijani separatists and making no move to leave Iran, and neither the Americans nor the British appeared to have any stomach for a confrontation with the occupying Soviets. Lacking any forces of his own and with his political position under constant attack from domestic rivals, Prime Minister Qavam negotiated with promises, the only weapons available to him: the promise of an oil agreement; the promise of an autonomous northwest Iran ruled by a pro-Soviet Democratic Party of Azerbaijan; and the promise of a Tehran government prepared to apply a policy of positive equilibrium, that is, to balance British influence with friendly Iran-USSR relations.

# 3

# The Oil Nationalization Crisis of 1951–53

*Tant pis pour nous.*
— Mosaddegh to American envoy Walter Levy, July 1951

Four years after the end of the Azerbaijan emergency, Iranians lived through another crisis, one that returned them to the forefront of world affairs. Once again, Iranians found themselves negotiating with a weak hand against powerful opponents for the highest of stakes— their national wealth, their sovereignty, and their destiny. In this case, the outcome for Iran was unfortunate, and their British and American adversaries won a Pyrrhic victory that would culminate in a disastrous defeat twenty-five years later.

In this crisis, the Iranians found themselves opposing the Anglo-Iranian Oil Company backed by the British government and, eventually, the American administrations of presidents Truman and Eisenhower. Once again, the Iranians had to negotiate against a backdrop of contentious domestic politics in which strong-willed individuals and opposing factions, many with powerful foreign backers, pursued competing objectives and made and unmade fragile alliances almost every day.

The events of that time have cast long shadows over Iran's foreign and domestic politics. Today, more than fifty years after this crisis, these incidents— and Iranians' perceptions of them—continue to bedevil both Iran's internal politics and its relations with the rest of the world.[1] In the long run, what happened in 1951–53—both its reality and the perception of that reality—had

---

1. For further discussion of the powerful mythology of the 1953 coup and its long-term effects, see the concluding chapter of this study, "Overcoming Mutual Myth-Perceptions."

the result of converting the United States, in many Iranians' eyes, from their friend to their enemy. The same powerful country that, less than a decade earlier, had supported Iran against Soviet attempts to detach one of its richest provinces and that many Iranians had believed would rescue them from centuries of British and Russian domination, now seemed to betray their hopes and became just another outside power determined to control Iran for its own purposes.

After August 1953, the United States became, for many Iranians, the new colonial master, the ultimate decider of their country's destiny, and the enemy of their hopes for achieving dignity and independence after so many years of humiliation. The same country that had urged Iran to reach a negotiated settlement with the AIOC had, in the end, short-circuited the negotiation and ignored Iranian sovereignty by staging the coup that removed a nationalist prime minister. The events of 1953 indelibly labeled Mohammad Reza Shah as an American puppet who owed his throne to his ability to please his foreign sponsors. The events also reinforced a deep cynicism in the nation's political culture. Many Iranians were now convinced that every evil in their society was the fault of the foreigner and that Iranians were not, and never could be, masters in their own house. Thus, as masters of nothing, they were responsible for nothing.

## Whose Oil? Whose Country?

The broad outlines of the oil crisis are well known. In the late 1940s, Iranian nationalists were expressing rising dissatisfaction with existing terms of the agreements between the Iranian government and the AIOC, the concession holder for Iran's southwestern oil fields since the original 1901 concession the Qajar rulers had given to the William Knox D'Arcy group. The group had discovered oil in Khuzistan, at Masjed-e-Soleiman, in 1908, and in 1914, on the eve of the First World War, the British government acquired a 51 percent share in what was then the Anglo-Persian Oil Company (APOC).

The APOC and the Iranian government, now in the hands of a new (Pahlavi) dynasty, renegotiated the terms of their agreement in 1933. That 1933 arrangement did not satisfy the Iranians, but with Reza Shah having personally approved its terms, there was little anyone could openly say against it. Even Hassan Taqizadeh, Iran's finance minister and leader of the delegation that negotiated the agreement, claimed that it was signed "under duress."[2] The main features of the 1933 agreement were as follows:

---

2. Bill, *The Eagle and the Lion*, 61.

- The area of the original concession was reduced from 500,000 to 100,000 square miles.
- Iran received a royalty of 4 shillings per barrel produced with an guaranteed minimum annual payment of £750,000.
- APOC was to pay 4 percent tax to Iran with a guaranteed annual minimum of 230,000 pounds.
- APOC agreed to move more Iranians into managerial and technical positions.
- APOC was exempted from all taxes not imposed in the original concession.
- The term of the concession was extended for sixty years (until 1993).
- AIOC lost its monopoly on the transportation of oil.
- APOC paid Iran £1 million as settlement of all past claims.

It is worth noting that Iran and the APOC signed this agreement at a time of worldwide depression, when low world oil prices, depressed demand, and general economic difficulties put strong pressures on the Iranians to settle for less than they could have gained a few years earlier. In 1928–29, APOC chairman Sir John Cadman and Iranian court minister Abdul Hussein Teymurtash had negotiated an arrangement that would have given Iran 25 percent of APOC shares—a revolutionary idea at the time. Although the British government approved that condition despite internal opposition, the Iranian side rejected it in the hope of getting a better deal.[3]

In any case, by the late 1940s the Iranians believed they were living with an oil agreement that was cheating them out of the benefits of their country's enormous natural resources. Even worse, the sixty-year extension of the agreement and the cumbersome procedures for resolving disputes made it appear that the Iranians had little recourse and were stuck with the terms of a bad bargain, made with AIOC under the most disadvantageous circumstances.

During and after World War II, the Iranians had played their oil card with some skill, particularly in the case of securing Soviet withdrawal from occupied Azerbaijan. In 1948, Venezuela signed a fifty-fifty oil profit-sharing agreement; in Saudi Arabia, ARAMCO was to do the same two years later. In Iran, the perceived injustice of the 1933 agreement remained a festering sore,

---

3. Ibid., 59–60. Bill's Iranian and British sources both considered the 1928–29 arrangement as a lost opportunity, which, had it been accepted, could have defused much of the subsequent bitterness.

and, in 1948, the Iranian government presented the AIOC with a document covering six major areas of concern:[4]

- increasing the amount of revenue accruing to Iran;
- supplying the British navy and air force with oil at a concessionary price;
- Iran receiving its share of profits from AIOC operations outside Iran;
- Iran gaining access to AIOC records and accounts;
- improving the status of Iranian employees at AIOC; and
- revising the length of the concession.

In response to these and other concerns, in July 1949 the British and Iranian governments signed the Gass-Golshayan Agreement, which became known as the Supplemental [to the 1933] Agreement. Although this new arrangement did raise Iran's royalty from 22 to 33 cents per barrel produced, it did little to address those underlying issues that, in reality, had little to do with oil prices, royalties, or tax rates and much to do with larger, complex, and symbolic issues of Iranians' sovereignty, national pride, and perceptions of personal and national respect. Most basic to the dispute was the Iranians' view, right or wrong, that the British looked down on them as a people. Noting the all-important human and psychological side of the crisis, the historian William Roger Louis writes:

> The Iranians knew that the British regarded them as inefficient if not incompetent—even more, that the British thought of them as inferior human beings. This was a psychological reality that bore as much on the actual negotiations as the abstract debate about the validity of the 1933 agreement and the practical amount of compensation to be paid to the company.[5]

## Enter Mosaddegh: The Person and the Problem

Experts advise negotiators to separate the people from the problem and to avoid letting emotional issues and misperceptions cloud judgment. As Fisher, Patton, and Ury remind us,

> … people get angry, depressed, fearful, hostile, frustrated, and offended. They have egos that are easily threatened. They see the world from their own personal vantage point, and they frequently confuse their

---

4. Ibid., 61.

5. Louis, "Britain and the Overthrow of Mosaddeq." In Gasiorowski and Byrne, *Mohammad Mosaddeq and the 1953 Coup in Iran*, 149.

perceptions with reality. Routinely, they fail to interpret what you say in the way you intend and do not mean what you understand them to say. Misunderstanding can reinforce prejudice and lead to reactions that produce counter reactions in a vicious circle; rational exploration of possible solutions becomes impossible and a negotiation fails. The purpose of the game becomes scoring points, confirming negative impressions, and apportioning blame at the expense of the substantive interests of both parties.[6]

In 1951–53, however, the British side (and eventually the Americans as well) came to see the person—in this case Iranian Prime Minister Mohammad Mosaddegh as the center of the problem. Thus the disagreement, as Fisher, Patton, and Ury would have foreseen, became unsolvable. The British—even those who saw justice in the Iranian objections to the existing arrangements with AIOC—became obsessed with Mohammad Mosaddegh the person and concluded that he and his personality—not issues of oil royalties, taxes, ownership, accounts, and so on—were at the center of the dispute. The result was exactly as predicted above—a vicious circle of clashing emotions, misunderstandings, and reciprocal misperceptions.

Mosaddegh himself, originally known by his Qajar aristocratic title of Mosaddegh al-Saltaneh came from the same wealthy patrician lineage as his cousin and five-time prime minister Ahmad Qavam. Born in 1882, he earned a law degree in France and Switzerland and served as minister of finance and governor-general of Fars and Azerbaijan provinces near the end of the Qajar period in the early 1920s. He was elected to the Fifth and Sixth Majleses, and, as a deputy in 1925, opposed Reza Khan's accession to the monarchy as Reza Shah.

Excluded from politics during the reign of Reza Shah (1925–41), Mosaddegh, like many other veterans of the pre-1925 political battles, returned to the arena after Reza Shah's abdication in 1941. Reentering the Majles, he sponsored the 1944 oil law, which forbade Iranian officials from discussing oil concessions with foreign governments or companies while foreign troops remained on Iranian soil. That law later was crucial to the outcome of the 1945–47 Azerbaijan crisis. Mosaddegh's legislation both helped to secure the departure of Soviet troops and gave the Iranian parliament a legal basis for rejecting Prime Minister Qavam's April 1946 oil deal with the Soviets.

In October 1949, Mosaddegh led a group of political figures protesting irregularities in the elections for the Sixteenth Majles. This group became the nucleus of the National Front (*Jebheh-ye-Melli*), a coalition of parties and

6. Fisher, Patton, and Ury, *Getting to Yes*, 19.

people centered on Mosaddegh and acknowledging his leadership. Mosaddegh himself avoided becoming the leader of a specific political party, but many key Front members came from Qavam's Democrat Party or from the Iran Party, a party of socialist ideology with a middle-class professional base. Although the former party became unimportant after 1949, the latter became a crucial element of the National Front. In its original demands, the Front did not mention oil or the AIOC but instead concentrated on domestic issues of free parliamentary elections, ending martial law, and freedom of the press.[7]

The National Front contained disparate elements of widely varying economic and social outlook. It included extreme nationalist groups, such as Mohsen Pezeshkpour's Paniranist Party and Dariush Foruhar's National Party; it included the social democrats and technocrats of the Iran Party; it included Mozaffar Baqa'i's Toilers' Party (*Hezb-e Zahmatkeshan*), which advocated an anti-Soviet leftist program; and it included Islamic groups (under the leadership of Ayatollah Kashani), which advocated support for Palestinian causes and for a greater role for religion in public life. Noting how the National Front combined contradictory (modern and traditional) trends in Iranian society—with widely differing values and outlooks—the scholar Ervand Abrahamian writes,

> The traditional middle class frequented bazaar teahouses, rarely wore Western ties, and colloquially used Arabic terms learned from the scriptures, whereas the modern middle class ate in European-style restaurants, dressed meticulously in Western clothes, and sprinkled their Persian with French expressions picked up from secular education and avant-garde publications. In short, one was conservative, religious, theocratic, and mercantile; the other was modernistic, secular, technocratic, and socialistic."[8]

Mosaddegh was to unite these dissimilar currents around opposition to the Pahlavi dictatorship, around opposition to the AIOC, and, most important, around his own personality and charisma. In a political culture notorious for corruption and for politicians ready to sell themselves to the highest bidder, Mosaddegh's appeal lay in his outspokenness, his patriotism, his absolute incorruptibility, and his record of long and consistent opposition to Pahlavi authoritarianism. He was particularly famous for his refusal to

---

7. See Abrahamian, *Iran between Two Revolutions*, 251–61, for an excellent account of the formation of the National Front. The author also provides a table (254–55) showing the background and activities of the founding members.

8. Ibid., 260. It is worth noting that these two groups have remained uneasy allies in Iranian reform movements since the constitutional period of the early twentieth century.

award positions to or otherwise favor members of his extended family. According to his grandson Hedayatollah Matin-Daftari, "When the person with whom he was dealing was a relative, that person was considered last."[9]

Yielding to National Front pressure, the authorities agreed to restart voting in the Sixteenth Majles elections. In the new balloting, the voters elected eight members from the Front, including Mosaddegh himself, Toilers' Party chief Baqa'i, and Iran Party leader Allahyar Saleh. Although Mosaddegh's coalition held only 8 of more than 130 seats in the new parliament, the Front—thanks to its nationalist platform, the broad popularity of Mosaddegh, and British miscalculations and ineptitude—was to wield influence over Iranian political life far beyond what the coalition's limited numbers in the parliament would justify.

## Challenging the AIOC

In June 1950, the government of Prime Minister Ali Mansur submitted the supplemental (Gass-Golshayan) agreement with the AIOC to the new parliament for its ratification. Opposition to the agreement became a rallying cry for the small National Front Majles delegation, and even the proroyalist and pro-British members (who together constituted a substantial majority) were reluctant to risk acting on what was becoming an explosive issue. The National Front, calling the original 1933 agreement illegitimate, demanded nationalization of the oil industry and accused AIOC of ignoring commitments to hire more Iranians, of shortchanging the Iranian government on taxes and royalties, and of interfering in Iranian domestic politics.[10]

Mosaddegh had tapped into a deep strain of anti-British resentment in the Iranian middle class. The royalist Prime Minister Ali Mansur (who had been Reza Shah's last prime minister in 1940–41) sensed the growing anti-AIOC and anti-British sentiment, and refused to push for ratification of the supplemental agreement. Mansur himself resigned on June 26, 1950, and the shah replaced him with the strong-willed and independent-minded General Ali Razmara, who was determined to secure approval for the agreement from the Majles. Razmara apparently supported the supplemental agreement, not on the basis of any principle but because his government desperately needed the oil income that even a flawed, one-sided agreement would produce. He

---

9. Cited by Bill, *The Eagle and the Lion*, 55.

10. Abrahamian, *Iran between Two Revolutions*, 263.

also believed his survival in office required appeasing the British, whose primary concern was protecting their Iranian oil interests.[11]

The situation was deteriorating for both parties. On the Iranian side, growing anti-British feeling was preventing the Iranians from reaching any agreement over oil. On the other side, the British appeared oblivious to the new strength of Iranian nationalism and how the Iranians were focusing their hostility on the AIOC, its existing agreements with Iran, and, by extension, on the British as a whole. Many British officials, including some most distinguished Persianists, seemed incapable of empathy, of understanding the Iranian sense of grievance against decades of what they believed was unjust and unequal treatment.

When in late 1949 the Iranian minister of finance asked the British to modify the supplemental agreement before he submitted it to ratification, the British refused. They believed a fair deal had been agreed on, and opposition to it appeared to come from only a small, noisy group of troublemakers in the Majles. A few months later, in February 1950, the British began to wake up to Iranian realities and offered Prime Minister Razmara a cash advance for his government's expenses and informed him they were ready to negotiate an entirely new deal for a fifty-fifty sharing of income. The Iranians might have accepted this British offer a few months before. Now, however, events had gone beyond such arrangements, and Razmara, although still opposing nationalization, knew he could not accept the new offer and survive politically.[12]

Writing of this turbulent period, the political scientist Richard Cottam notes how mythology and wishful thinking had overtaken and obscured reality and good sense among all parties concerned.

> Modern Iranian history has more than its share of mythology; and Iran, the Soviet Union, and the Western powers seem to have been in wild competition for top honors in self-delusion. Since interpretations of the Razmara regime reflect this massive confusion, the objective historian of the period has great difficulty sifting the fact from the fiction of the various interpretations. Razmara was called reformist-minded, but the men whose elections to the Sixteenth Majlis were engineered by the Army, of which Razmara was chief-of-staff, were among the most reactionary in the Majlis. Razmara was called pro-West, but he did far more to accommodate Iranian policy to the USSR than did Dr. Mossadegh.[13]

---

11. Cottam, *Iran and the United States*, 90–91.

12. Ibid., 91.

13. Cottam, *Nationalism in Iran*, 209–10.

In response to Razmara's support for the supplemental agreement, the National Front attacked the prime minister and called for immediate nationalization of the oil industry. In so doing, the pronationalization forces were able to intimidate or convince enough members of parliament to oppose the prime minister's efforts and block ratification. Mosaddegh told a rally in Tehran that Razmara was not demanding enough of Britain and that "the conflict would not be resolved until the entire oil industry was nationalized." Ayatollah Kashani encouraged his followers to support nationalization, and, on March 7, 1951, a member of the Feda'iyan-e-Islam, a group associated with Kashani (but not with the National Front), assassinated Razmara in a Tehran mosque.[14]

Within two weeks of Razmara's death, both houses of parliament had approved an oil nationalization law. In April, after a six-week interlude during which the new Prime Minister Hossein Ala, although selected with National Front support, refused to execute the newly enacted law. Ala stepped aside, and with the approval of both the parliament and the shah, Mosaddegh became prime minister with a mandate to implement oil nationalization. In its pessimistic commentary on these events, *The Times*, reflecting the prevailing, condescending British view of Iranian politicians as utterly corrupt and self-serving and of Mosaddegh as obsessed by relentless and irrational Anglophobia, described the situation as follows:

> The inner tension of Persian society—caused by the stupidity, greed, and lack of judgment by the ruling class [presumably including the aristocrat Mosaddegh]—has now become such that it can be met only by an acceleration of the drive against the external scapegoat—Britain.[15]

## Positions Harden; Mediation Fails

Now the British and Iranians were moving into a classic downward spiral in which the objective for each side became not achieving gains through agreement but imposing its will and inflicting maximum damage on the other party. In July 1951, Mosaddegh broke off negotiations with the oil company in response to what he saw as AIOC threats. In September, the company withdrew its technicians and shut down installations, including the refinery at Abadan, and imposed an informal but effective boycott that prevented other companies from buying nationalized Iranian oil. The British

---

14. Abrahamian, *Iran between Two Revolutions*, 265–66. The author discusses the Feda'iyan-e-Islam on 258–59.

15. *The Times*, April 14, 1951. Cited by Abrahamian, *Iran between Two Revolutions*, 267.

government threatened military action, reinforced its naval presence in the Persian Gulf, and brought complaints against Iran to the United Nations Security Council.[16]

Thus by the end of 1951, Iran's dispute with the AIOC had become a full-scale international crisis in which both sides were dug into inflexible (and ultimately self-defeating) positions. The Iranians and the British had descended into what Roger Fisher calls "positional bargaining," in which each side tenaciously holds to a position, raises the emotional temperature, attempts to defeat or humiliate an opponent, and neglects to identify its own or the other side's underlying interests that could form the basis of a mutually beneficial accord. Fisher has noted that these kinds of sterile exchanges usually degenerate into one side's telling the other (in effect), "We may both suffer, but I will win in the end because there will be more flowers at my funeral than at yours."

Rather than dealing with issues and essential interests, Mosaddegh and the British chose to view each other as uncompromisingly hostile and then react accordingly. Each saw the other as an infinitely devious, crafty, and ruthless adversary that was determined at any cost to impose its will and humiliate the other side. In so doing, they both confirmed negative preconceptions and created self-fulfilling prophecies. For Mosaddegh and his National Front allies, the centuries-old British tradition of manipulating Iranian politics and politicians was an insidious, festering evil that they, as Iranian nationalists and patriots, were determined to end. For their part, the British believed that by Mosaddegh's insisting that the 1933 oil agreement—the basis of AIOC operations in Iran for almost twenty years—was illegitimate, he had become almost an existential threat. Not only was he ignoring signed agreements, but he was also, in effect, calling into question every aspect of the British political and commercial presence in Iran. Thus he was, they believed, threatening Britain's position in the entire region.

In July 1951, President Truman—in the face of both British and Iranian opposition—sent the veteran diplomat and troubleshooter Averell Harriman and the oil specialist Walter Levy to Tehran in a fruitless attempt to mediate this dispute between two of America's friends who seemed bent on mutual destruction. When Harriman met Mosaddegh, the former seemed caught off-guard by the depth of the Iranian's resentments and by his anti-British

---

16. According to Mary Ann Heiss in "The International Boycott of Iranian Oil and the Anti-Mossadegh Coup of 1953" (in Gasiorowski and Byrne, *Mosaddeq and the 1953 Coup*, 178), "The AIOC's boycott was part of a larger plan to destroy the Iranian government economically. . . ."

tirade (as recounted by interpreter Vernon Walters): "[Mosaddegh] looked at Harriman and said, 'You do not know how crafty they [the British] are. You do not know how evil they are. You do not know how they sully everything they touch.' " Harriman, perhaps unaware of the Iranian stockpile of historical grievances against the British, seemed to miss or deliberately ignore the prime minister's point. He replied that the British he knew were, like most people, a mix of good, bad, and in-between. Mosaddegh, who could not have cared less whether individual Britons were good or bad, continued, "You do not know them. You do not know them."[17]

The British, for their part, concluded that resolution of the crisis and preserving Iran's interests (as London interpreted them) would come only with Mosaddegh's removal from office. British Ambassador Sir Francis Shepherd, who held a low opinion of Iran and Iranians in general, saw Mosaddegh sitting on the fringe of irrational and lunatic behavior. Driven by stereotypes of decadent Orientals, Shepherd dismissed Iranian nationalism as a sham and seemed to believe that the country's shortcomings originated in a combination of innate character defects and a lack of sufficient British tutelage (i.e., direct colonization), an inadequacy that had prevented Iranians from developing a respectable (i.e., British-inspired) nationalist movement.[18]

Of greater consequence was that Shepherd's ignorance was the blindness of the British Persianists—knowledgeable scholars and observers who, through long study of Iran's history, culture, and language thought they understood the country better than its own people did. Although the analyses of this group—and Louis cites the names of Ann ("Nancy") Lambton, R. F. G. Sarell, Sam Falle, and Robin Zaehner—were more subtle that Shepherd's crude paternalism, the Persianists were breathtaking in their arrogance, and, in the last analysis, quite wrong. Implicit in their views was the assumption that they—along with a group of pro-British Iranian contacts they considered patriots—knew what was best for Iran and Iranians. These British experts admitted Mosaddegh's genuine nationalism, recognized the sources of his popular appeal, but also wrote him off as dangerously irrational and pathologically anti-British—characteristics that would, in their view, do damage to both Iranian and British interests. With all their knowledge and skill, these experts convinced themselves that the British government needed to help

---

17.   Walters, *Silent Missions*, 247–48. According to Walters' account, neither did Mosaddegh trust his own countrymen. When the British government sent a representative to negotiate, Mosaddegh, trusting neither a British nor an Iranian interpreter, insisted that Walters be the interpreter for those meetings as well, 256.

18.   Gasiorowski and Byrne, *Mosaddeq and the 1953 Coup*, 135–36.

reasonable, civic-minded Iranians (i.e., patriots) restore sanity and rid Iran of this unstable, troublesome, and demagogic leader.

Foreign Secretary Morrison appointed Zaehner acting counselor at the British Embassy in Tehran with the assignment to work for Mosaddegh's downfall, and the scholar Ann Lambton gave her advice from outside. The historian William Roger Louis summarizes Lambton's views as follows:

> Lambton believed that revolution might be averted because certain patriotic and intelligent Iranians held views that coincided with British concepts of national self-interest based on effective and responsible government, professional integrity, and respect for the rule of law. Yet they would be regarded as traitors if they publicly denounced Mosaddegh. Hence there was a need for covert cooperation with those public-spirited Iranians who would work toward reform in concert with the British.[19]

Louis also notes how this academic's views of Mosaddegh influenced those Foreign Office officials. In particular, he cites the anti-Mosaddegh opinions of Eric Berthoud, the assistant undersecretary of the foreign office supervising economic affairs.

> [Berthoud's opinions] usually reinforced the judgment of Nancy Lambton, who characteristically urged the Foreign Office to boycott Mossadegh as far as possible and to deal with him only when necessary to preserve public order … She still held, as she had from the time of Mosaddegh's ascendancy, that it was impossible to negotiate with him because his entire position was based on anti-British sentiment.[20]

Such attitudes die hard. A participant at a 2002 UK conference on the Mosaddegh period said he found some of the elderly British participants had not changed their patronizing views of Iranians. Their views, he noted, had remained unchanged since 1951. They knew what was best for Iranians at that time; and fifty years later, they still did.[21]

## Collision Course: From Rigidity to More Rigidity

All sides became victims of competing and contradictory pressures. Some Iranian opponents of Mosaddegh urged their British Embassy contacts not to make any settlement with him because doing so would increase his domes-

---

19. Ibid., 131.

20. Ibid., *Mosaddeq and the 1953 Coup*, 137.

21. Malcolm Byrne, personal interview, Washington, D.C., February 25, 2008.

tic popularity and strengthen his political position.[22] Mosaddegh himself was torn between his desire to claim a victory over Britain and his fear that members of his own coalition would denounce any agreement he reached as a betrayal. For its part, Washington urged restraint on both sides but was unable to find a settlement and unwilling to apply serious pressure on Britain to be more flexible in the face of Iranian nationalism. If the United States had applied such pressure, it is unclear how long London could have resisted.

In the end, however, it became irrelevant who was at fault in these futile exchanges. The rigidity of one side reinforced that of the other, and it became impossible for either side to retreat from its most extreme demands. Mosaddegh must have been well aware that the British regarded him as an irrational, xenophobic, and mendacious representative of a degenerate Iranian aristocracy. Beyond all that, he and many of his countrymen also understood how the British had long regarded Iran and most Iranians with contempt. Those patronizing attitudes (or Mosaddegh's perception of them) strengthened his certainty that Iran's salvation lay less in the details of a new oil agreement than in freeing itself politically and psychologically from British domination, specifically in breaking the economic and political power of the AIOC and in undoing its immoral and illegitimate agreements with previous Iranian governments. Therefore, there could be no settlement until Britain recognized, implicitly or explicitly, that the existing arrangements ignored the just claims of Iran.

On the British side, what they thought they saw in the Iranian nationalists made them more inflexible. The Iranian prime minister's vitriolic anti-British rhetoric, his refusal to accept what they considered a reasonable compromise settlement with AIOC, his refusal to negotiate in good faith, and, perhaps above all, his ingratitude for Britain's positive historical role in Iran, all made stronger their determination to insist on their maximalist demands. Furthermore, Mosaddegh's ("mad Mossy's") attitude convinced them that this xenophobic Iranian leader's remaining in power not only prevented a settlement, but constituted a danger to Britain's vital interests in Iran and the entire region. Such an obvious and irrational ingrate had to go. As James Bill writes:

> The British felt their influence in Iran was benign and that without English technological support Iran would have remained a backward desert land. Their many interventions in the past had served to protect Iran from its aggressive Russian neighbor to the north. Therefore, even some of the

---

22. Katouzian, "Mosadegh's Government in Iranian History," in Gasiorowski and Bryne, *Mosaddeq and the 1953 Coup*, 6.

most learned of the "old Persian hands" in Britain professed horror at the
ingratitude displayed by Mosaddegh and the Iranian nationalists.[23]

Prime Minister Clement Attlee's socialist government, which had nationalized much of British heavy industry, could not well oppose the Iranian oil
nationalization on principle. Neither Attlee's foreign secretary, Herbert
Morrison, nor AIOC chairman Sir William Fraser, however, were able to
understand the new realities in Iran or the underlying Iranian resentments
against what many saw as centuries of spiteful, overbearing British behavior. Nor could these officials look beyond the law book or the balance sheet
to understand how their attitudes were fueling anti-British feelings among
Iranians. Bill describes Fraser as having "the background of an accountant
and the mindset of a ledger."[24] They simply could not accept the fact that
Iranians could hold, based on more than a century of history, legitimate
grievances against the British or that the AIOC might need to bend in the
face of Iranian nationalism.

Britain would not back down from its insistence that Iran accept one of
two principles: either retreat from nationalization and negotiate a new concession, or compensate AIOC for oil the company would have extracted until
1990, only three years short of the original expiration of the 1933 agreement.
As for the first principle, once nationalization was approved, it became impossible for the Iranians—of any political stripe—to return to a concession
agreement, no matter how favorable. In fact, the British envoy Richard Stokes,
in the summer of 1951, offered (and Mosaddegh rejected) terms of a new
concession that were more favorable than the consortium agreement the
Iranians were eventually to sign in 1954. As for the second (compensation)
principle, although the Iranians were willing to pay compensation for AIOC
assets, they would never accept the terms of the detested 1933 agreement as
its basis.[25]

Against this unpromising backdrop of mutual suspicion and hostility,
Mosaddegh came to the United Nations in the fall of 1951 to argue Iran's
case. He also met with American officials, including President Truman and
Secretary of State Acheson. Neither he nor the British, however, were in any
mood to propose a settlement that the other side would accept. Working with

---

23. Bill, *The Eagle and the Lion*, 64.

24. Ibid., 74. Citing U.S. Assistant Secretary of State George McGee, Bill also reports,
Fraser's assertion that "one penny more and the company [AIOC] goes broke," 72.

25. Katouzian, "Mosaddeq's Government in Iranian History," in Gasiorowski and Byrne,
*Mosaddeq and the 1953 Coup*, 7–9.

Assistant Secretary of State George McGee, Mosaddegh drew up a proposal to the British that specified

- forming a national Iranian oil company responsible for exploration, production, and transportation of crude oil;

- selling the Abadan refinery to a non-British firm that would recruit its own technicians;

- AIOC's establishing a purchasing organization to buy, ship, and market Iranian oil;

- establishing a fifteen-year life of the contract and setting a minimum annual production of 30 million tons; and

- setting the price of crude by Iranian-British negotiation, with a maximum of $1.10 per barrel.[26]

By this time (November 1951), the British had changed governments, and the now-ruling Conservatives, fearing the loss of British influence implicit in the above terms, rejected the McGee proposal. A proposal for World Bank mediation by restoring production and export of Iranian oil collapsed when the Iranian side, fearing its domestic opponents would accuse it of selling out to the West, insisted the Bank should state in such an arrangement that it was acting as an agent of the government of Iran. The British side would never agree to such a condition, which would require it to recognize implicitly the legality of the nationalization before there was a compensation agreement. In New York, Harriman sent Vernon Walters to visit Mosaddegh in the Premier's Hotel for a last-ditch effort to persuade Mosaddegh to agree to a settlement. Walters told Mosaddegh that, despite all the hopes raised by his visit, he would be returning to Iran empty-handed. Walters records Mosaddegh's response as follows:

> He looked at me shrewdly and said, "Don't you realize that, returning to Iran empty-handed, I return in a much stronger position than if I returned with an agreement which I would have sell to my fanatics." I was satisfied that he simply did not want to reach an agreement at that time.[27]

---

26. Gasiorowski and Bryne, *Mosaddeq and the 1953 Coup*, 77. According to Stephen Kinzer (*All the Shah's Men*, 129–30), the proposal came from McGee and Acheson, and both Mosaddegh and the British rejected it—the former because it kept operations and management in foreign hands; the latter because it seemed to legalize expropriation of British property.

27. Walters, *Silent Missions*, 262.

## Endgame: A Desperate (and Losing) Bet

There are multiple questions around Mosaddegh's negotiating stance. Did he believe that his interest and his political survival lay in prolonging the crisis and avoiding a settlement? Did he believe that his National Front coalition would fracture if he agreed to a settlement that was anything less than a complete British surrender? Did he believe the British, desperate for Iranian oil, would eventually give in to Iranian demands? Did he misread the American government's position and believe that the United States would back Iran indefinitely (or at least remain neutral) and would eventually pressure Britain into accepting Iranian terms?

Did Mosaddegh in effect commit political suicide by refusing to settle? The scholar Mark Gasiorowski believes that "[Mosaddegh's] foolish actions in 1951 caught up with him in 1953."[28] In reality, the prime minister's calculations may have been more perceptive than they appear. Whatever his motivations for not settling the dispute, the failure of American mediation and the stalemate of 1951 did not, in the short term, bring about his government's collapse. His domestic position remained strong, and the British, despite their oil boycott and threatening moves, did not resort to military action against what they considered the illegal seizure of a British company's property. After his empty-handed return from the United States, he continued in power for nearly two more years. During that time he survived in office despite an intensified British (and later American) campaign against him, defections from within his National Front coalition, an abortive attempt to replace him as prime minister (by his cousin, the veteran Ahmad Qavam) in July 1952, and growing economic dissatisfaction from the country's loss of oil revenue.

In March 1953, Mosaddegh rejected a proposal by American Ambassador Loy Henderson—a proposal that still called for compensation until 1990. In response, Mosaddegh did retreat from his previous call to base compensation on the market value of AIOC property and agreed to World Court arbitration if the British would declare its maximum compensation demand in advance. The two sides remained far apart, and the British rejected this proposal.[29]

---

28. Private communication, February 2008.

29. Katouzian, in Gasiorowski and Byrne, *Mosaddeq and the 1953 Coup*, 9. It is worth noting in that same month President Eisenhower gave his blessing to America's joining the British project to overthrow Mosaddegh (Kinzer, *All the Shah's Men*, 157–58).

By the time of the infamous coup of August 1953, by all calculations Mosaddegh should have fallen easily, given the economic and political problems he confronted. His oil cards were a pair of deuces—the world oil markets had found other (mostly Arab) sources to replace the missing Iranian oil. Mosaddegh himself had been playing a dangerous and ultimately losing game with the Americans who, having failed to mediate a settlement, told the British in March 1953 that the CIA was ready to discuss a joint operation to overthrow Mosaddegh and the National Front. In early April the CIA allotted a million dollars for its Tehran station to use in any way that the station chief and the ambassador agreed to bring about the fall of Mosaddegh's government.[30]

Mosaddegh, unable to exploit American interest in Iranian oil to break the power of the AIOC, must have perceived Washington's growing hostility. He made a bad situation worse, however, when, in a desperate bet, he posited an implicit threat of a Communist takeover of Iran in a May 28, 1953, letter to President Eisenhower. The latter's coldly worded response, broadcast on the Voice of America, seemed clear evidence of what many suspected: that the Americans had already come around to London's position that Mosaddegh was dangerously unstable and had joined the British in working for his downfall. After Eisenhower's letter was published, Richard Cottam describes Mosaddegh's situation as follows:

> All Iran knew that Mosaddegh gambled and lost in his attempt to force the United States into active support. Here was the cue for the fence sitters to leap as far from Mosaddegh as possible ... Still he persisted with the gamble he had already lost.[31]

The Americans were now privately working for Mosaddegh's overthrow and publicly announced they had lost confidence in him. The shah and his allies, for their part, were concerned by the prime minister's efforts to limit royal prerogatives and suspected he was working for the complete abolition of the monarchy. Mosaddegh also faced defections of some crucial National Front allies—including Ayatollah Kashani, Toilers' Party leader Baqa'i, and nationalist Hossein Makki. The British Embassy claimed that their agents, the Rashidian brothers, were responsible for these key defections.[32] Beset on

---

30. Wilber, "Overthrow of Premier Mosaddegh," 3. According to one veteran U.S. foreign service officer, the State Department's political officers in Tehran were reporting vicious, personal attacks on Mosaddegh in the Iranian press without realizing that their colleagues in the CIA station had planted those very stories.

31. Cottam, *Nationalism in Iran*, 224–25.

32. Kinzer, *All the Shah's Men*, 159.

multiple fronts and with his National Front coalition weakening, Mosaddegh grew more suspicious and autocratic. His support in the streets seemed to come increasingly from pro-Tudeh demonstrators, a development that further increased alarm in Washington. The continuing oil boycott was crippling the Iranian economy, and the government was unable to pay its bills or meet its payrolls.

On May 20, 1953, the American administration specifically authorized the Tehran station, in addition to the general authorization noted above, to spend up to a million Iranian riyals a week (about $11,000) to buy the cooperation of members of the Seventeenth Majles.[33] As these efforts continued through the summer of 1953, Mosaddegh found himself facing increasing problems from the legislature. The prime minister became embroiled in a dispute with the Senate and opposition delegates in the Majles over his reform proposals and extension of emergency powers that had allowed him to rule by decree for six months. In response to this resistance, the National Front deputies resigned en masse and thereby deprived the lower house of a quorum and its power to legislate. In July 1953, in the absence of a functioning Majles, Mosaddegh called for a national referendum to ratify his various reform measures. The results of the voting were a suspicious 99.99 percent favorable. Faced with many enemies determined to overthrow him, Mosaddegh was no longer the moderate who insisted on upholding the law and the constitution. Abrahamian describes the new, radical, and populist Mosaddegh as follows:

> Mosaddegh, the constitutional lawyer who had meticulously quoted the fundamental laws against the shah, was now bypassing the same laws and resorting to the theory of the general will. The liberal aristocrat who had in the past appealed predominantly to the middle class was mobilizing the lower classes. The moderate reformer who had proposed to disenfranchise illiterates was seeking the acclaim of the national masses.[34]

## Failure and Success

When his opponents struck in August 1953, however, Mosaddegh, despite all that both his foreign and domestic enemies had done to undermine him, was not an easy victim. The first actions of the coup plotters—a coalition of army officers, pro-British politicians, royalists, and American CIA operatives—went badly awry. Colonel Ne'matullah Nasiri, who was supposed to deliver the shah's decree dismissing Mosaddegh and replacing him with General

---

33. Wilber, "Overthrow of Premier Mosaddegh," 18–19.

34. Abrahamian, *Iran between Two Revolutions*, 274.

Fazlollah Zahedi (and arrest the former) on the evening of August 14, did not act until the following evening, by which time Mosaddegh's government had learned about the coup and acted to stop it. Instead of arresting Mosaddegh, Colonel Nasiri found himself under arrest when he attempted to deliver the shah's decree.[35]

On the morning of August 16, it appeared that the coup attempt had collapsed. Pro-Mosaddegh forces patrolled the streets of the capital and began arresting those suspected of involvement in the attempt. Zahedi went into hiding at the house of a CIA officer. Zahedi's son and other plotters took refuge at the American Embassy. The shah himself, fearing for his life, fled the country without telling either Zahedi or the CIA team, travelling first to Baghdad and then to Rome. National Front Foreign Minister Hossein Fatemi and other Mosaddegh supporters called for the shah to abdicate. The next day, Kermit (Kim) Roosevelt, head of the CIA's coup team in Tehran, received instructions from CIA headquarters to leave Iran as soon as possible. He began to make plans for his own departure and for that of Zahedi and some other participants in an American defense attaché aircraft.

Despite these initial setbacks, the foreign and Iranian coup makers did not give up. By August 19, they had organized anti-Mosaddegh elements in the army and among Tehran street mobs. It is also believed that provocateurs had encouraged pro-Tudeh mobs to tear down statues of the shah and demand an end to the monarchy. The CIA reportedly channeled money to Ayatollahs Kashani and Behbehani and publicized the shah's original decree dismissing Mosaddegh and appointing Zahedi in his place. The notorious gang leader Sha'ban Ja'fari ("Sha'ban the brainless") also organized anti-Mosaddegh demonstrations among the mobs of south Tehran. Pro-Mosaddegh and pro-Tudeh demonstrators were nowhere to be seen that day, and by late afternoon, anti-Mosaddegh army units had defeated those units that remained loyal and had continued guarding the prime minister's home. By the end of the day, Zahedi had broadcast a message on state radio, and Tehran was firmly in anti-Mosaddegh hands. The shah returned to Tehran on August 22.[36]

---

35. This account follows that of Mark Gasiorowski, "Coup d'Etat Against Mosaddegh," in Gasiorowski and Byrne, *Mosaddeq and the 1953 Coup*, 227–60.

36. There are differing versions of exactly what happened and what led to the turnaround between August 16 and 19. I have followed Gasiorowski's account, Gasiorowski and Byrne, *Mosaddeq and the 1953 Coup*, 251–56, appropriately subtitled "From Failure to Success."

## The Person Is Gone: The Problem Remains

The British, the Americans, and their Iranian friends had now removed the person they saw as the cause of their difficulties. Just overthrowing Mosaddegh, however, still did not resolve the dispute over control of Iran's oil resources. That resolution would come only after very tough two-stage negotiations: first between American oil companies and the AIOC (now renamed British Petroleum [BP]); then between the combined foreign interests (called the consortium) and the Iranians. An Iranian source described the former set of talks as "a tug of war between the avarice of William Fraser [chairman of BP/AIOC] and the acquisitiveness of the major [non-British] oil companies."[37] By forming a consortium—an idea that Walter Levy had presented in the summer of 1951—the companies could, in effect, address (or appear to address) a major Iranian grievance—the AIOC's monopoly control of Iranian oil and that company's identification as an instrument of British policy in (and domination of) Iran.

When the American expert and later Undersecretary of State Herbert Hoover Jr. first approached the Iranians in the fall of 1954, he urged that BP retain a majority share of the consortium. The Iranian negotiators—including Manuchehr Farmanfarmaian and Dr. Hosein Pirnia—rejected this proposal. Given the history of AIOC in Iran, they argued, the Majles would never approve such an arrangement.[38] Eventually, the original consortium included the following members: British Petroleum (40 percent); five American major companies (8 percent each totaling 40 percent); Royal Dutch Shell (14 percent); and Compagnie Française des Pétroles (6 percent). Later, independent American companies protested, each of the five majors gave up 1 percent of its shares to a group of independents collectively known as Iricon.

Representatives of the international consortium and Iranian negotiators—this time led by Finance Minister Ali Amini (another Qajar aristocrat who would become prime minister in 1961)—met in Tehran in April 1954 and reached an agreement in August. The negotiations centered on three principles: (1) With or without Mosaddegh, the nationalization of Iranian oil could not be reversed. Nationalization was a fait accompli of enormous symbolic importance. (2) AIOC-BP's monopoly control of the Iranian oil industry could not continue. As noted above, diluting that company's preeminent position was also of great symbolic importance for the Iranian side. (3) The Iranians

---

37. From Fathollah Naficy, cited by Bill, *The Eagle and the Lion*, 105.

38. Farmanfarmaian and Farmanfarmaian, *Blood and Oil*, 302.

should pay some form of compensation to the British company for its facilities and its lost revenue.[39]

As for the settlement itself, it was a mixed outcome for Iran. Its main features, as outlined by James Bill, were as follows:

- The basic ownership rights of the National Iranian Oil Company (NIOC), originally claimed after the original nationalization in 1951, were recognized.

- The NIOC was put in charge of the distribution of all petroleum products—gasoline, kerosene, and so on—in Iran's domestic market.

- NIOC took over operations at the small western Naft-e-Shah oil field and the nearby Kermanshah refinery.

- The consortium operating companies managed operations within the rest of the agreement area—basically the area of original APOC-AIOC concession.

- Foreign trading companies bought from NIOC all oil produced except what Iran used for domestic consumption.

- Complex royalty and tax arrangements brought the Iranian government, in effect, 50 percent of the profit on oil sold abroad.

- Iran would pay AIOC-BP about $70 million compensation over ten years, and the other participating foreign companies would also reimburse AIOC-BP for their shares of former AIOC holdings.[40]

## Judging the 1954 Agreement

Given the events that preceded the agreement, it is doubtful that Iranian nationalist opinion would have supported any deal signed by the government installed by the August 1953 coup. The consortium agreement, however, did provide some important benefits to Iran. It ended the British boycott, brought increased government revenue, and preserved the important principle of Iran's nationalization and control (albeit incomplete) of the country's resources. The importance of the last became apparent in the years

---

39. Bill, *The Eagle and the Lion*, 105–06.

40. Ibid., 108. According to Farmanfarmaian and Farmanfarmaian (*Blood and Oil*, 306–07), BP made out very well on the compensation deal, receiving more than $600 million from the other partners in the consortium for their 60-percent interest.

after 1954, when the NIOC was able to negotiate agreements for areas outside the consortium's limits with terms more favorable for Iran.

On the negative side, although appearing to break the AIOC's monopoly, the agreement left a group of foreign oil companies in control of a large part of the Iranian oil industry. Many Iranians believed that NIOC's ownership of Iran's oil resources was purely symbolic, and the real power over these resources remained in foreign, if not entirely British, hands. As one Iranian expert noted, the agreement gave "NIOC the impression it was somehow involved, even though it really wasn't."[41] Although the hated label "concession" was gone, the new consortium, for all intents and purposes, still operated like a traditional concession even though the resources the consortium extracted, transported, and sold officially belonged to the NIOC. This feature did not escape the notice of Iranians. As James Bill observes,

> From the Shah on down, the Iranians were not pleased with this agreement. Even Ali Amini often admitted that the consortium agreement was not what Iran deserved or needed, since the control still existed in the hands of foreigners. On the other hand, it was the best agreement Iran could have gotten given the time and circumstances.[42]

In the longer term, creation of the NIOC had some very positive consequences for Iran. The company hired and trained Iranians in management and technical positions, a subject that had been a festering Iranian grievance against the AIOC. Within a few decades, manpower in the oil sector was almost entirely Iranian, operating with a high level of expertise and competence. Beginning in the late 1950s, NIOC also provided scholarships—by competitive examination—for young Iranians to study technical subjects abroad (mostly in the United States). These students were to become a highly trained cadre who contributed to Iran's development in the 1970s. The economist Feridoun Fesharaki writes of NIOC:

> Perhaps the most significant consequence of the nationalization was the creation of the NIOC. The NIOC was the first national oil company in a major oil-producing country. Its immediate task of taking over the domestic distribution of the oil products in Iran … contributed greatly to the material well-being of the country and its economic development by providing cheap energy and expanding its distribution network. As a young company, it observed the operations of the Consortium and gradually obtained a great deal of experience and knowledge.[43]

41. Farmanfarmaian and Farmanfarmaian, *Blood and Oil*, 313.

42. Bill, *The Eagle and the Lion*, 109.

43. Fesharaki, "Development of the Iranian Oil Industry," 59–60. Cited by Bill, *The Eagle and the Lion*, 110.

## The Lessons: Dealing with History and Preconceptions

In the last analysis, however, almost everyone lost in this sorry history of the oil nationalization crisis and the August 1953 coup. Whatever the objective merits of the subsequent agreement, Iranians would always see the 1954 oil agreement as tainted by its association with foreign intervention in Iranian politics and by the view that the great powers were determined, by means fair or foul, to prevent Iranians from taking control of their own resources and their own destiny. Many Iranians concluded that powerful outsiders and their self-interested Iranian allies had frustrated yet another Iranian effort to assert national dignity, limit absolutism, and put the country on the road to democracy.

The effects of the events on American-Iranian relations were profound and tragic, as the United States had, in Iranian eyes, betrayed their country's hopes. For their part, Britain and Russia had never pretended to be anything but the semicolonial masters of Iran. The United States, however, had pretended otherwise and had then revealed a treacherous face when it went from being a supporter of the country's independence to a new master (albeit an inept one), dictating to Iranians according to Washington's (and some would say London's) requirements and demands.

In the years after the CIA coup, American officials seemed blind to the implications of their actions. They seemed unaware how the United States had discredited both itself and those Iranians—from the shah on down—with whom it associated. Now everything the shah did, for good or evil, was interpreted as done in obedience to American commands. Even when the shah apparently opposed an American position, a cynical public opinion dismissed his actions as a charade. Subsequent American administrations seemed oblivious to how Iranians viewed these events and to the resulting resentments that simmered below a surface of smiles and politeness. When, for example, the Americans pressed the Iranian government for what the former called a technical modification of the existing Status of Forces Agreement in 1963–64, the issue exploded into a major domestic crisis that Ayatollah Khomeini, until then a marginal figure in Iranian political life, skillfully exploited to establish credibility among the nationalist heirs to Mosaddegh's tradition. Addressing this issue in a speech of October 22, 1964, Khomeini said,

> A law has been put before the Parliament according to which we are
> to accede to the Vienna Convention, and a provision has been added
> to it that all American military advisers, together with their families,

technical and administrative officials, and servants—in short anyone in any way connected to them—are to enjoy legal immunity with respect to any crime they may commit in Iran.

If some American servant, some American's cook, assassinates your senior clergyman in the middle of the bazaar, or runs over him, the Iranian police do not have right to apprehend him! The dossier must be sent to America, so that our masters there can decide what is to be done.

[The Iranian government has] reduced the Iranian people to a level lower than that of an American dog. If someone runs over a dog belonging to an American, he will be prosecuted. Even if the Shah himself were to run over a dog belonging to an American, he would be prosecuted. But if an American cook runs over the Shah, the head of state, no one will have the right to interfere with him.[44]

Provoked by this explicit defiance, the shah sent Khomeini into exile eight days later. Inspired by this cleric's outspoken defense of Iranian honor and sovereignty, many Iranian nationalists—for whom the events of August 1953 were still fresh—were willing to ignore the antidemocratic and obscurantist strains in their new hero's rhetoric. For that oversight they would later pay a very high price when the Islamic Revolution—soon after its victory—turned against them and their values.

However all sides deal with this bitter legacy of 1953, there are important lessons for negotiators in these events.

**Inequalities between the two sides created contradictory perceptions**. What one side saw as a negotiation, the weaker (Iranian) side saw as an attempt to dictate conditions. In this case any agreement or compromise for the Iranians became surrender. During the oil nationalization crisis, the Iranians were well aware that they could not deal on equal terms with the AIOC and the British government. Nor did the British see the Iranians—whom they had dominated for centuries—as equals who could expect a major change in traditional arrangements. Noting how the British insisted the Iranians accept at least one of two unacceptable conditions—granting a new concession or paying compensation until 1990—Homa Katouzian writes,

Neither of the two alternative British demands—another concession or compensation for operations until 1990—would have been made, let alone succeeded, if Britain's dispute had been with Holland, Sweden, or any other small European country. It was clear that Iran's position was weak, not on legal grounds, but in terms of the country's relative world power.[45]

---

44. For the full text of Khomeini's speech, see Khomeini, *Islam and Revolution*, 181–88.

45. Katouzian, in Gasiorowski and Byrne, *Mosaddeq and the 1953 Coup*, 10.

The British also seemed genuinely confused when the Iranians refused to behave as a weaker side should and insisted on remaining ungrateful for past British beneficence. The British, including even some distinguished scholars of Iran who should have known better, could only explain the Iranians' attitude as a defect in their national character, as further evidence that Mosaddegh and his colleagues needed to be replaced by responsible Iranians, and as yet another manifestation of oriental mendacity.

**History matters**. In this case negotiators ignored it with disastrous results. The Iranian side approached this dispute not only as an effort to obtain better terms from AIOC but as an attempt to address grievances and correct the historical wrongs stemming from centuries of British domination. The British, in Iranians' view, had long meddled in Iran's domestic affairs and had cheated and exploited Iran both in the original 1901 D'Arcy oil concession and, later, in the oil agreement of 1933. When Mosaddegh made his famous characterization of the British to Harriman ("you don't know them"), he was not criticizing individual Britons but giving his view of Britain's negative place in Iran's unfortunate past. In that sense, Mosaddegh and his allies were seeking not only to negotiate a better oil deal but to realign the whole Iranian-British relationship and thereby correct the injustices of Iranian history. Such an attitude appeared to lead Mosaddegh into insisting on a settlement that was absolutely fair (in his view) instead of one that reconciled the interests of the two sides.

For the British—and to some extent for the Americans—there seemed to be almost no empathy for how Iranians' saw their own history and for how they saw the British role in that history. The British, and eventually the Americans, came to write off Mosaddegh as dangerous, as a captive of his own anti-British rhetoric, and as obsessed with the British to the point of irrationality. In that sense, Harriman's reaction to Mosaddegh's blanket condemnation reveals a larger failure: the failure to understand how the Iranians' view of their past was shaping their actions and pushing them into unreasonable positions.

**The Iranian side sought an abstraction called justice**. The parties were unable to find objective criteria as a basis for negotiations. The two sides in this dispute were working from completely different starting points, and, for that reason, could not establish the all-important objective criteria, acceptable to both sides and free of emotional overtones, against which to measure a settlement. Neither side could accept the standards of the other. The British side emphasized compensation for lost revenue and carrying out existing agreements. The Iranian side's criteria were achieving justice by correcting historical wrongs. In such a setting, it should have been expected that American mediation would fail. The two sides' positions were too far apart and based on different assumptions.

The British side, and eventually the American mediators, came to see the Iranian insistence on justice as too subjective and too absolute to be a basis for a settlement. After all, what did justice mean? It was too imprecise a term for Western lawyers and accountants. The British came to see it as a cover for unreasonable Iranian demands and for Mosaddegh's desire to use Britain as a scapegoat for Iran's troubles. In the accounts of the crisis, there are few indications that the British side attempted to get behind this language and deal with the Iranians' sense of grievance. Nor did the Iranian side realize that by insisting on justice as a goal it was putting a negotiated settlement beyond reach. Finally, there is little evidence that either side made an effort to move beyond its initial positions—which became more inflexible over time—and work with the other to establish those objective standards essential for a successful negotiation.

**The parties ignored Roger Fisher's principle. They could not separate the person from the problem**. Both sides in this dispute came to personalize the issues between them to an extent that reaching agreement became impossible. Each side saw the other as the embodiment of evil and duplicity. For the British, Mosaddegh himself was the problem. How, they asked, could one deal with him when he refused to see reason, rejected any compromise settlement, ignored signed contracts, reneged on yesterday's agreements, used Britain as the scapegoat for his own failures, and played to the extremists in his National Front coalition? In a strange symmetry, Mosaddegh, expressing the sentiments of many of his countrymen, saw the British in a similar way. How, he asked, could one reach an agreement with those who would not negotiate in good faith, refused to acknowledge the simple justice of Iran's position, insisted on maintaining their stranglehold on Iran's wealth, bought and sold Iranian politicians, and used all means fair or foul to dominate Iran as it would its colonized territories?

Holding such views, both sides became trapped in a vicious circle of misperceptions, emotions, and distortions. Strong feelings of mutual dislike and distrust blinded both Britons and Iranians to their own interests. Both sides missed opportunities for settlement because their goal became not securing their interests but humiliating the other side, whom they had demonized beyond all recognition or rationality. In fact, humiliating the other side and forcing it to submit to unacceptable conditions—not negotiating a beneficial agreement—became the goal of the whole encounter.

In this contest in which all sides were eventually losers, the increasing distrust and negativity became a self-fulfilling prophecy. Each side understood well how the other saw it. The Iranians were smart enough to know that many British officials viewed them with contempt, as corrupt, uneducated, emotional savages, for whom reason, truth, rationality, and law were alien concepts. Similarly the British certainly perceived how Mosaddegh and the nationalists were painting them as infinitely evil, duplicitous, patronizing, domineering, greedy, and the source of all of Iran's problems. These views would feed on each other. Understanding the other side's perception (or misperception), each side would harden its position and rationalize its self-destructive actions by saying: "You see what they are like? You see how they hold such a distorted view of us? They are evil, and we are obviously right not to trust them."

## Turning Over the Board

Little good could emerge from such an impasse brought on by the parties' shared blindness. The crisis of 1951–53 was not only a failure of negotiations; the events contained many tragic subplots, large and small. One tragedy was that the British side felt it had the option and the right to go outside the process of negotiation to overthrow an Iranian government it regarded as intransigent and on which it could not impose an agreement. Fisher might say that because the British negotiators' BATNA included eliminating Mosaddegh and the National Front, they could insist on conditions they knew the Iranians would never accept. Rather than play the game by the rules, the British would turn over the board. An even greater tragedy was that the British convinced their American allies—who early in the crisis seemed to understand Iranian nationalism and to be making a good-faith effort to resolve a dispute between two of Washington's friends—to join London's efforts against the Iranian nationalists.

The result was that after the 1953 CIA coup, the American government and the shah—for better or for worse—were stuck with each other. After 1953 many Iranians, particularly those who had supported Mosaddegh's nationalist coalition, came to see the United States as their enemy responsible for all the shah's excesses and all they disliked about his regime. Analy-

zing the anti-American currents in 1970s Iran and the anti-American fury
that boiled over during and after the Islamic Revolution, the scholar Homa
Katouzian writes:

> What mattered most was the very strong emotional conviction—for
> which the starkest and the most deprecated evidence was the 1953
> coup—that western imperialism was behind every decision of the
> modern arbitrary state [i.e., the Pahlavi monarchy] . . . .

> The reality of the deep anger against the United States in particular can
> hardly be underrated. And there were many reasons for it. But the central
> reason was that it was known as the power that overthrew Mosaddegh's
> government in 1953, and it was wrongly perceived to be the real power
> behind, and the daily instructor of the absolute and arbitrary state.[46]

Overthrowing Mosaddegh may have helped solve the oil nationalization
crisis and rid America and her British friends of an Iranian annoyance. But
so doing also would poison relations for decades to come between Iranians
and Americans—now no longer identified as Iran's beneficiaries but as the
new colonizers and powerful supporters of the shah's arbitrary rule.

---

46. Gasiorowski and Byrne, *Mosaddeq and the 1953 Coup*, 23–24.

# 4

# The Embassy Hostage Crisis of 1979–81

*It is useless to attempt to reason a man out of what he was never reasoned into.*

—Jonathan Swift

When Americans and Iranians deal with each other today, there is symmetry in their respective views of recent history. Each side sees itself as the injured party, as victim of the other's unacceptable actions, which it may denounce as treachery, terrorism, hegemony, or by some other uncomplimentary name. Two crucial events have created this persistent mutual hostility. In the Iranian view, the central event, described in the previous chapter, is the oil nationalization crisis and its climax in the CIA-sponsored coup d'etat that overthrew Prime Minister Mosaddegh in August 1953. That action gave Iranians twenty-five years of royal dictatorship, more than fifty years of grievance, and the conventional wisdom that America, which Iranians once regarded as their supporter against historical colonial powers, had assumed Britain's traditional role as the controller, the puppet master of Iran and Iranians.

In the American case, the comparable event is the hostage crisis of 1979–81. Like the 1953 episode for Iranians, that crisis still casts its long shadow over how America and Americans view Iran. The event lurks behind some American analysts' Nazi metaphors for Iran and descriptions such as rogue state, axis of evil, Iranian threat, and world's number-one state sponsor of terrorism. Ask many Americans what they associate with the terms "Iran" and "Iranian," and, even if they are too young to remember the hostage crisis, they will recall images and stereotypes associated with it: fanaticism, violence, irrationalism, self-destruction, and disregard for the norms of international relations. In response, many Iranian-Americans now identify themselves as "Persians," preferring an association with carpets, culture, and cats (putting the purr into Persian) to all the awfulness that Iranian suggests.

One may question the similarity of these two events. Many Iranians would argue that there are few parallels. The embassy hostage crisis, they claim, was merely a speed bump for the United States—albeit one exaggerated by incessant media coverage that one observer called a combination of soap opera and freak show. On the other hand, they say that the 1953 coup had profound, long-term effects for Iranians. That episode, they argue, solidified the power of an absolutist regime, provided fifty years of grievance, and frustrated—for the umpteenth time—Iranians' attempts to gain control of their national destiny.

There is considerable merit in this argument. The crises of 1953 and 1979 were not the same. Such a comparison, however, misses a crucial point. Whatever the reality of these two events and whatever their relative importance in the cosmic scheme, both still influence, in the most negative way, how the United States and Iran view each other. The two crises have created national mythologies and explain much of the hostility, mistrust, fear, and suspicion that today pervade each side's view of the other.[1] The events also account for why it has been so difficult for the two governments to begin serious discussions, even on issues where interests coincide. For how can the two countries talk when the starting point for each is demonization of the other? And how can two sides talk when one side trivializes the other's sense of being victimized. Claiming "my disaster is worse than your disaster" is never a promising way to begin a dialogue.

Whoever has right on its side in this pointless argument over victimization, the events of 1979–81 illustrate how reciprocated misconceptions, misuse of intermediaries, failure to appreciate history, ignoring a BATNA, mistaking rhetoric for reality, and overplaying a hand can both create a crisis and prolong and intensify it when events pass out of the control of those nominally in charge of a country's affairs. Negotiation under such conditions becomes extremely difficult.

In the chaotic aftermath of Iran's revolution of February 1979, some crisis in Iranian-American relations may have been unavoidable. What was not inevitable, however, was that a series of mistakes and misjudgments would transform what began as a minor incident—a 1970s-style student protest and

---

1. Chapter 7 discusses how these perceptions affected a group of American undergraduates with no firsthand knowledge of these events.

sit-in—into a perfect storm, a major international crisis that would poison the atmosphere between Iran and the United States for at least three decades.

## Caught by Surprise

For twenty-five years, the United States had taken for granted Iran's status as an ally and semiclient state. Despite misgivings about Pahlavi repression, corruption, economic mismanagement, and brutality, for official Washington the shah remained the linchpin of America's anti-Soviet efforts in the Middle East.[2] At the beginning of 1978, there were few visible clouds on the shah's horizon. Despite some internal disaffection, to foreign eyes Iran appeared stable, and the shah's position appeared secure. Although poor planning and overspending of the crude oil windfall of 1973 caused economic setbacks, shortages, and imbalances, the country was still enjoying the benefits of high world oil prices, economic development was proceeding, and education was expanding. In her international relations, Iran had virtually no enemies. She had settled her boundary disputes with Iraq (at the expense of the Iraqi Kurds) and enjoyed good relations with all of the world's major powers, whose representatives flocked to Iran seeking lucrative commercial and military contracts. Israel had good relations with the shah's government, and Tehran's relations with her Arab and other neighbors, if not warm, were at least correct.

Of course there were signs of trouble, but the shah had faced worse problems before (notably the violent uprisings of 1963) and had survived. What escaped the notice of outsiders in the late 1970s was the shah's deteriorating health. Although French specialists had first diagnosed the shah's leukemia in April 1974, the American administration did not learn of his illness until October 1979.[3] More than a year before that revelation, reports that the shah was suffering from cancer or some other blood disease were circulating among diplomats in Tehran. In July 1978, a Soviet Embassy political officer asked his American counterpart about these rumors, and the latter dismissed

---

2. According to William Green Miller, a former foreign service officer who served in Iran from 1959 to 1964, there were many American officials with reservations about the shah both within the Tehran embassy and in Washington—particularly during the Kennedy administration. The linchpin argument, however, overcame all these misgivings. Interview, March 17, 2008, Washington, D.C.

3. Shawcross, *The Shah's Last Ride*, 230–32. According to Shawcross, at the insistence of the shah's Iranian physician, the French specialists at that time did not use the words "leukemia" or "cancer" but told the shah he had a blood complaint called Waldenström's disease—another name for the same thing.

them in his subsequent report, noting, "This rumor has abounded in many quarters and may be of Soviet inspiration."[4]

When the shah's downfall came, it came quickly. President and Mrs. Carter spent New Year's 1978 in Tehran. On New Year's Eve, the president toasted his royal host in the most flattering terms and referred to Iran as an island of stability in one of the more troubled areas of the world. Iran may have appeared to be that island, but just more than a year later, fierce political storms had shattered its surface calm. On January 16, after a year of escalating demonstrations and violence that his demoralized security forces could no longer control, the shah left Iran to the jubilation of most citizens.[5] Millions of Iranians were calling for the end of the monarchy, and just two weeks later they welcomed the return of the exiled Ayatollah Khomeini with massive demonstrations of support. Ten days later, on February 11, 1979, the last units of the armed forces supporting the monarchy collapsed, and the revolution had triumphed.

## A New Reality for Washington

*I'm sorry for the interruption, but this is a revolution.*

—Lawrence Ferlinghetti

On February 12, 1979, the party was over, and Washington woke up with a collective hangover. The shocks of the Iranian revolution—how such a strong ally could fall so far and so fast—seemed to knock American officials off balance and cloud their judgment about what was to follow. Although American analysis of Iran had never been very profound, after the revolution it became even more confused, congealing into a thick stew of wishful thinking and unalloyed hostility. Having failed to see the simmering discontent that lay below the placid surface and pseudodevelopment of the Pahlavi system, many American observers now missed the rage and the thirst for

---

4.  John Stempel, Memorandum of Conversation, Tehran, July 18, 1978. In Moslem Student Followers of the Line of the Imam, *Documents from the U.S. Espionage Den*, vol. 48, 76. Henceforth known as *Documents*.

5.  An enterprising real estate agent in Morro Bay, California, saw a chance for profit in the shah's troubles. In a letter to Ambassador William Sullivan dated December 7, 1978, the agent wrote, "In light of recent events in your area, it occurred to us that His Royal Highness [sic] might be interested in purchasing a **large** [emphasis in original] parcel of land (with home) in this country. . . ." *Documents*, vol. 7, 253. Included in the package was a brochure describing an estate of more than 9,000 acres near San Luis Obispo. I could find no record of whether Ambassador Sullivan ever passed the agent's letter to the shah.

revenge for real or imagined grievances that pervaded revolutionary Iran. The country's new masters were not in a forgiving mood.

Iranians of widely opposing political views—nationalists, Marxists, religious ideologues, and others—had formed a fragile coalition for the sole purpose of removing the shah. Now that he was gone, the real battle would begin. Americans, many of whom shared their Iranian friends' hopes for a more open society without the self-aggrandizing monarchy, failed to recognize the true balance and inherent conflicts among the forces that had made the victorious coalition.

American policy reflected the prevailing confusion. At one level, that policy, as stated by Washington's official representatives in Tehran and elsewhere, was to accept Iran's revolution and to build a new relationship with whatever regime succeeded the monarchy. The new leaders were hearing this message from multiple American sources. As late as the end of October, National Security Adviser Zbigniew Brzezinski, meeting with senior provisional government figures in Algiers, told them (in essence), "We will accept your revolution. We will recognize your country. We will recognize your government. We will sell you all the weapons that we had contracted to sell the shah. We have a common enemy to the north. We can work together in the future."[6]

Behind all this seeming pragmatism was a view that, given historical American interests in Iran and the country's wealth and strategic importance, something had to be salvaged from this new and chaotic situation. Iranian-American relations could never again be what they once were, but they could continue on a different basis if the two sides recognized that certain fundamental common interests had not changed. In the background of these ideas also lay imperial and Cold War rivalries—stated explicitly by Brzezinski—which for centuries had made Iran a major prize in great power competitions. In 1979—in the midst of the Cold War—for the United States to give up on relations with Iran was almost unthinkable. Doing so would have meant not only surrendering all American economic and cultural interests but abandoning more than three decades of anticommunist policy, declaring defeat, and leaving the political field to the Soviet Union.

On another level, however, the matter was not so clear. If Iranians were not going to forget the past, neither were many Americans. The shah had been Washington's ally for three decades. In that time, he had made many

---

6. From the speech of Defense Secretary Robert Gates, September 29, 2008, The National Defense University, Washington, D.C.

powerful American friends, some of whom he had rewarded generously for their support. These friends were ready to join his cries of "sellout" and "betrayal." At best, these friends argued, the shah was a victim of the Carter administration's ineptitude and its inability to formulate a coherent foreign policy. At the worst, the president had deliberately abandoned the shah in his time of need. At the same time, conditions in Iran did not encourage those Americans arguing for a fresh relationship with the new government. Seen from Washington, the view of Iran was not promising. The prevailing chaos, the vitriolic anti-American tirades, the dubious revolutionary justice and summary executions, and the suppression of women and ethnic minorities all made it hard to advocate a policy of patiently building connections based on the new realities.

## Extremists Raise Their Voices

Although some on both sides advocated restraint and patience, harsher, more dogmatic voices were drowning out voices of reason. In May–June 1979, Washington asked Tehran to approve officially (grant agreement) the nomination of career diplomat Walter Cutler as a new American ambassador. The nearly simultaneous congressional approval, however, of the nonbinding Javits resolution condemning the summary executions and other harsh practices of the Iranian revolutionary courts put another nail in the coffin of rapprochement. The Javits resolution provoked a firestorm in Tehran, where the provisional government reversed its early informal acceptance and rejected Cutler's nomination.[7] Having been turned down once, the Carter administration was in no hurry to name another ambassador. Bruce Laingen, American chargé d'affaires in Tehran, did not give up. Writing in early October, he reminded Washington that it was crucial to show unambiguously America's accepting the outcome of the revolution. He urged Washington to appoint a new ambassador as soon as possible and to seek, with or without an ambassador in Tehran, an early meeting with Imam Khomeini. Laingen told Washington,

> … As this embassy has recommended earlier, we believe we can and should find ways to speak publicly and positively more than we have to date about having accepted the change in Iran … What we need to say,

---

7.   The fact that Senator Javits's wife had worked for the Pahlavi Foundation did not escape the attention of the Iranians, who saw the resolution as directly tied to the shah's attempts to regain his power.

> in ways that we have not done, is that we have long-term interests in Iran that continue and which we believe can be preserved in an Islamic Iran.
>
> … There is the very large importance of the symbolic acts of seeing Khomeini and naming an ambassador. These actions are long overdue; they are central to the way [Foreign Minister Ebrahim] Yazdi and indeed most Iranians see our attitudes toward the revolution. If a new ambassador is to be further delayed, we recommend that we seek a meeting with Khomeini now at the chargé level. The timing will never be totally right; the action should no longer be delayed.[8]

Throughout the summer and fall of 1979, the situation in Iran was deteriorating on multiple fronts. The coalition that had made the original revolution was fracturing, and the heirs of Mosaddegh's National Front—many of whom held high positions in the provisional government—were losing influence day by day to parallel figures in a shadowy collection of Islamic groups. On one side power was falling into the hands of neighborhood *komitehs* (local vigilantes who maintained a sort of security); radical provincial clergy centered around Friday prayer leaders in the major cities; a so-called revolutionary council in Tehran; the revolutionary courts; imam's representatives and Islamic councils in universities, factories, ministries, and other institutions; and goon squads and street gangs ready to use direct methods of persuasion against misled rivals who thought that democratic rules might apply in postrevolutionary Iran.[9] Bands of vigilantes were seizing businesses, occupying buildings, intimidating opponents, and the nationalists and intellectuals of the provisional government were powerless to stop them. On another side, leftist groups were urging the authorities to take still more draconian measures against those considered feudals and counterrevolutionaries. There were violent clashes in many provincial areas, particularly in the Sunni regions of Kurdistan and Turkman-sahra.

The atmosphere in Tehran became increasingly toxic and hostile to those seeking some form of normality. The shouts of extremists on left and right were drowning out the voices of those who saw Iran's interest in establishing some kind of organized society and preserving orderly relations with the outside world. Calls to protect Iran's economic stability provoked Khomeini's scorn. In a speech of September 1979, he told Iranians, "Some have told me that the revolution is over and we must now protect Iran's economic infrastructure. But we did not revolt for economic infrastructure; we revolted for

---

8.   Laingen to State Department, Tehran Cable No. 10891, October 12, 1979. *Documents,* vol. 63, 126–27.

9.   In October 1979, at the University of Mashhad the saying was, "The [National Front] chancellor resigned; the [Islamist] vice chancellor refused to accept his resignation."

Islam." Khomeini and many of his closest allies saw such calls as a cover for policies that would allow traditional Iranian elites to keep their privileges at the expense of the deprived (*mostaz'afin*)—those in whose name Iranians had made their revolution.

Perhaps recalling Mosaddegh's failure to rally his followers in the streets against the coup makers in August 1953, these extremists now encouraged continuing turmoil on Tehran streets and in the provinces, believing that such ongoing chaos represented their best chance for neutralizing any attempt at a counterrevolution, for eliminating the old social order, and for consolidating their own power. Attempts to negotiate settlements in the Kurdish regions collapsed when thousands of armed non-Kurdish volunteers, in response to calls for popular action against so-called counterrevolutionaries, flooded into Kurdistan and destroyed delicate compromises with local groups. Those seeking to profit by ongoing turmoil continued stirring the pot and encouraging popular hysteria against real or imagined enemies.

This internecine contest over the future of the revolution was in reality never a contest. As faction battled faction, that group of religious radicals and ideologues who were closest to Khomeini's own thinking easily defeated their rivals. First to go under were the religious intellectuals and the nationalists, who had been useful during the revolution (particularly in talking to foreigners) but now found themselves outfought and outmaneuvered by radical clerics and their gangs of supporters. When it came to a test of strength, the middle-class and upper middle-class nationalist leaders had neither the stomach nor the talent for the violent and brutal street fighting that wins revolutionary struggles. These nationalists could write penetrating analyses, publish lively newspapers, and speak eloquently to their supporters of a new, pluralistic Iran free of the corruption and absolutism of the monarchy. Such talents, however, did not matter in the decisive street battles that would determine the fate of the revolution. Mosaddegh's heirs lacked the necessary organization and ruthlessness. They could not throw acid at uncovered women, beat up demonstrating students, or organize mobs to trash opposition newspaper offices. Their more brutal opponents, however, could and did do all of those things.

# Lighting the Iranian Tinderbox:
# It Seemed Like a Good Idea at the Time

By the early autumn of 1979 the situation in Iran was not calming down. It was getting worse. As instability grew, one could discern these trends among the conflicting political currents:

- The victorious revolutionary forces were turning on each other. Shadowy groups, such as the anticlerical Forqaan, were carrying out assassinations and other terrorist actions.[10] There were ongoing problems among ethnic minorities, particularly in the majority Sunni regions near the frontiers.

- The so-called spring of freedom (*bahar-e-azadi*), the euphoric period of open debate and discussion that immediately followed the revolution, was coming to a close. Whoever was in authority was tightening the circle of permitted speech and debate. Whatever system was going to emerge from Iran's political contest, it was unlikely to be open, democratic, or pluralistic.

- The National Front veterans and Muslim intellectuals who occupied the key posts in the new provisional government of Iran were losing their grip. Ministers held almost no authority beyond the doors of their own offices. Extremists on both left and right were challenging the provisional government's authority with impunity, and Ayatollah Khomeini himself seemed to have lost interest in supporting Prime Minister Bazargan and his nationalist ministers.

- Members of Iran's educated middle class were very uneasy about what they were witnessing. They sensed the hostile direction of the political winds. There were long lines of middle-class, well-educated visa applicants, including many members of clerical families, outside the American Embassy. Whatever their ostensible reasons for travelling, in reality many of these applicants were finding Iran increasingly inhospitable to their values. Even those serving in major government posts were considering leaving and were looking for the insurance policy of an American visa in their passports.

---

10. For more on the violent, anticlerical group Forqaan, see an interview with the former judge Abd al-Majid Ma'adikhah in *Shahrvand-e-Emruz*, April 2008. Ma'adikhah claims he was the chief judge of a panel that sentenced the leaders of Forqaan to death.

- The revolution had not brought Iranians the promised paradise. Some-one had to be responsible for its failure to arrive and for the continuing turmoil, shortages, and other difficulties faced by ordinary citizens. All of these failures created the need for scapegoats. The conspiracies of American imperialism and its Iranian agents were obvious ones, and the media, especially state radio and TV under the leadership of Sadeq Qotbzadeh, produced a regular drumbeat of anti-American tirades. Even the so-called moderates of the provisional government, seeking to validate their credentials as true revolutionaries, joined the anti-American chorus.[11]

If American policymakers were counting on the office-holders in the pro-visional government—such as Foreign Minister Ebrahim Yazdi and Prime Minister Mehdi Bazargan—to moderate the harsh spirit of the times, Yazdi's October 1979 performance in New York in meetings with his American coun-terparts should have dispelled any such notions. Those talks made it clear that the provisional government officials were riding the back of an angry tiger—one that would eventually devour them. Describing Secretary of State Cyrus Vance's talks with Yazdi, Assistant Secretary of State for Near Eastern Affairs Harold Saunders writes,

> The conversations with Foreign Minister Yazdi in New York brought home to the American participants the difficulty of communicating with Iran's new leaders. Yazdi had spent almost a decade in Texas. Those of us who sat … with Secretary Vance and the Foreign Minister anticipated an Iranian polemic, but we thought that it might be possible, because of Yazdi's American experience, at least to communicate with him in private conversations. In the conversation with Secretary Vance, he returned again and again to the theme of American culpability for all that Iranians had suffered under the regime of the Shah.
>
> Later, in a private conversation with Yazdi and his colleagues … for two hours we heard out Iranian views about the causes of the revolution and repeatedly asked, "How can we develop our relationship now?" Yazdi and his colleagues turned every issue into a litany of complaints about the past sins of the United States.[12]

---

11.  State Department to Embassy Tehran, State Cable 253952, October 8, 1979, and Lain-gen to State Department, Tehran Cable No. 10091, October 12, 1979. *Documents*, vol. 63, 122. Writing about Foreign Minister Yazdi's abrasive performance at the United Nations, Laingen notes, "Yazdi's purposes [were] to create, for his own psychic and personal political purposes the impression of the Islamic revolutionary as a new breed of man demanding to be heard on the world stage."

12.  Harold Saunders, "The Crisis Begins," in Christopher, *American Hostages in Iran*, 55–56. Vance was reportedly so disgusted at Yazdi's attitude that he did not, as planned, present the Iranian with the name of America's new ambassador-designate, the Persian-speaking William Miller.

Given the conditions of the time, developing the relationship was not, in Roger Fisher's memorable phrase, a yessable proposition. Even if doing so were to Iran's long-term benefit, dealing with American representatives on the basis of shared interest in a continuing relationship exposed the already vulnerable Iranian negotiators to charges of sellout and betrayal. Yet Fisher's principle still worked, although at a different level. Saunders noted that when the Americans asked Yazdi to meet with experts to discuss American military supplies to Iran, Yazdi readily agreed and conducted those meetings in a professional manner free of the rhetoric and posturing that had marred his earlier political exchanges with Vance and Saunders.

In October 1979, was anyone with authority in Washington aware of the dangerous realities in Tehran? Apparently not, judging by the decisions made at the time. Such had not been the case, however, eight months before. As early as February 22, 1979, while staying in Morocco, the shah had formally expressed interest in travelling to the United States. Perhaps affected by the mid-February armed attacks and seizures of the Tehran Embassy and the Tabriz Consulate, President Carter rejected National Security Adviser Brzezinski's advice and denied the shah's request. American ambassador William Sullivan gave his counsel from Tehran, saying that admitting the shah would destroy any hope of relations with the new Iran and "would confirm the worst suspicions of those Iranian revolutionaries who assumed that the U.S. was plotting to restore the shah to power."[13]

Throughout the spring and summer of 1979, the shah's American friends maintained the pressure on the Carter administration to admit the monarch. On July 26, the Department of State sought Tehran Chargé Bruce Laingen's views. Two days later, in a detailed and thoughtful message, Laingen told the Department:

> For us now to give refuge to the Shah would almost trigger massive demonstrations against our embassy. With luck, they may stop at that, without a physical assault of the kind we experienced last February. But there could be no assurance of that, since Iran's regular military and police forces remain largely demoralized and cannot yet be relied on to apply the force that might be needed to prevent violence against us.

Noting the political issues involved, Laingen continued:

> It is of the utmost importance, in my view, that we not involve ourselves in that process [establishing the authority of the provisional government] with any premature gesture toward the Shah, with all the suspicions

---

13. Cited by Harris, *The Crisis*, 164. Bill, in *The Eagle and the Lion*, 328–78, provides a detailed examination of the Pahlavi informal American network, which was able to bring consistent pressure for the shah's admission.

about our attitudes and about USG interference that this could arouse and the opportunity it would provide for those revolutionary hotheads who would probably like nothing better than a chance to frustrate the political timetable and take a crack at us at the same time.[14]

So there it was. Given the prevailing instability in Iran, the United States had a clear choice. It could continue the difficult work of reestablishing a relationship or it could admit the shah and say goodbye to its Tehran embassy, the provisional government, and the chance of establishing orderly American-Iranian relations on any basis.

In late September 1979, Joseph V. Reed, David Rockefeller's senior aide and liaison to the State Department, called Undersecretary of State David Newsom to report that the shah was seriously ill in Mexico and might need treatment in the United States. At the time Reed did not know the exact nature or gravity of the shah's condition. He sent to Mexico a physician and family friend, parasitologist Benjamin Kean, who at first could learn nothing about the shah's true condition. A few weeks later, however, Kean returned to Mexico and met for the first time the French cancer specialist Georges Flandrin, who had been treating the shah since 1974. On October 17, just before Kean's second trip to Mexico, Reed again called Newsom to say that the shah's condition had worsened and that he might have cancer. Kean's view—which Flandrin did not share—was that the shah's condition was so serious that he should come to the United States for treatment. On the night of October 18, Kean gave his opinion to the State Department's medical officer, and Reed made a parallel call to Under Secretary Newsom.[15]

The next day the president's advisers, now aware for the first time of the shah's medical condition, urged Carter to admit the shah. Even Secretary of State Vance, who had consistently opposed such a move, argued for admission on humanitarian grounds and as a matter of principle. The president found himself standing alone against those who argued for the shah's admission based on political principle, humanitarianism, and domestic political concerns. Although he gave in to the opinion of his advisers, Carter well understood the risks. Famously, he asked them, "What are you guys

---

14.  Laingen to State Department, Tehran Cable No. 7930, July 28, 1979. *Documents*, vol. 7, 273–74.

15.  The implication of Shawcross's and other accounts is that the shah's condition had remained secret from all but a very tight circle—his wife, his personal physician, and the French specialists—until October 1979. Not only were Carter administration officials ignorant of the illness, but the shah's American allies such as Kissinger, Rockefeller, and John McCloy were equally in the dark. Shawcross, *The Shah's Last Ride*, 242–49.

going to advise me to do when they overrun our embassy and take our people hostage?"[16]

The account of presidential adviser Hamilton Jordan makes it appear that President Carter did not make his final decision to admit the shah on that day but waited until after he had received a response from the Iranian provisional government, via the embassy in Tehran, guaranteeing the safety of our mission if the shah was admitted. The October 20 instructions from the State Department to Tehran on this subject were ambiguous, but the implied message was that Laingen was to inform the Iranians of the president's decision. The last paragraph reads,

> Report when message delivered via flash [highest priority] cable. Given deteriorating medical condition, we are planning for Shah's arrival here as soon as possible but will await your notification of delivery of message and Bazargan's reaction prior to making final decision.[17]

Despite the apparent hesitation in those words, in reality the U.S. government was telling both its own representatives and the Iranians that the final decision had been made. Laingen himself read the message that way, and on October 21, when he met (simultaneously) with Prime Minister Mehdi Bazargan, Foreign Minister Ebrahim Yazdi, and Deputy Prime Minister Abbas Amir-Entezam, he presented the Iranians with a fait accompli and told them, "[We] concurred in medical judgment that shah's condition required admission soonest to U.S. medical facilities." As for ensuring the security of the American mission in Tehran, the chargé received the less-than-reassuring response from PM Bazargan that "We will do the best we can."[18]

In reality, by this time the Iranians' opinion (and the opinion of Laingen and the American mission) didn't matter. If the administration had weighed (as Jordan's account implies) the Iranian reaction and the provisional government's commitment to provide mission security as factors in its decision, then it misread the following three important points:

---

16. Jordan, *Crisis*, 32. Almost all accounts of the events include Carter's question. I personally first saw it in an issue of *Time* that I was reading while tied to a chair in the embassy on November 6. You can imagine my reaction at that moment.

17. State Department to Laingen, State Cable No. 275001, October 20, 1979. *National Security Archives*, IR 03344.

18. Laingen to State Department, Tehran Cable No. 11135, October 21, 1979. *Documents*, vol. 7, 281. Bruce Laingen, in a March 2008 conversation, confirmed this version of events. In an October 20, 1979, memorandum to the president, Brzezinski had insisted that the Iranian government simply be informed of the U.S. government decision and that there should be no "implied request for permission from the Bazargan Government."

- The situation on the ground in Tehran—as reported clearly both by the embassy and the media—demonstrated that power had passed out of the hands of the provisional government into the hands of vigilantes and so called "revolutionary" institutions. Under those conditions, the assurances of provisional government officials were worthless.
- Although Prime Minister Bazargan had publicly complained to Iranian audiences that he was powerless ("a knife without a blade"), the officials of the Iranian provisional government—whatever their true capabilities— would never admit officially to American representatives that they were unable to protect the embassy. Asked a direct question about their ability to do so, rather than admit the uncomfortable truth, they would give an answer that would make it appear they were members of a functioning government capable of affecting events in the Tehran streets.
- Given the history of American-Iranian relations, the prevailing suspicions of American motives, the ongoing turmoil throughout Iran, and the perception that the United States had run Iran as a virtual colony for the past quarter century, few Iranians at any level were going to believe that Washington was acting from purely humanitarian motives to aid a critically ill shah. There were too many factors suggesting other, more devious motives. Thus, when Laingen informed the provisional government officials of the decision, he encountered great skepticism, particularly from Foreign Minister Yazdi. In the days that followed, the Iranian reaction would become increasingly negative.[19]

In making this decision, events suggest that officials of the Carter administration either did not understand the Iranian response or, having understood it, decided to ignore it.[20] In any case, in the early morning of October 23, 1979, the shah and his party arrived in New York. Twelve days later, on November 4, a mob overran the embassy as the provisional government officials watched helplessly and the police guards the Iranian government had assigned to protect the embassy disappeared. On that day, calls for help from the embassy to the foreign ministry and the prime minister's office elicited visa requests but no relief. President Carter's misgivings turned

19.  *Documents*, vol. 7, 281. See also Laingen to State Department, Tehran Cables No. 11371, October 28, 1979, and 11515, October 31, 1979, 288–90. Almost thirty years later, at a March 28, 2008 conference at Columbia University, I asked Yazdi directly, "At that time, did you believe the Americans' explanation about humanitarian motives?" His answer was simply, "Not for a minute."

20.  In late October 1979, Bazargan and his colleagues responded to Brzezinski's assurances in Algiers (see above) with the simple message, "Give us the shah." Robert Gates at National Defense University, September 29, 2008.

out to be correct, and now he and his administration were to pay the price of having ignored and misread Iranian reality.

## A Perfect Storm

What followed the embassy takeover was, in a sense, the culmination of decades—if not centuries—of Iranian humiliations real and perceived, of misunderstandings and misinterpretations by both sides, and of bitter factional struggles among Iranians holding competing visions of their own society and their own interests. By their own accounts, the students who overran the embassy had not intended to stay there for long. They planned to depart in a few hours or in a day after staging a sit-in and issuing defiant anti-American communiqués. The provisional government's Foreign Minister Yazdi himself assumed that his government, with the backing of Khomeini, could repeat its actions of February 1979 when it had expelled a group of leftist invaders from the embassy compound after a few hours.

In November, however, circumstances had changed, and they now conspired to create a very complicated state of affairs. Forty-eight hours after the initial attack, Khomeini had endorsed the takeover, Bazargan's provisional government had collapsed, and embassy staff members were still captives. The American side now found itself without anyone in authority in Tehran with whom it could negotiate, and the Iranian side found itself captive of its own angry rhetoric and unable to extricate itself from a situation that was doing serious damage to Iran's internal and external political standing. In Iran, these events gathered momentum, and a student sit-in, which should have lasted a few hours, now became a political tsunami from which no one was safe.

The components of this perfect storm were as follows:

- On November 5, the day after the attack, large crowds gathered outside the embassy walls to voice support for the occupation. Whether these demonstrations were staged or spontaneous, the students' act did strike a responsive chord in Iranian popular opinion. That response in the streets went much deeper than the shah's presence in the United States and the desire to bring him home for punishment. It was as though Iranians, long humiliated in their own country, were finally standing up for themselves after centuries of foreign domination and decades of American overlordship. Under such circumstances, the niceties of international law and the immunities of diplomats meant very little to those who saw themselves as historical victims and instruments of revenge.

- Ayatollah Khomeini, fearing that leftists—such as the Mojahedin-e Khalq Organization—would move to seize power and hijack his beloved revolution, sent his son Ahmad to the embassy compound to identify the students and their orientation. Khomeini did not want leftists to gain popular support through an anti-American action. Although leftist groups had been part of the original revolutionary coalition, in the summer and fall of 1979 they and the religious extremists were coming into increasingly open conflict both in Tehran and the provinces.

- Foreign Minister Yazdi visited Khomeini in Qom and argued that no government could function if this occupation were allowed to continue. According to Yazdi's account, Khomeini agreed and told the foreign minister to kick them out.

- When Khomeini learned about the crowds of demonstrators at the embassy and when his son told him that the occupiers were not the detested *jujeh-komunist* (mini-commies) but rather sincere young believers, he reneged on his instructions to Yazdi. On November 5, reassured that he was not facing a leftist power grab, unwilling to oppose what appeared to be a popular movement, with intense dislike for the American presence in Iran, and perhaps persuaded that he and his closest allies could exploit the attack to redirect the course of events in revolutionary Iran, Khomeini endorsed the takeover, calling it a second revolution perhaps greater than the first.

- Khomeini was willing to sacrifice the provisional government for the sake of revolutionary purity and mobilization. After Khomeini's endorsement of the students' action, Bazargan and his provisional government—now publicly discredited and powerless—resigned. Iran now lacked a functioning government and the United States—with its embassy staff captive in Tehran—had no one within the revolutionary power structure with whom it could communicate.

## A Message Undelivered

The American response to these events was to send a mission led by former Attorney General Ramsey Clark and Persian-speaking Senate staffer William Miller to Tehran with a letter from President Carter to Khomeini. That letter read,

> I ask that you release unharmed all Americans presently detained in Iran and those held with them and allow them to leave your country safely

and without delay. I ask you to recognize the compelling humanitarian reasons, firmly based in international law, for doing so.

I have asked both men [Clark and Miller] to meet with you and to hear from you your perspective on events in Iran and the problems which have arisen between our two countries. The people of the United States desire to have relations with Iran based upon equality, mutual respect, and friendship.[21]

Miller and Clark never reached Tehran and never delivered the president's letter. Their secret mission soon became public knowledge, and by the time they reached Istanbul, conditions in the Iranian capital had further deteriorated. Working through their contacts in Tehran and through the three American embassy officers sheltering at the Iranian foreign ministry, Clark and Miller were first told that the Iranians, fearing some kind of Entebbe-style rescue operation, would not allow the envoys' large presidential plane to land in Tehran. When they procured a smaller, U.S. military aircraft, they were told that no American plane could land. When they next arranged to fly to Tehran on a Turkish aircraft, they learned that their party was not welcome and that Khomeini had issued orders that no Iranian official could meet with them.

Miller and Clark did not give up and remained in Istanbul until November 15. From there they would call the offices of revolutionary council members Mohammad Beheshti, Sadeq Qotbzadeh, and Abu Al-Hassan Bani Sadr. Although those Iranian officials, following Khomeini's instructions, would not speak directly to the Americans, they conducted indirect conversations through secretaries and telephone operators who would give messages to their superiors (who were often sitting next to the phone). Although in terms of resolving the crisis these conversations led nowhere, they did convince Miller that Khomeini's action had started a new chapter in the ongoing power struggle in Tehran and that the situation with the captives would remain unresolved until that struggle had worked itself to a conclusion.[22]

## The Iranian Side: A Hand Overplayed

Now neither side could talk to the other. For the Americans, there was no one to negotiate with but Khomeini, and Khomeini was not interested in negotiating. The Iranian side could not resist the temptation to pursue

---

21. Quoted in Saunders, "Diplomacy and Pressure," in Christopher, *American Hostages in Iran*, 75–76.

22. Interview with William Miller, March 31, 2008, Washington, D.C.

*mard-e-rendi* behavior (see chapter 6) that is, outsmarting itself by tenaciously seeking short-term gains while ignoring larger issues and long-term consequences. In this case, the short-term gain was the opportunity for an extreme religious faction within the revolutionary coalition to use the embassy occupation to crush its opponents—be they nationalists, leftists, or traditional conservatives. The opportunity was simply too tempting to ignore.

By supporting and exploiting the takeover, this extreme faction could deploy its demagogues to stir up the populations' worst political instincts. The extremists proudly claimed to be publicly defying and insulting the United States. They denounced their Iranian opponents and anyone who questioned the takeover as liberals and compromisers who were ready to sell out Iran's interests to foreigners. These hated liberals and moderates, the demagogues insisted, were not going to stop Iranians from having their sweet revenge against America for decades of humiliation.

For their own purposes, the extremists and their student allies at the American Embassy organized a carefully measured political campaign. Cheered on by leftist groups (who thought they could ride an anti-American wave and failed to recognize that their turn would come very soon), they stirred up popular frenzy and made selective use of the documents found in embassy files to discredit their domestic enemies. In books and in the media, the students published dozens of volumes of their *Documents from the U.S. Espionage Den*, in which any Iranian opponent's contact with an American official—even on the most innocuous of subjects—elicited hysterical calls for his dismissal and worse. It soon became obvious that the United States was only an incidental target of the takeover, and that the real target were those Iranians who did not share the extremists' political views.[23]

In one sense, in the short-term the extremists' strategy of exploiting the takeover for domestic political purposes was successful. By the end of the crisis, they had mobilized a network of support and driven their Iranian rivals, both moderates and leftists, into the political wilderness. They pushed the Mojahedin-e Khalq into open opposition beginning in 1980 and defeated them in bloody street battles in 1981–82. In early 1981 President Bani Sadr—who, the Revelations showed, was the subject of an attempted CIA recruitment—was in retreat and a few months later, having been deposed, would flee for his life. A few months later Ali Khamene'i, a cleric and member of

---

23. For a detailed look at how the extremists used these documents, see John Limbert, "Nest of Spies." The selective revelations carefully targeted the hated liberals and omitted mention of important figures such as Ayatollahs Montazeri or Beheshti, who had also met with American officials.

the ruling inner circle, became president of Iran, and the clerical extremists were able to solidify their control over both revolutionary and republican institutions in the new Islamic Republic.

These domestic political gains for one Iranian faction, however, came with serious long-term losses for the majority. Although an elite of radical clerics and their allies consolidated power in Tehran, Iranian society as a whole paid a heavy price for this faction's success. On one side, the event created a pervasive climate of lawlessness, from which Iran has yet to recover. By supporting mob rule on the streets of Tehran, the authorities guaranteed that Iran would face decades of domestic turmoil in which the prevailing law would be mostly the rule of brute force.[24] The long-term effects have been corrosion of the norms of society and degradation of justice and security to the point that individuals and factions with the right political connections could get away with almost anything. They could murder, imprison, terrorize, and attack opponents with impunity. Almost twenty years after the takeover, when Mohammad Khatami was elected president in 1997, he and his administration's officials—for all of their brave talk about civil society and the rule of law—found themselves powerless against rivals who, guaranteed impunity by powerful backers, murdered intellectuals, journalists, and opposition politicians.[25] The extremists were playing by their own rules, and their message to fellow Iranians and the world was clear: "The president and his allies may say what they like about democracy and such things; real power, however, remains with us. Any questions?"

The event also created enduring instability in Iran's relations—both political and economic—with the outside world, particularly the United States. Although Khomeini defiantly proclaimed, "Why do we need relations with America?" the continuing abnormalities of no war, no peace with much of the world have put Iran at a permanent disadvantage in its foreign relations. Through its short-sighted actions, Iran needlessly made itself a dangerous long-term adversary—one that has remained consistently hostile and suspicious for thirty years. If not openly attacking Iran, the United States has done its best to make life difficult for the Islamic Republic and has made no secret of its desire for some other kind of regime in Tehran.

---

24.  Some historians have suggested that Khomeini himself encouraged continuing disorder to prevent a repeat of August 1953, when Mosaddegh had kept his supporters off the streets and thus left the field to his enemies and the pro-shah street mobs (see Chapter 3).

25.  In a further irony, some of President Khatami's reformist supporters—including his own brother—were among those who had attacked the embassy and had loudly denounced those who questioned their actions.

Iran, on one hand, demands respect from the world community based on its ancient glories and culture. As the writer Barbara Slavin points out, Iran believes it has become the Rodney Dangerfield of the Middle East—it gets no respect and can only watch with frustration as the Arabs get that respect that rightly belongs to Iranians.[26] At the same time, however, Iran seems not to care how it deals with at least some important members of that community from which it demands respect. When Iran has sought to do international business for important industrial projects, its isolation and unsavory recent past have meant that it has often had to pay premium rates to the shadier characters of world commerce and to second-rate contractors and financiers. Many of the respectable partners Iran sought for her development projects would have nothing to do with the country, and those that would do business with Iran were often those with whom Iran would normally not have chosen to deal. Open hostility from the United States—and reservations by other countries with advanced technology—have made Iran's developing its vital gas and oil resources more difficult and complicated than it would have been if Iran had not thumbed its nose at international respectability. American support for the Baku-Cayhan oil pipeline, which brings Caspian basin oil to international markets by a circuitous route that avoids Iranian territory, is just one example of the long-term costs of Iran's picking fights with Washington and others.

During the 1980–88 Iran-Iraq war, the Iranian people paid a steep price for their leaders' being *mard-e-rendi*, indulging in a collective temper tantrum, and showing their contempt for norms of international behavior. Likewise they paid heavily for their leaders' short-term pleasure at getting away with outrageous statements and actions. Although Iran, despite its provocative acts against Iraq, was clearly the aggrieved party and the victim of Iraqi aggression in 1980, almost no other country was willing to take Iran's side. With the Islamic Republic having made gratuitous enemies not only of the United States but of its own wealthy Arab neighbors, Saudi Arabia, Kuwait, and the UAE all became important financial backers of Iraq. Although the leaders of those Sunni Muslim countries did not admire Saddam Hussein and his brand of Arab nationalism, they feared the excesses of revolutionary Shiite Iran more. Choosing the lesser of two evils, they found themselves enrolled on Iraq's side as defenders of the Arab cause against a revolutionary and Iranian threat.

---

26. Slavin, *Bitter Friends, Bosom Enemies*, 13.

The same factors—particularly the Islamic Republic's diplomatic ineptitude—made other countries lukewarm at best to the Iranian cause. The Soviet Union, France, and other countries became major arms suppliers for Saddam, who was willing to spend his rich Arab neighbors' money for the cause. There was no rush to condemn the original Iraqi aggression in the United Nations. Nor did Iraq face strong international condemnation for using chemical weapons against Iranian troops or even its own Kurdish citizens. Prolonging the hostage crisis to achieve domestic political ends and for its symbolism of defying the United States became emblematic of Iran's lack of diplomatic skill and of its attitude that it could ignore international opinion. By the end of the war, an isolated Iran found itself fighting not only Saddam's Iraq but an international coalition that came to include the United States.

## The American Side: No Cards to Play

While the Iranians were overplaying their hand almost to the point of self-destruction, the Americans found themselves holding no cards at all. Whoever was in authority in Tehran was refusing to negotiate on any basis. The American administration knew what it wanted the Iranians to do, but it did not know how to persuade them to do it. The usual combination of pressure and incentives seemed to have no effect other than to provoke further gestures of defiance. In Assistant Secretary of State Harold Saunders' words,

> The President and his top advisers on November 4 and for months following were faced with the challenge of how to move those other human beings who were leaders in Iran—leaders with their own agenda and their own world view—to do what we wanted them to do. Our textbooks picture presidential decision-making in an international crisis as relating to major decisions involving such forces as balances of power. It is easy to decide in the abstract what ought to be done; it is much harder to move human beings to do it.[27]

Harvard Law School professor and negotiation specialist Roger Fisher, who himself spoke to Ayatollah Mohammad Beheshti during the crisis, has reconstructed the Iranians' decision alternatives in a way that suggests how they saw themselves having few incentives to settle and many not to settle. In Fisher's analysis of the Iranians' view of their situation, when the Iranian

---

27. Saunders, "The Crisis Begins," in Christopher, *American Hostages in Iran*, 47.

leaders posed the question, "Should we release the American hostages now?" their choices appeared as follows:[28]

**If we say yes:**
- We sell out the revolution.
- We will be criticized as pro-American.
- Iran backs down to the United States and looks weak.
- Iran gets no shah and no money.
- We do not know what the United States will do next.

**But**
- There is a chance that economic sanctions might end.
- Our relations with other nations, especially in Europe, may improve.

**If we say no:**
- We uphold the revolution.
- We will be praised for defending Islam.
- We get fantastic TV coverage to tell the world about our grievances.
- Iran stands up to the United States and looks strong.
- We have a chance of getting something (at least our money back).
- The hostages provide some protection against U.S. intervention.

**But**
- Economic sanctions will no doubt continue.
- Our relations with other nations, especially in Europe, will suffer.
- Inflation and economic problems will continue.
- There is a risk that the United States might take military action.

**However**
- The United States may make further commitments about our money, nonintervention, ending sanctions, and so on.
- We can always release the hostages later.

---

28. Fisher, Patton, and Ury, *Getting to Yes*, 46–47. Fisher calls these alternatives the perceived choice of an Iranian student leader. In fact, these were the choices not of the students but of those with the highest authority in Iran, including Ayatollahs Beheshti and Khomeini themselves.

With such a decision tree—or anything remotely like it—it is understandable why the crisis went on so long and why it was so difficult to influence the Iranians' course of action. To borrow another of Fisher's usages, the Iranians' saw their BATNA as more attractive than a settlement. In such a case, Washington saw any American action, such as a blockade or direct military action that might have influenced (i.e., lowered) the Iranian BATNA, as too dangerous and politically unacceptable. Whatever was acceptable—including appeals and attempts at mediation—seemed to confirm to the Iranian side the rightness of their position and give Khomeini the chance to indulge in some crowd-pleasing taunts, such as his famous "America can't do a damn thing"—an expurgated translation of a very vulgar Persian original.

For Washington, with few opportunities to influence those with authority in Tehran, downplaying the crisis, minimizing its importance, backing away from the controversy, applying quiet pressure and persuasion on Iran, and simply waiting out the Iranians might have been the best alternatives. In the setting of an Iranian bazaar, feigning indifference is usually a good tactic, and showing too much interest in a product will usually make the seller hold to his original price. Some analysts at the time recommended America adopt the Iranian practice of *qahr*—that is, of showing displeasure through refusing to communicate. In the American political and media context, however, such detached and reasoned approaches may not have been possible. Saunders argues that they were not.

> Members of the crisis team would later acknowledge that this argument [to downplay the crisis] may have some validity, but they also insist on recalling the mood in those first days after the takeover. Could the President have walked away from a crisis that had so thoroughly captured national attention? If President Carter were to have had the option of downplaying the crisis, media leaders would have had to find a way to reduce television coverage of events in Tehran . . . .
>
> Against this background, President Carter in his initial reaction may simply have been acting as Jimmy Carter—an outraged and concerned American who happened to be President.[29]

---

29. Saunders, "The Crisis Begins," in Christopher, *American Hostages in Iran*, 48–49. It is worth noting that President Reagan later attempted to minimize in public the importance of the American hostages held in Lebanon. That strategy, however, worked no better than his predecessor's.

## Stalemate and Frustration:
## From Zero Cards to a House of Cards

Until late summer of 1980, American attempts to affect events in Iran remained immobilized on the shoals of Iranian domestic politics, mis-judged attempts at mediation, and, in the case of the failed rescue mission of April 1980, faulty planning, bad luck, and poor weather. The American side's inability—whether imposed or self-imposed—to distance itself from the events meant that it was unwilling to wait out the ongoing political drama in Tehran. Instead, Washington could only grasp at straws and eventually found itself relying on intermediaries who were too far from the turbulent Iranian political mainstream to affect the course of events. When the frustrated mediators were unable to deliver on their promises, President Carter—feeling out of other options—approved a rescue mission (Operation Eagle Claw) with only the remotest chance of success.

In mid-January 1980, presidential adviser Hamilton Jordan learned through Panamanian contacts of two Paris based-lawyers—the Frenchman Christian Bourguet and the Argentinean Hector Villalon—who had been negotiating with Panama on behalf of Iranian foreign minister Sadeq Qotbzadeh. The ostensible subject of these negotiations was the shah's extradition from Panama, where he had taken refuge after leaving the United States in December 1979. Jordan learned, however, that when Panamanian officials visited Tehran to continue discussions with the two lawyers and meet with Qotbzadeh himself, they found that the Iranian minister quickly changed the subject from extraditing the shah to resolving the hostage crisis. According to the Panamanians, Qotbzadeh saw three possible ways of ending the standoff.[30]

- Through the death of the shah. Although Qotbzadeh believed the shah was dying, such an event could be months or even years away.

- Through a UN channel. If the United Nations organized an international tribunal on the crimes of the shah and recognized Iran's right to seek his extradition, such a step might be enough to allow Iran to claim victory over the United States and release the hostages.

---

30. Harris, *The Crisis*, 274. Qotbzadeh also told the Panamanians he would like to meet secretly with Jordan himself. Perhaps he could do so when he came to Panama to deliver personally Iran's extradition request. Although Jordan could not reply immediately, the two were eventually to meet during February 1980 in Paris to discuss the ill-fated scenario that was supposed to end the crisis.

- Through an Iranian-Panamanian channel. If the Panamanians simply initiated a process of extradition at Iran's request, that itself could give Khomeini the cover he needed to declare victory and order release of the hostages. The Panamanians judged that the shah was not the real issue in the crisis. They told Jordan that Qotbzadeh had said he knew they would never give up the shah; furthermore, in their judgment, the Iranians did not really want the shah returned.

Throughout January and early February, Jordan and Assistant Secretary of State Saunders met with Bourguet and Villalon to devise a scenario of timed reciprocal steps that would lead to a resolution of the crisis. As Saunders describes the agreement,

> The scenario that emerged from the talks with Bourguet and Villalon was a series of paired reciprocal steps, each pair including a move by Iran and a move by the United States, with the built-in opportunity to abort the process if either side elected. The first steps would be defined precisely; later steps could be outlined at the beginning but might have to be refined or changed as the situation evolved.[31]

The eventual scenario negotiated had three stages, each of which included several reciprocal actions and statements. The first stage would establish a United Nations Commission of Inquiry whose stated purpose was to visit Tehran to hear the grievances of the Iranians, meet with the hostages, and report to the secretary-general. In the second stage, the commission would take Iranian evidence in Tehran, meet with the American hostages, and prepare its report. When the report was ready, the commission would notify Iran's Revolutionary Council that the hostages should be released or at least moved out of the students' control. In the final stage, triggered by the transfer or release of the hostages, the commission would return to New York and submit its report. Then the hostages would depart, and Iran and the United States would both release prepared statements.

In late February, this elaborate house of cards began to collapse as soon as the parties attempted to put it into action. Perhaps the Americans should have been suspicious when Qotbzadeh remained evasive and noncommittal in response to Jordan's direct question about whether Khomeini had approved the negotiated scenario. Like the American rescue mission attempted three months later, the scenario was too complex for its chaotic environment. UN Secretary-General Kurt Waldheim began the cascade of

---

31. Saunders, "Diplomacy and Pressure," in Christopher, *American Hostages in Iran*, 122.

missteps when he departed from the agreed script, which had called for his presenting the commission as a response to Iranian demands that the international community hear its grievances. Instead, he announced that he had established the commission at American insistence. Thus, at the very outset, he had raised Iranians' suspicions of the group and its mission. To the Iranians, accepting it now took on the appearance of a diplomatic surrender to American pressure.

To make matters worse, on February 23, while the commission members were in the air between Geneva and Tehran, Khomeini's office issued a statement concerning the future elections for parliament. In that statement, Khomeini insisted it would be the people's representatives in the still nonexistent Iranian parliament who would have responsibility for resolving the issue of the hostages. Such a process could (and did) take months while Iranians held the required two-stage elections and the new parliament organized itself and chose a prime minister. The statement caught the Americans and both Iranian president Bani Sadr and foreign minister Qotbzadeh by surprise, but there was little choice but to let the work of the commission—about to land in Tehran—go forward.

Matters did not improve when the commission arrived in Tehran. It turned out that the UN secretary-general had left its members in the dark about the Iranian-American scenario, the real purpose of their visit, and the role of Villalon and Bourguet. The commission members expected to meet the American hostages on their third day in Tehran, but the students holding the embassy kept postponing the visit and resisting Qotbzadeh's demands that they allow the commission to make the scheduled calls. Qotbzadeh counterattacked by denouncing the students for defying the Revolutionary Council (Iran's acting government) and creating a state within a state. The frustrated commission members were prepared to leave March 5, but Qotbzadeh persuaded them to stay another twenty-four hours in the hope of rescuing the mission.

The next morning (Thursday), it appeared that the dam had finally broken. The students announced that they were yielding to pressure and asking the Revolutionary Council to take control of the hostages. If the students' gesture was a bluff, Qotbzadeh immediately called it and managed to receive what he thought was the endorsement of the imam and the council for the transfer. With the council unable to act on March 7 (a Friday holiday), the students used delaying tactics (e.g., demanding a letter from the president's office) while their supporters in the streets around the embassy launched noisy demonstrations opposing the transfer.[32]

The delays and the apparent popular opposition to the move—broadcast on national radio and television—undermined the imam's fragile support for the transfer. He dealt the whole tottering arrangement a deathblow on March 9, when his son Ahmad informed the Foreign Ministry that his father's silence on the transfer did not mean consent. The next day the imam issued a statement saying only that the commission could meet with the hostages after it had issued its report and if the report was judged satisfactory by Iran. He made no mention of transferring control of the hostages from the students to anywhere else. On March 11, the frustrated commission members left Tehran for New York, while in their wake Qotbzadeh and some of the student leaders engaged in a shouting match and a scuffle at Tehran airport.[33]

## Breaking the Stalemate: The Right Persons and the Right Time

The crisis continued without resolution through the spring and summer of 1980. The American rescue attempt failed in April of that year, and inside Iran the turmoil continued. In the two-stage parliamentary elections of February–May, the hard-line and ideological Islamic Republican Party (IRP), led by Ayatollah Mohammad Beheshti, won a strong majority and outmaneuvered President Bani Sadr, who found himself increasingly isolated. In response to what they claimed were fraudulent elections, the Mojahedin-e Khalq Organization accused the IRP of monopolizing power and of setting up a fascistic one-party dictatorship. In May, after the elections, the organization began a thirteen-month campaign against the Islamic Republic that reached its climax in assassinations, bloody street fighting, and executions in June 1981.[34] Tensions with Iraq continued to mount, and in July 1980 the authorities announced they had foiled a coup plot among officers of the Iranian Air Force. A bitter and disillusioned Sadeq Qotbzadeh resigned as foreign minister in August 1980.

---

32. A personal note: During February and March, using a stolen radio, I could follow the fiasco of the commission from inside the embassy. The demonstrations outside the embassy on the 7th and 8th (Friday and Saturday) had a hysterical tone and seemed much less disciplined than those we had heard previously. My guess was that there was considerable leftist presence among the demonstrators on those days.

33. The account of the aborted UN mission is taken from Harris, *The Crisis*, 305–17.

34. Abrahamian, *The Iranian Mojahedin*, 206–07.

At some time in August—after the death of the shah in Egypt—Khomeini decided that enough was enough. He reportedly told his closest confidants—excluding President Bani Sadr—to fix the problem. Many Iranian analysts now believe that Khomeini was never happy about the hostage taking, although he was certainly willing to exploit it. He believed that the students and their allies had painted him into a corner by mobilizing what appeared to be popular support for their action. Confronted by a wave of emotion, Khomeini decided to ride it rather than resist it. By August—with the shah no longer alive and with Khomeini's ideological allies gaining unchallenged control of the Islamic Republic's institutions—he apparently now felt he could quietly put his prestige behind a settlement.[35]

As he usually did, Khomeini left it for others to work out the details of a settlement, a process that was to take about five months of negotiations once Khomeini had made his decision. On September 9, the German ambassador in Washington told Secretary of State Edmund Muskie that Sadeq Tabataba'i, brother-in-law of Khomeini's son Ahmad, had contacted the German ambassador in Tehran seeking to enter into negotiations with American representatives to arrange the release of the hostages. According to Tabataba'i, only he, Khomeini, Ahmad, and Parliament Speaker Ali Akbar Hashemi-Rafsanjani were aware of this contact. If the German ambassador's report was accurate, this time the Americans were dealing with a different and more serious group that might be able to deliver on its commitments.

The German ambassador conveyed to Secretary Muskie three Iranian demands for release of the hostages and asked for a response within 48 hours. The three demands were

- unfreeze Iran's assets;
- commit to a policy of nonintervention in Iranian affairs; and
- attempt to return the assets of the late shah.

---

35. There are varying accounts of Khomeini's instructions. Although he is vague about the dates, former Iranian official Mohsen Sazegara told Voice of America Persian TV (in a November 4, 2007, special on the hostage crisis) that Khomeini told members of his inner circle—including his son Ahmad, Prime Minister Mohammad Ali Raja'i, and adviser Behzad Nabavi—to resolve the crisis because it was no longer in Iran's interest to prolong it. Nabavi—who was Sazegara's source for the account—said he told Khomeini that "we were stuck with the problem and that if we were going to solve the issue, we would need to soften some of our demands." Khomeini reportedly responded, "I don't know anything about that. Just solve it."

Notable for its absence from the list was any demand for an American apology for past events—a condition that the Iranians had previously insisted on and which Carter had adamantly rejected. The West German ambassador in Tehran had apparently convinced Tabataba'i to delete that last condition, persuading him it would lead to failure of the negotiations.[36]

The president authorized Deputy Secretary of State Warren Christopher to deal with this latest approach and to confirm that it was genuine. Recalling Khomeini's ambiguous attitude, which had led to the earlier collapse of the Jordan-Qotbzadeh scenario, Christopher told the German intermediaries he was willing to meet with the Iranian emissary, but before doing so he wanted an assurance that the Iranian representative would be speaking with full authority from the imam. The response from the Germans was that the Iranian contact (Tabataba'i) had told them within a few days Khomeini would publicly announce the following four conditions for the hostages' release:

- an American pledge not to intervene in Iran's internal affairs;
- return of frozen Iranian assets;
- cancellation of American claims against Iran; and
- return of the shah's wealth to Iran.

On September 12, Khomeini laid out exactly these four conditions as seeming afterthoughts to a long, rambling speech that had dealt mostly with domestic affairs.[37] After ten months of frustration, the American side finally seemed to be talking to the right people. On September 15 and 17, Christopher and Tabataba'i held secret meetings in Bonn, at which the two exchanged positions on such matters as commercial claims, resumption of military supplies, and transfer of the shah's assets. None of the specific issues presented insurmountable problems, and, on the issue of commercial claims, the American side proposed submitting both sides' claims to an international tribunal for arbitration. The talks were free of polemics, and the two envoys agreed to meet again in late September after consultations in their respective capitals. Christopher at that time believed that the Iranians were ready to settle with a minimum of formality.[38]

---

36. The account of this September 9 contact is from Harris, *The Crisis*, 384–85.

37. Roberts B. Owen, "Final Negotiation and Release in Algiers," in Christopher, *American Hostages in Iran*, 301–02.

38. Author's interview with Warren Christopher, December 13, 2007. Also Owen, "Final Negotiation and Release in Algiers," in Christopher, *American Hostages in Iran*, 306. Telephone interview.

The outbreak of the Iran-Iraq War on September 22, 1980, ended the Christopher-Tabataba'i contact, but the two had laid the groundwork for the eventual settlement. In Tehran, a parliamentary committee began work on the hostage issue, but there was little progress through the rest of September and October. On November 2, just before the American presidential elections, the parliament approved its version of Khomeini's conditions for the release. The Iranian government asked Algeria, its protecting power in Washington since U.S.-Iranian relations had been broken in April, to deliver its conditions. On November 3, the Algerian ambassador Redha Malek brought the Iranian conditions to the State Department in a diplomatic note. Roberts Owen, Secretary Muskie's legal adviser, describes the American reaction as follows:

> The news was both bad and good. The Majles resolution was disappointing on its face, because it seemed to ignore several of the fundamental problems that Christopher had painstakingly explained in Bonn and that stood in the way of U.S. compliance with the Ayatollah's four conditions. . . .

> The heartening aspects were that, despite its preoccupation with other matters (including particularly the war with Iraq), the erratic Iranian government seemed to be continuing on a relatively steady course toward active negotiations and had selected as an intermediary a government [i.e., Algeria] whose diplomatic corps enjoyed a very high reputation.[39]

The next two and a half months featured a series of proposals and counterproposals leading to the eventual agreement that freed the hostages on January 20, 1981—Jimmy Carter's last day in office and Ronald Reagan's first. Christopher notes how helpful the Algerians were in advising the American side to find the yessable proposition and to frame its ideas in language that the Iranians could accept. For example, Christopher recalled that his negotiating team, acting on the Algerians' advice, reduced its original proposal for the claims arbitration tribunal from twenty-five to three pages. Although Christopher says he had no special insight into the Algerian-Iranian interaction, he believes that the Algerian team was particularly helpful in explaining to the Iranians the limits of American executive power and why the president could not simply transfer assets on his own authority. Christopher also recalled how the Algerians visited President Carter at Camp David in late 1980 and gave him the advice, "Don't give up."[40]

---

39. Owen, "Final Negotiation and Release in Algiers," in Christopher, American Hostages in Iran, 307.

40. Christopher interview, December 13, 2007.

# The Lessons: Dealing with the Unthinkable

- **American officials needed to expect the unusual and avoid the easy assumption.** The American side found itself in difficulty when it made assumptions about likely Iranian reactions to admitting the shah. It ignored clear and well-informed advice from its own diplomats in Tehran, it ignored reports in the media that described the prevailing anarchy in Iran and the growing power of extremists there, it misread the situation of Iran's provisional government and overestimated its ability to control events, and it assumed the authorities in Tehran would calculate their national interest in a certain way. Finally, it made the tacit assumption that "the Iranians would never be so foolish as to do X." Such an assumption—in the prevailing confusion—became almost a guarantee that the Iranians would do precisely X. In this particular case, the Iranian authorities, for their own purposes, encouraged anarchy rather than attempt to control it.

- **Officials should have listened to those who knew (even a little). They should have remembered the lessons of history and understood the other side's perceptions of that history.** American diplomats in Tehran had repeatedly advised against admitting the shah, noting how doing so would mean the end of Bazargan's fragile provisional government, the end of chances for a normal U.S.-Iranian relationship, and the end of the U.S. mission in Tehran. When the American administration decided to admit the shah in October 1979, how could it have expected the Iranians to believe the story about his illness and Washington's humanitarian motives? Even if that account was true, the weight of history and perception was against it. In the prevailing atmosphere of October 1979—with their revolution beset on all sides by enemies real and imaginary—Iranians were not about to believe Washington's explanations. As then-Foreign Minister Yazdi later recalled, "When the American chargé told me [on October 21, 1979] the reasons for Carter's decision, I didn't believe him for a minute."[41]

- **Officials should have respected the power of ghosts.** In this crisis, the American government and its mission in Tehran were engaged in an losing and unequal struggle with a long line of historical ghosts. Their opponents were the ghosts of the treaties of Gulestan (1813) and Turkmanchai (1828), the D'Arcy concession (1901), the Anglo-Russian agreement of 1907, the tripartite occupation of WWII, the CIA coup of 1953, the American SOFA

---

41.  Yazdi statement at Columbia University, March 28, 2008. See above, footnote 19.

controversy of 1963–64, the thoughtless and insulting Richard Helms appointment as American ambassador in 1973, and other humiliations inflicted on Iran over the last centuries. In the end, the struggle was no contest. The ghosts were too many and too powerful.

- **Patience and timing were everything.** The Iranians were eventually prepared to settle for a deal that they could have had months earlier. If they had settled earlier—particularly before the U.S. broke relations in April 1980—it is possible (although by no means certain) that the American-Iranian military supply relationship could have been reestablished on some basis and the Iranians would have been much better equipped to resist Iraq's aggression.

  Why did it take the Iranians ten months even to propose such a settlement? Warren Christopher suggests it might have been then-Parliament Speaker Hashemi-Rafsanjani who persuaded Khomeini it was time to settle.[42] Algerian contacts have suggested that Iranian Prime Minister Raja'i's cold reception at the 1980 session of the UN General Assembly convinced the Iranians of the toxicity of the hostage crisis and demonstrated their country's diplomatic isolation even when it had been the victim of a neighbor's aggression. A major factor was Khomeini's view that a settlement should wait until those Iranian politicians closest to his way of thinking had triumphed over their rivals. Once he and his allies had driven their clerical rivals, the secular nationalists—the hated liberals—and the leftist Mojahedin—whom Khomeini ridiculed as baby Communists and hypocrites—into the political wilderness, there was little reason for them to prolong the crisis.

  The Algerians' advice to President Carter ("Don't give up") was very valuable. In the weeks and months of negotiation that led to the eventual Algiers agreement, the American side had to remain patient and focused on its objectives. It did not let apparent setbacks, such as new Iranian demands, derail the process. With the help of the Algerians, the Americans preserved that delicate process and kept working for a consistent goal—an effective agreement that would bring a release.

- **The parties had to find serious intermediaries.** The lawyers Bourguet and Villalon, who helped devise the ill-fated scenario of February–March 1980, and other intermediaries may have been well-intentioned, but they (and Foreign Minister Qotbzadeh) could not deliver an agreement under the prevailing conditions in Tehran. By engaging in such an exercise the

---

42. Warren Christopher interview, December 13, 2007.

Americans not only endured the humiliation of public failure but also showed themselves overeager for an agreement—a tactic that hardened the adversary's position. Although doing so would not have been easy, in this situation it might have been better for the American side to pull back, impose what coercive measures were possible, and wait for the Iranians to do what they eventually did—offer to enter serious negotiations.

Khomeini's original decision to endorse the takeover had converted a disorganized student sit-in into an international crisis. Because Khomeini had created the crisis, he was the only person who could, either tacitly or explicitly, bring the standoff to an end. Whatever Foreign Minister Qotbzadeh's motives, he simply did not speak for the imam when he was negotiating with Hamilton Jordan in early 1980. When the Germans approached the Americans in September with the Iranian offer to make contact, it was soon clear that this time something important was in process. Warren Christopher's insistence on a sign of Iranian good faith was a wise step. Once Khomeini had confirmed in his speech the original conditions carried by his emissary Tabataba'i, the whole matter was essentially settled, although months of difficult negotiations lay ahead. In those negotiations, the professionalism and the credibility of the Algerian intermediaries were to prove crucial.

# 5

# Freeing the Lebanon Hostages

*Why, sometimes I've believed as many as six impossible things before breakfast.*

—Lewis Carroll, *Alice in Wonderland*

Iranian-American relations did not improve after the hostage crisis ended in January 1981. Resolving that crisis failed to bring a resumption of official Iranian-American contact or open channels of negotiation. On the contrary, the hostage crisis left such a bitter taste that subsequent American administrations preferred to put Iran and Iranian affairs into an isolation chamber. Iran was simply too dangerous for American officials to touch. If they thought about Iran at all, they would put it into their too-hard-to-do boxes. The Islamic Republic had already brought down one American president and during the Iran-Contra scandal of 1985–86 almost brought down a second. The American bureaucracy relegated Iranian affairs to its most distant corners until the State Department delivered the ultimate insult of combining Iranian affairs with those of Iraq (under the label of Northern Gulf affairs) and then, even worse, with the Arabian Peninsula states. Iran expertise and Persian language skills within the bureaucracy were allowed to wither, and officials showed little interest in training a new generation of either Iranian or Afghan Persian speakers.

Try as it might, however, Washington could not ignore Iran. Although the United States may not have wanted to have anything to do with Iran after January 1981, Iran continued to impose itself on American attention. In the eighties, Iranian protégés in Lebanon seized and held Western hostages, including Americans, and officials of the Reagan administration seemed as impotent as their predecessors had been in either forcing or negotiating the captives' freedom. Those years saw the bizarre Iran-Contra scandal and George H. W. Bush's statement that goodwill begets goodwill, which brought very little goodwill to either side. There was also the tanker war in the Persian Gulf during which the United States became a virtual ally of the Iraqis in their war with the Islamic Republic.

These encounters were not fortunate for either side. There was too much lingering hostility and suspicion for any productive negotiations to occur. Because each side assumed that the other was implacably hostile, it could not judge an offer or statement by the other side on its merits—that is, how it might serve national interests. As the Iranians and British had done during the 1951–53 oil nationalization crisis, each side approached contact with the other not as a negotiation but as a death struggle against unalloyed evil.

That attitude could extend to denying reality. In May 1987, for example, after an Iraqi aircraft had attacked the destroyer USS *Stark* in the Persian Gulf, President Reagan simply ignored the facts of the incident and stated that Iran "is the real villain in the piece." In a press conference, he went on to refer to Iran as "this barbaric country."[1] In February 1990, after President Bush as a conciliatory gesture notified Iranian President Hashemi-Rafsanjani through the UN secretary-general that the White House had received a telephone call from someone impersonating an official in the Iranian president's office, the Iranians responded intemperately and called the president's reference to the bogus caller "unclear."[2]

If the United States or Iran itself was the problem for the other side, then the only way to resolve that problem would be by completely eliminating or humiliating its source. In this situation, negotiators came to neglect their own underlying interest in favor of doing maximum harm to the adversary. Negotiators forgot how to say "yes." They would reject any offer or agreement that was less than a complete surrender by the other side. When there was no agreement, officials on each side would shrug and say, "How can one negotiate with such [unreasonable, fanatical, devious, arrogant] people?"

After 1979, posturing, name-calling, finger-pointing, and repeating sterile slogans replaced negotiation. For the American side, the Islamic Republic became suicidal, a rogue state, a regional hegemonic power, a threat, and the world's number-one sponsor of terrorism. For the Iranian side, America became the great Satan and the leader of world arrogance calling for military action against Iran and for regime change in Tehran by subversion,

---

1. Bill, *The Eagle and the Lion*, 307.

2. Picco, *Man Without a Gun*, 120–23.

bribery, and ethnic strife. How, each side asked, can one negotiate under such conditions?

## Part One: People in Funny Hats

In this most unpromising setting, the Iran-Contra scandal 1985–86 revealed the depths of misunderstanding and misjudgment on both sides. With Americans and Iranians not communicating, almost everything said and done could be (and was) misinterpreted. As the anthropologist Bill Beeman writes,

> Communication between Americans and Iranians has been multichannel and indirect … Intermediaries handled most messages. Alternatively, communications were delivered through public speeches as "signals" to the other party. The diffuseness of this kind of communication created enormous confusion. Since official communiqués were sparse, almost *anything* [emphasis in original] could be treated as a significant message by observers of the other nation.[3]

## Who Misled Whom? Who Misled Themselves?

The Iran-Contra episode originated during the mid-1980s in tripartite maneuvering among Iranians, Israelis, and Americans. Each party had something the others wanted. Iran wanted American-made arms and spare parts to continue fighting an increasingly destructive war against Saddam's Iraq; Israel wanted to weaken the most extreme elements within the Islamic Republic and restore at least part of its former relationship with Tehran, particularly after Iraqi Foreign Minister Tariq Aziz, in late 1983, had refused to accept an Israeli letter offering cooperation against Iran; and the United States began by wanting what Israel said it wanted and ended up seeking freedom for the American hostages held by Iran's allies in Lebanon.[4]

In 1985, Iran remained frustrated in its attempts to approach the United States directly. In June of that year, after Lebanese Hezbollah members hijacked TWA Flight 847, Parliament Speaker Hashemi-Rafsanjani and Foreign Minister Ali Akbar Velayati both directed Iranian Ambassador to Syria Mohtashemi-Pour to work for release of the captives. Although the TWA hostages were eventually released, thanks in part to Iranian intervention, the United States still rejected overtures from Iran, including those by the

---

3. Beeman, *The "Great Satan" vs. the "Mad Mullahs,"* 43.

4. Parsi, *Treacherous Alliance*, 113.

arms dealer Manouchehr Ghorbanifarr, a person reportedly close to speaker Hashemi-Rafsanjani and his allies.[5]

On their own, the Americans had little interest in any rapprochement with Tehran, and Secretary of State George Shultz was particularly hostile to the idea. Nor did it help Ghorbanifarr's case that American intelligence officers had considered him unreliable since 1980–82. In 1984 the CIA ordered its officers to have nothing to do with him (through a burn notice). He was still on the scene in 1986, however, when he failed an agency lie-detector test by showing "deception in all relevant questions."[6]

One of Ghorbanifarr's associates—the Saudi businessman and arms dealer Adnan Khashoggi—advised him that the only way to approach Washington for his purposes was through the Israelis, who were looking to improve their relations with the Islamic Republic and who might be able to win American support for their goal. Most Iranian officials, for their part, apparently had no such improvement in mind—certainly not with Israel and probably not with the United States. Their thinking was almost entirely short-term: procuring the American arms they needed to survive in what looked like an endless war with Iraq. But the Iranians were (or at least Ghorbanifarr was) willing to bait the hook for their Israeli contacts—including David Kimche of the Labor Party and Yaacov Nimrodi, former Israeli defense attaché in Tehran—with promises of better future relations in return for Israel's good offices in Washington.

In the midst of this maneuvering, it is difficult to know if Ghorbanifarr was speaking for anyone but himself. At crucial times, he would bring purportedly influential Iranians into meetings, and these persons, for reasons of their own, would reinforce Ghorbanifarr's arguments about the need to strengthen purportedly moderate groups and individuals inside Tehran. What remains uncertain is whether Ghorbanifarr and his associates were representing factions in Tehran or just improvising based on their own reading of how the Israelis (and Americans) would respond. In any case, Ghorbanifarr was able to persuade the Israelis Kimche and Nimrodi on the need to approach Washington, and they in turn convinced Israeli Prime Minister Shimon Peres to support the effort. Peres put his prestige behind continuing the contacts and helped gain the support of American National Security Adviser Robert McFarlane after he had originally shown no interest in the arguments Ghorbanifarr and Khashoggi presented.

---

5. The following account mostly follows Parsi, *Treacherous Alliance*, 114 ff.

6. Bill, *The Eagle and the Lion*, 308.

# Goals Real and Imagined

Although some Reagan administration officials worried about yellow ribbons appearing for America's Lebanon hostages—a symbolic reminder of Jimmy Carter's seeming impotence against Iran during the 1979–81 hostage standoff—others constructed an anticommunist fantasy about a battered and chaotic Iran's collapsing into a Soviet puppet state. They jumped easily from that imaginary threat to the need for American action—such as supporting (nonexistent) moderate Iranian opposition politicians who would prevent such a catastrophe. On June 17, 1985, McFarlane wrote to the secretaries of state and defense about a CIA document that "makes clear that instability in Iran is accelerating, with potentially momentous consequences for U.S. strategic interests [i.e., keeping the Soviets out]. It seems sensible to ask whether our current policy toward Iran is adequate to achieve our interests."[7]

In a draft National Security Decision Document (NSDD) accompanying his note, McFarlane (more precisely, NSC staffers Donald Fortier and Howard Teicher) wrote ominously of growing instability in Iran and observed,

> The Soviet Union is better positioned than the U.S. to exploit and benefit from any power struggle that results in changes in the Iranian regime, as well as increasing socio-political pressures. In this environment, the emergence of a regime more compatible with American and Western interests is unlikely. Soviet success in taking advantage of the emerging power struggle to insinuate itself in Iran would change the strategic balance in the area.[8]

At the end of the draft NSDD's rambling discussion of Iran, the Soviet Union, and the United States, one finds the following recommendation (among others) described as a "component of U.S. policy."

> [The administration should] encourage Western allies and friends [i.e., Israel] to help Iran meet its import requirements so as to reduce the attractiveness of Soviet assistance and trade offers, while demonstrating the value of correct relations with the West. This includes provision of selected military equipment as determined on a case-by-case basis.[9]

---

7. McFarlane memorandum to Shultz and Caspar Weinberger, June 17, 1985. National Security Archives.

8. Draft NSSD, ca. June 11, 1985, accompanying memorandum cited in footnote 7 above. From Kornbluh, *The Iran-Contra Scandal*, 221.

9. Kornbluh, *The Iran-Contra Scandal*, 225. Secretary of Defense Weinberger's reaction was "This is almost too absurd to comment on."

The authors argued that their recommended policy would somehow advance American influence and minimize that of the Soviets in Iran. In an amazing non sequitur, the authors presented what was actually their starting point (selling arms to the Islamic Republic) as their reasoned conclusion.

Almost twenty years later, McFarlane admitted that this reasoning that a Soviet threat to Iran justified arms sales had no basis in any evidence. He told the scholar Trita Parsi, "It was created among ourselves [the Cold Warriors of the Reagan administration] and had no foundation in fact of contemporary events or intelligence material."[10]

At some level, administration officials must have known that they were operating in total ignorance and were relying on the views of a collection of arms merchants, con men, hustlers, and others pursuing their own political and personal goals. Knowing that their line of reasoning would not survive close examination, these officials never consulted anyone who might have pointed out the obvious flaws and unproved assumptions in the scheme. Instead, they compounded the growing fiasco by putting Michael Ledeen, a part-time consultant to the National Security Council, in charge of investigating the purported Iranian approach. Ledeen, who was to become Ghorbanifarr's strong supporter, requested and received a meeting with McFarlane on July 13, 1985, to deliver a message from Prime Minister Peres saying that the Iranians were interested in exchanging hostages for American-made weapons.[11]

Now the American goal was shifting. Although Reagan's men may have seen themselves as strategic thinkers and players of the great game against Russia, in reality their professed goals of countering Soviet influence in Iran, encouraging Iranian moderates, and helping establish a more congenial regime in Tehran became less important to them. Instead, the immediate goal of freeing American hostages carried enormous symbolic power in Washington and effectively clouded the judgment of those who should have known better. For who could oppose the most absurd schemes if they had even the slightest chance of winning freedom for the imprisoned Americans in Lebanon? Yet the confusion of goals continued, and the Iranian side seemed to sense that it could play different melodies for different audiences until it found the tune that elicited the best response. For example, in July 1985

---

10. Parsi-McFarlane interview, October 13, 2004, cited by Parsi, *Treacherous Alliance*, 117.

11. Kornbluh, *The Iran-Contra Scandal*, 214 and 254 (memorandum requesting the meeting). According to Parsi, *Treacherous Allies*, 117, McFarlane told Ledeen to keep both CIA and State in the dark about his activities. Presumably McFarlane's better judgment told him how State and CIA would react to these ideas.

Ghorbanifarr arranged a meeting in Hamburg between his three Israeli associates and a certain Hassan Karoubi, purportedly an Iranian clergyman and trusted confidant of Khomeini. Karoubi told the Israelis exactly what they wanted to hear: that Iran needed American and Israeli support to prevent its further descent into chaos and to prevent a Soviet takeover.[12]

In this meeting, as in so much associated with the entire episode, among both Israeli and American participants there was an absence of skepticism and a willingness to accept statements as fact without looking for inconsistencies or hidden motives. Khashoggi introduced Ayatollah Karoubi to the Israelis as a key leader of a moderate faction in the Iranian government. According to a purported transcript of the Hamburg meeting, however, Karoubi offered the Israelis little new information beyond what was already the usual fare of journalists and the Tehran gossip circuit: that within Iranian ruling circles there were extremists, moderates, pragmatists, and opportunists. But the combination of extreme secrecy, the lack of independent reporting from inside Iran, and the desire for self-delusion prevented those listening to Karoubi's purported analysis from seeking basic confirmation about what they were hearing. Certainly all should have been suspicious of Karoubi when, in a follow-up memorandum, he asked the Israelis for money to "properly entertain ... some of the people who support the clergy in Qom, the merchants of the bazaar, and extreme line." He also noted that "a few rials for activity among the clergy in Qom, the merchants of the bazaar, and in South Tehran, under camouflage contributions to the Martyrs' Foundation could be very productive."[13]

What had happened to good sense? Why did no one smell a rat? Who exactly was Hassan Karoubi? For whom did he speak? What was his association with the self-interested intermediaries Ghorbanifarr and Khashoggi? In reality, Karoubi seemed to have no political base of his own. His chief credential was that he was brother of the influential Mehdi Karoubi, at that time deputy speaker of Iran's parliament and chief of the Martyrs Fund—and later to be speaker of parliament and unsuccessful candidate for president of Iran in 2005. Did no one realize that Karoubi was playing a classic Iranian political game of seeking foreign support (i.e., money) to further his own po-

---

12. Parsi, *Treacherous Allies*, 118–19. One suspects that the Israelis had become, in the late Justice William O. Douglas's words, "suckers for people in funny hats."

13. Segev, *The Iranian Triangle*, 154–63. Segev includes what he claims is a transcript of the meeting between Karoubi and the Israelis. Although Mehdi Karoubi has remained an influential figure in Iranian politics since the revolution, his brother Hassan disappeared from the political stage after his brief emergence in 1985–86.

litical fortunes and those of his allies? To attract that support he was prepared (apparently in league with Ghorbanifarr) to exaggerate his own importance, to tell his listeners whatever they wanted to hear, and to persuade them that he and his allies were ready to reshape the Iranian political system into a form more acceptable to their foreign backers.

Karoubi, aided by his association with Ghorbanifarr, apparently convinced the Israelis that he and his allies in Tehran could deliver something—perhaps freedom for Western hostages, anti-Soviet policies, better relations with Israel and the United States, or more moderate Iranian policies. Three months later NSC consultant Ledeen joined Kimche, Nimrodi, and Peres ally and businessman Adolph Schwimmer to meet Karoubi and Ghorbanifarr in Geneva. As the reporter Segev describes the October meeting:

> Karoubi claimed that he and his men were now in key positions and that they could influence their country's policy and bring about the release of the five remaining American hostages—with Khomeini's knowledge. He said that he and his fellows were ready to commit themselves to halting terrorist actions against the U.S., and could also put pressure on the Hezbollah faction in Lebanon to refrain from further kidnappings once the current hostages were released.[14]

In return, Karoubi asked for 150 Hawk antiaircraft missiles, 200 air-to-air Sidewinder missiles, and 30 to 50 long-range air-to-air Phoenix missiles. His main area of disagreement with Ledeen was whether Iran should pay for these weapons. Ghorbanifarr, hardly a disinterested party in the matter, persuaded Karoubi to agree to pay.[15]

## Everything Goes Wrong

Such a house of cards—built on greed, duplicity, confusion, wishful thinking, and ignorance—could not stand for long. On August 9, 1985, President Reagan authorized shipping American-made TOW antitank missiles from Israel to Iran. When the first shipment (96 of 504) arrived at Tehran airport less than two weeks later (with Ghorbanifarr accompanying the shipment), there were no Iranian moderates in sight. Instead, Prime Minister Mir Hossein Mousavi (whom Hassan Karoubi had put into the extremist and leftist faction) ordered the missiles turned over to the Iranian Revolutionary Guard Corps, which was not part of any agreement involving hostages. The Iranians, in effect, pocketed the shipment of TOWs and did nothing about freeing any hostages.

---

14. Segev, *The Iranian Triangle*, 183.

15. Ibid., 184.

Ghorbanifarr reported from Tehran that he was certain the Iranians would keep their promises once they had received the remaining missiles.[16]

The remaining 408 missiles from Israel arrived in Tehran on September 15, and the same day one of the Beirut hostages, Reverend Benjamin Weir, was released. Now the Iranians had their missiles and had released only one American hostage. In all of this dealing, however, there was no trace of any Iranian moderation nor of any improved relationship with either Israel or the United States.

The Iranians, however, now understood perfectly how valuable the captive Americans were. The deal had shown the Iranians that the unfortunate hostages were the means for the Islamic Republic to obtain the weapons it so desperately needed to continue its war against Saddam. For the Americans, the outcome of this first exchange was not satisfying, but they did have at least something (one freed hostage) to show for it. That outcome was just enough to draw Washington deeper into the swamp—for it showed that the Iranians could use their influence over the Lebanese hostage takers. As the historian Theodore Draper describes the outcome:

> It was a foretaste of what was to come…The men in power in Iran cared about one thing—arms with which to fight Iraq. All other issues, such as a change in the long-term relationship with the United States, were at best to be left to an indefinite future . . . .

> The one thing that Iran had to trade for arms was the American hostages. But they were in Lebanon, not under direct Iranian control. Just what hold Iran had on the Lebanese who held the hostages was never satisfactorily established. Yet the release of the Reverend Weir showed that Iran could use its influence in Lebanon **if the price was right** [my emphasis].[17]

This dubious outcome of the these first transactions should have raised immediate red flags and warned the American participants exactly what kind of swindle was going on: that the talk of improving relations, assisting Iranian moderates, and countering Soviet influence was just that—empty talk. Perhaps there was someone important in Tehran who believed such policies were the right ones for Iran; or, as is more likely, these themes were a refrain composed by Ghorbanifarr, Karoubi, and their friends to bait the hook for Tel Aviv and Washington.

Now American officials, knowing President Reagan's strong feelings on the matter of the captives in Lebanon, had implicitly accepted the principle

---

16.  Ibid., 174–75.

17.  Draper, *A Very Thin Line,* 171.

of trading arms for hostages. Given Tehran's intense need for arms, however, making that principle effective required that Iran always have hostages to be traded. Instead of backing out of what promised to be an endless trading cycle, however, the Americans marched deeper into the morass. Marine Lieutenant Colonel Oliver North, McFarlane's deputy at the National Security Council, gradually assumed a larger role in the operation, pushing Ledeen into the background. Although Ledeen continued to back the Ghorbanifarr connection, he believed that arms-for-hostages could be a trap and that the Americans should pursue the course originally presented by the Israelis—selling arms to improve relations with Tehran and strengthening (purported) Iranian moderates. He told Schwimmer and Nimrodi, "If we don't unlink the supply of weapons from the release of the hostages, we ourselves will become hostages of the hostages."[18]

North's entry into the affair also made an already complex scheme completely unworkable. Now that Iran had its 500 TOW missiles, it asked for improved Hawk missiles in addition to (air-to-air) Sidewinders and Phoenixes to use against enemy planes flying at high altitude. Although Karoubi—in his October meeting with Ledeen and the Israelis noted above—had linked supply of these antiaircraft weapons to more moderate policies in Tehran, another Ghorbanifarr contact, Deputy Prime Minister Mohsen Kangarlou, explicitly linked the weapons to release of American hostages, even providing (through Ghorbanifarr) a schedule of hostage releases tied to arms deliveries.[19]

There were too many parts and too many conflicting interests for such a complicated plan to work. Just getting the first shipment of 18 Hawk missiles from Israel to Tehran became a logistical nightmare that North and all his covert associates could unravel only after several aborted attempts and days of delay. When the plane carrying these missiles finally reached Tehran on November 24, it turned out that the Israeli Ministry of Defense had sent older missiles that could not hit enemy aircraft at high altitudes. An Iranian army officer, who before the revolution had been at the American factory that manufactured the missiles, examined them and confirmed that the serial numbers showed they were older even than those the United States had supplied Iran during the time of the shah. Prime Minister Mousavi was furious and suspected both his own deputy Kangarlou and Ghorbanifarr of

---

18. Quoted by Segev, *The Iranian Triangle*, 188.

19. Ibid., 185.

taking Iranian money in return for supplying Iran with outdated American-made military junk.[20]

Despite this temporary setback, the follies continued. Iran was still desperate for weapons, and the United States was still desperate for its hostages. At another level, the United States and Israel still hoped for an Iran that would moderate its hostile policies against the United States and its friends. No one would accept the reality that intermediaries had oversold both sides on the deal. Iran was expecting more and better American weapons than could be supplied, and the United States was expecting a new and reformed Islamic Republic that would both see the error of its past ways and give up the only cards in its hand. Locked in secrecy and ignorance and prepared to hear what they wanted to hear from a collection of self-interested middlemen, the American officials simply refused to accept the reality that they were engaged in nothing but a shady arms-for-hostages deal in which the Iranians would drive a very hard bargain.

## Into the Swamp

In November 1985, National Security Adviser MacFarlane submitted his resignation and recommended that the Americans pull out of the entire operation. Rather than take such a rational step, however, the Reagan administration increased its direct involvement, took over the Israeli role as supplier, and decided to sell American arms directly to Tehran. On January 17, 1986, new NSC director John Poindexter argued as follows in a memorandum to the president prepared by Oliver North:

> I do not recommend that you agree with the specific details of the Israeli plan. However, there is another possibility. Some time ago Attorney General William French Smith determined that under an appropriate [presidential] finding you could authorize the CIA to sell arms to countries outside of the provisions of the laws and reporting requirements for foreign military sales. The objectives of the Israeli plan ["the strategic goal of a more moderate Iranian government"] could be met if the CIA, using an authorized agent as necessary, purchased arms from the Department of Defense under the Economy Act and then transferred them to Iran directly after receiving appropriate payment from Iran.

---

20. Ibid., 204–07. It turned out that the Israeli Air Force had improved these older missiles. The problem was that the Iranians wanted missiles to use against high-flying aircraft and Ghorbanifarr had told them the improved Hawks would do what they wanted. In fact, there were no such Hawk missiles in anyone's inventory. The Iranians were still not satisfied, and on subsequent flights the Americans took the missiles out of Iran.

> The Israelis are also sensitive to a strong U.S. desire to free the Beirut
> hostages and have insisted that the Iranians demonstrate both influence
> and good intent by an early release of the five Americans. Both sides [it
> is unclear just who both sides are] have agreed that the hostages will be
> immediately released upon commencement of this action.[21]

So there it was. North and Poindexter claimed to agree with the Israeli objectives of using arms sales to push Iranian policy toward moderation. In reality, however, they were looking at the release of American hostages in return for 4,000 American TOW missiles shipped to Iran.

As recommended, President Reagan signed the intelligence finding attached to the North-Poindexter memorandum. According to that document, the United States would supply weapons to "moderate elements" in Iran to establish the credibility of these elements in defending their country against Iraq and Soviet intervention. The stated policy goals of the actions approved were: (1) establishing a more moderate government in Iran, (2) obtaining new intelligence about Iran and Iran's intentions, and (3) "furthering the release of American hostages held in Beirut."[22]

Now the Americans had completed a shift of both the focus and the personnel of this operation. Ledeen and Kimche, who had both pushed the original plan for a realignment of Iranian-Israeli-American relations by means of arms sales, were now out of the picture. The lead operators were now Oliver North at the White House and Amiram Nir, Peres' adviser on terrorism. The members of this new team—perhaps with more modest ambitions than their predecessors—were going to negotiate arms-for-hostages rather than new relationships with the Islamic Republic. Of course, if the release of hostages also meant better relations with a more moderate Islamic Republic, so much the better. But such was not the main goal.

In February 1986, the Iranians received 1,000 American TOW missiles in two shipments. There was no corresponding movement on hostage releases, however, and it was clear that Ghorbanifarr had promised more to each side than the other was going to deliver. The Americans were expecting the immediate release of all hostages and at least some hints of a new relationship with Iran; the Iranians were expecting delivery of high-grade American intelligence on Iraq and sophisticated antiaircraft weapons.

A late-February Frankfurt meeting with Iranian deputy PM Kangarlou descended into low farce. Because North had no idea what Ghorbanifarr was saying to Kangarlou in Persian, the American insisted that arms mer-

---

21. Quoted in Kornbluh, *The Iran-Contra Scandal*, 232–33.

22. Ibid., 235.

chant (and business partner of retired U.S. Air Force General Richard Secord) Albert Hakim be present as interpreter. Ghorbanifarr, perhaps seeing his commissions melting away, objected, saying that Hakim was so disliked by Iranian officials that his presence would sink the whole deal. Then North had Hakim—introduced as the Persian-speaking Turk Ibrahim Ibrahimian—put on heavy makeup, a wig, and sunglasses so that Ghorbanifarr and Kangarlou would not recognize him. When Ghorbanifarr left the room, Hakim and Secord slipped Kangarlou their Washington telephone number so the Iranian could deal with them directly instead of through Ghorbanifarr.[23]

## The Final Collapse

The parties could not escape the path to failure. They seemed to forget their objectives. Some were exclusively concerned with protecting their profits; some were determined to exclude others whom they saw as unreliable or as competitors; the brokers were determined to keep the process going beyond any political purpose for the sake of their commissions; and the Israeli representative Nir was determined to keep Ghorbanifarr in the game because his presence kept the Israeli connection alive. The American side prepared to send a delegation to Iran (the first destination mentioned was Kish Island) for a meeting to discuss the future of the bilateral relationship.

North gave Ghorbanifarr a powerful weapon when he instructed the Iranian to prepare for the American delegation's trip to Iran. In Segev's words, "[North] had given [Ghorbanifarr] the means with which to blackmail the administration—if the Americans continued to work with him, Ghorbanifarr would keep his mouth shut; if they tried to shake him off, he could make the whole affair public."[24]

Throughout the spring of 1986, events moved to their inevitable and disastrous climax. In April, Ghorbanifarr relayed new Iranian demands for Hawk missile spare parts instead of TOWs and for shifting the meeting with the American delegation from Kish Island to Tehran. The Iranians also refused to release all the hostages to the American delegation but insisted on first receiving the Hawk parts and then releasing the captives in sequence. Poindexter's instructions to Oliver North, written about a month before the latter's trip to Tehran, shows bluster, frustration, and every expectation of failure.

---

23. Segev, *The Iranian Triangle*, 246.

24. Ibid., 253.

You may go ahead and go, but I want several points made clear to them. There are not to be any parts delivered until all of the hostages are free in accordance with the plan that you layed [sic] out for me before. None of this half shipment before any are released crap. It is either all or nothing. Also you may tell them that the President is getting very annoyed at their continual stalling. He will not agree to any more changes in the plan. Either they agree finally on the arrangements that have been discussed or we are going to permanently cut off all contact. If they really want to save their asses from the Soviets, they should get on board. I am beginning to suspect that [Kangarlou] doesn't have such authority.[25]

The question remains: If Poindexter (and President Reagan) were as adamant and as frustrated as appears in this memo, then why did they agree to North and McFarlane's travel? Poindexter appears both resigned to the mission's failure and to realize how the Iranians were exploiting the Reagan administration's Cold War obsessions.

When the American delegation—including McFarlane, North, Nir, Teicher, and Persian-speaking retired CIA officer George Cave—reached Tehran on May 25, they began three days of talks with mid-level Iranian officials—talks that satisfied no one. It is clear from accounts of those meetings that each side had expected what the other was not willing or able to deliver. Nor were the Americans able to meet any high-ranking Iranian officials—such as Parliament Speaker Hashemi-Rafsanjani, Prime Minister Mir Mousavi, or President Ali Khamene'i, who—Ghorbanifarr had hinted—were all waiting to receive them.

The American plane had carried a partial shipment of Hawk missile parts, but the Iranians were apparently expecting much more than this piecemeal delivery, including arrangements for a long-term and steady supply of needed weapons and parts. As for releasing hostages, the Iranians claimed that the captives were not under Tehran's control and then offered to release some after further arms deliveries. The American side was torn between its explicit instructions (see above) from Poindexter to execute an all-or-nothing exchange and its desires not to leave Tehran empty-handed. Although the details of accounts differ, the Americans (or at least North and the Israeli Nir) were apparently willing to send a second planeload of Hawk spares provided the Iranians released two hostages immediately and two more in the (indefinite) future. McFarlane, however, instructed the second plane

---

25.  Poindexter to North, April 16, 1986. Quoted in Kornbluh, *The Iran-Contra Scandal*, 294.

to turn back, and when it was clear that no hostage release was imminent, ordered his delegation to leave Tehran on the morning of May 28.[26]

Beginning in July 1986—after the failure of the MacFarlane visit to Tehran—North, Secord, and Hakim attempted to cut Ghorbanifarr out of the action by opening a second channel to Iran through contacts of Hakim. On the Iranian side, the links were reportedly Ahmad Khomeini's brother-in-law Sadeq Tabataba'i (who had opened the original negotiating channel with Deputy Secretary of State Warren Christopher in 1980), Mehdi Bahremani, a son of the powerful parliament speaker Hashemi-Rafsanjani, and two of the speaker's brothers, Mohsen and Mahmoud.[27]

Even after the Tehran fiasco, the Americans felt they were in too deep to back out. On July 26, the Lebanese captors released American hostage Lawrence Martin Jenco. On August 3, the Iranians received another load of Hawk parts sent through Israel. In September–October, three more Americans (Frank Reed, Joseph Ciccipio, and Edward Tracy) became hostages in Lebanon, perhaps to replace those being released and to provide Iran with continued leverage to obtain American arms. On October 3, after negotiations with intermediaries of the so-called second-channel (excluding Ghorbanifarr and Kangarlou but including Hashemi-Rafsanjani intimates), Iran received its last arms shipment, including 500 Israeli TOWs and Hawk spare parts. On November 2, a third American hostage, David Jacobsen, was released.

The futile maneuvering and the misjudgments continued to the end. American attempts to escape the trap of arms-for-hostages bargaining came to nothing. As Draper writes:

> For all the brave talk about a "strategic dialogue," an arms-for-hostages deal was all that North was capable of making. From time to time he tried to inject his larger vision of future U.S.-Iran relations into the discussion. ... North cited what McFarlane had tried to tell them at Tehran: "Think big. Think beyond the hostages. Think economic aid. Think of all kinds of ways in which we can help you ... ."

> But the Iranians were not interested in "thinking big." They wanted to think about weapons, the fate of Iraq's Saddam Hussein, and the release of the Da'wa (Shi'a) prisoners in Kuwait. On these points the Americans could not satisfy them ... As Cave put it, "there were no real concrete proposals from the Iranian side on a strategic and political relationship."

---

26. There is a detailed account of the Tehran meetings in Draper, *A Very Thin Line*, 315–31. Kornbluh's document collection includes George Cave's mission report to McFarlane. *The Iran-Contra Scandal*, 295–99.

27. Segev, *The Iranian Triangle*, 296–97.

> Whenever this kind of relationship came up, the Americans virtually
> talked to themselves.[28]

At the end of October 1986, North, Secord, Cave, and Hakim met in Mainz with the second-channel Iranian Bahremani-Rafsanjani and a certain Ali Samii, who seemed to work with both channels. In reality, the Iranian intermediaries of both channels were reporting to the same Tehran officials, who might be variously represented as moderates, leftists, hard-liners, and so on depending on the Iranian side's needs at the moment. At this meeting, the Iranians reported that Ayatollah Hossein Ali Montazeri's supporters in Tehran, especially his son-in-law Hadi Hashemi and Hadi's brother Mehdi, had inspired radical students to distribute leaflets exposing and denouncing McFarlane's trip. A few days after the Mainz meeting, the small Lebanese weekly *Al-Shiraa*—tipped off by the imprisoned Mehdi Hashemi's allies— also reported the story of the Americans' visit under the guise of analyzing the reasons behind Mehdi Hashemi's arrest in May 1986 (at the time of Mac-Farlane's visit).[29]

Although the story of the American visit and the arms-for-hostages deal had been circulating for months, the *Al-Shiraa* story became front-page world news and ended the whole dubious proceeding. The Iranians gave their own version of events, pretending that the arms-for-hostages deals never happened. Hashemi-Rafsanjani claimed that the Americans had come to Tehran uninvited seeking Iran's intercession on behalf of the captives in Lebanon. He painted a picture of the Americans pleading for Iranians' goodwill and the latter remaining standoffish but willing to consider a humanitarian gesture. "[We told them] if your governments prove to us in practice that they are not fighting against us, if they prove in practice that they do not engage in treason against us, if they prove in practice that they do not confiscate our assets through bullying tactics … then the Islamic Republic in a humanitarian gesture is prepared to announce its views to its friends in Lebanon." Prime Minister Mir Mousavi was blunter. He claimed that the American came to Tehran seeking better relations and that the Iranians turned them down: "[We told them] negotiations with the United States in the light of its crimes against the Islamic Revolution will never take place."[30]

---

28.  Draper, *A Very Thin Line*, 455–57.

29.  For more on the Mehdi Hashemi case, see Abrahamian, *Tortured Confessions*, 162–67. Abrahamian believes Hashemi was arrested in 1986 and executed in 1987 because he had leaked the story of MacFarlane's visit in an attempt to embarrass Ayatollah Montazeri's political enemies, particularly Hashemi-Rafsanjani.

30.  Quoted by Draper, *A Very Thin Line*, 457–58.

The American side had more difficulty whitewashing the matter. Two weeks after the *Al-Shiraa* story appeared, after some attempts at cover-up and denial, the revelations had created a sensation and a full-blown scandal that nearly brought down the Reagan administration. That administration's policy ineptitude and clownishness were bad enough (although not necessarily against the law), but the issue moved from stupidity to criminality when it was discovered that North and company had secretly diverted funds from the covert arms sales to Tehran to finance weapons supplies to the Nicaraguan Contras—an act explicitly forbidden under American law.

Beyond all the political misjudgments was the sense that skillful, double-dealing Iranian negotiators had outfoxed the simple Americans, who had agreed to a most unequal bargain. As Secretary of State Shultz told congressional investigators, "Our guys … got taken to the cleaners."[31] On the surface, it certainly appeared that way. Between August 1985 and October 1986 Iran received six shipments of arms including more than 2,000 TOW antitank missiles, Hawk missile system spare parts, and Hawk missiles—although the Iranians canceled the Hawk sale and returned the missiles to Israel, claiming the weapons were obsolete. In return, the Lebanese captors, presumably under pressure from Tehran, released three American hostages—Benjamin Weir (September 1985), Lawrence Martin Jenco (July 1986), and David Jacobsen (November 1986). As noted above, however, they also abducted three other Americans (Reed, Ciccipio, and Tracy) in September–October 1986.

Even if we accept Secretary Shultz's judgment of the outcome, in the longer term, the deal brought the Iranians few advantages. Although they received some weapons, which might have had short-term military benefits, the Iranians did not get what they were seeking—a long-term and reliable supply of American arms that could have affected the outcome of the war with Iraq. The weapons that the Iranians did get were insignificant in comparison to Iraq's expensive purchases of upgraded weapons. In August 1988, less than two years after the last shipment of American arms in October 1986, an exhausted Islamic Republic was on the brink of collapse and was forced to accept a humiliating cease-fire after rejuvenated and resupplied Iraqi forces inflicted decisive defeats on the Iranian military.

But the political cost of such a renewed, consistent supply of American weaponry—an entirely new relationship with the United States—was more than the Iranians were prepared to pay. Ali Hashemi, Hashemi-Rafsanjani's nephew who was involved in the second-channel dealings, told an Iranian

---

31. Quoted by Kornbluh, *The Iran-Contra Scandal*, 252.

journalist in 2008 that "at the end of the matter, the issue was selling arms to Iran and nothing else."[32] Perhaps the Iranians believed that Washington would never moderate its hostility and that the best they could do was bargain for piecemeal shipments of American weapons. Whatever their motives, the Iranians became captives of their own rhetoric, their short-term thinking, and their refusal to think big (in MacFarlane's words). By relying on an endless supply of hostages to obtain American arms, the Iranians fell victim to the *mard-e-rendi* trap of outsmarting themselves and ignoring any long-term implications of what they were doing.

After the complex and bizarre trading arrangements became public knowledge in November 1986, Washington had no excuse of building a relationship with Iranian moderates with which to cover its shady dealings with the Islamic Republic. With a scandal breaking in Washington and with Tehran's contacts there in disgrace, the hostages in Lebanon suddenly lost their trading value, and the Iranians discovered that they had, once again, overplayed their hand. Now they were not only cut off from the American arms they so desperately needed, but by April 1988, they were facing a direct military threat from United States naval and air forces now, to all intents and purposes, openly allied to the Iraqis. In the Persian Gulf, the United States no longer even pretended to be neutral.

In the mid-1980s, the idea of restructuring Iranian-American relations was an appealing one to at least some officials in both Washington and Tehran— although not to either the American secretary of state or secretary of defense. Those two powerful figures—as well as American public opinion—would have probably opposed any arms supplies to the Islamic Republic, no matter what their purpose.

In the prevailing atmosphere of bitterness and suspicion, rebuilding bilateral relations was probably beyond the negotiating and political skills of officials on either side. Like the Iranians, the Americans involved in these inept transactions suffered from their own short-term thinking. Their objective—following President Reagan's own preferences—became liberating the hostages in Lebanon. Perhaps going beyond that goal and rebuilding the Iranian-American relationship was just too hard to do, particularly given both the American domestic political climate and the fact that the Iranian side thought it did not need to improve relations to obtain the weapons it needed. For that purpose, the Iranians believed, American hostages were currency enough. On the American side, ignorance, amateurism, ideology,

---

32. Interview in *Shahrvand-e-Emruz,* June 15, 2008.

excessive secrecy, and self-delusion guaranteed failure. As James Bill de-scribes the American actions,

> Yet the methodology of the plan to establish this communication [with the Islamic Republic] was poorly, clumsily, and unprofessionally conceived. It involved the wrong people (MacFarlane, North, Teicher) advised by the wrong "experts" (Ledeen, Ghorbanifarr) supported by the wrong allies (Israel); they went to the wrong place (Tehran) at the wrong time (during the month of Ramadan and after the United States had tilted to the Iraqi side in the Gulf War) carrying the wrong tactical plan.[33]

## Part Two: Goodwill Begets (Some) Goodwill

*Attention must be paid.*

—Arthur Miller, *Death of a Salesman*

After the fiasco of Iran-Contra, the American administration was in no mood to engage the Islamic Republic, even to pursue the worthwhile (if imaginary) goal of keeping Iran out of the Soviet grasp. The previous inept efforts to do so had brought Washington only embarrassment and ridicule and had nearly brought down an American president. For the last year of his term in office, President Reagan was badly wounded, some said fatally. Officials in Wash-ington might have preferred for Iran simply to go away—but of course it would not. Iran continued to demand American attention, and the encoun-ters continued to be difficult and unsatisfying for both sides.

George H.W. Bush, the new American president, took office in January 1989, having avoided being stained by the disaster of the arms-for-hostages scheme. Bush still faced the reality, however, that American hostages re-mained captive in Lebanon and that the previous, clumsy attempts to release them had ended very badly. As president, Bush was now responsible, and he had to do something to resolve the situation. He could no longer say, as he had when asked about Iran-Contra, that he was "out of the loop."

Other aspects of the political landscape were changing, and these changes opened new possibilities. In August 1988, Iran and Iraq accepted a United Nations brokered cease-fire to end their eight-year war. Thus, the Islamic Republic was no longer in desperate and immediate need of weapons to feed its war machine. Furthermore, in those difficult cease-fire negotiations, UN Secretary-General Pérez de Cuéllar had earned new credibility with the Islamic Republic.

---

33.  Bill, *The Eagle and the Lion*, 313.

In June 1989, Ayatollah Khomeini died, although not before dropping a final bombshell on the world by issuing (in February 1989) his *fatwa* (religious opinion) calling for the death of the British writer Salman Rushdie. The outgoing president and long-time regime insider, Ali Khamene'i, replaced Khomeini as supreme leader. In July 1989, Ali Akbar Hashemi-Rafsanjani became Iran's new president. Like Khamene'i, Hashemi-Rafsanjani was a founding member of the Islamic Republic's ruling inner circle. He also had a reputation—deserved or not—as a pragmatist and had reportedly been one of the key figures behind the arms-for-hostages negotiations. Unlike his American counterparts, however, he had not suffered political damage from his involvement. On the contrary, he had vanquished his rival and Khomeini's first designated successor—Ayatollah Hossein Ali Montazeri—and had eliminated one of that figure's main supporters, Mehdi Hashemi, the person responsible for exposing the Islamic Republic's highest officials' dealings with the Reagan White House.

At his inauguration on January 20, 1989, Bush spoke to the hostage issue and made the Iranians a clear, if indirect, offer of better relations. "There are today Americans who are held against their will in foreign lands, and Americans who are unaccounted for. Assistance can be shown here and will be long remembered. Goodwill begets goodwill. Good faith can be a spiral that endlessly moves on." So here was an explicit offer to break the downward spiral that had characterized American-Iranian relations for ten years.

## United Nations Officials Act

At the end of 1988, even before Bush's offer, Assistant UN Secretary-General Giandomenico Picco began building on the relationships he had created during the Iran-Iraq cease-fire negotiations. He started talking to those Iranian officials he had gotten to know about progress on the hostages in Lebanon. His first contact was with Cyrus Nasseri, the Iranian ambassador to the United Nations in Geneva. At a meeting in Geneva on December 14, 1988, Nasseri agreed to raise the hostage issue in Tehran and told Picco that Washington should make a gesture to encourage a reciprocal gesture by those holding the hostages. Looking for some yessable proposition, Picco asked that an observer be permitted to visit the hostages and verify their good health.[34]

---

34. Picco, *Man Without a Gun*, 103–04. Picco notes (107–09) how, as he continued to work on the hostage issue, he had to keep his activities secret from most of his colleagues and nominal superiors at the United Nations headquarters.

Although Picco and Secretary-General Pérez de Cuéllar had decided that the key to movement in Lebanon was in Tehran, progress was slow. Iranian officials had to maintain the appearance of distance between themselves and the Lebanese hostage-holders. In late May, six months after his meeting with Nasseri, Picco was in Tehran to meet again with Nasseri and with Foreign Minister Ali Akbar Velayati. Although the Iranians attempted to maintain the façade of separation, their involvement was clear. The Iranian minister referred to the Lebanese people and told the envoy that there could be a meeting between Picco and the Lebanese in Damascus at an undetermined date in the future. When Picco noted that the Syrians should be informed, Velayati replied that issue was not his (Picco's) problem.[35]

After Khomeini's death and Hashemi-Rafsanjani's becoming president of Iran, there were indications of changes in Tehran. In August, the Iranian president told the Pakistani foreign minister that he was prepared to assist in efforts to release the hostages in return for some gesture from Washington. Also significant was the Iranian president's elevating young diplomats who took a professional approach to their work. One of these was Picco's contact Nasseri; another was Javad Zarif, who during this period was adviser to the foreign minister and later Iran's deputy permanent representative to the United Nations in New York.

What were the new Iranian president's motives? Although many observers referred to Hashemi-Rafsanjani as a pragmatist or a moderate, the reality was not that simple. Above all, he had been the consummate regime insider since the earliest days of the Islamic Revolution and as such closely associated with its excesses and nastiness—the terrorism, the brutality, and the diplomatic ineptitude that had made Iran into an international pariah. The analyst Kenneth Pollack explains the new president's motives and actions as follows:

> ... Rafsanjani may be a true moderate, but his policies have consistently been subordinated to what is best for his career. Rafsanjani is wildly ambitious. . . . He is also a thoroughly unprincipled political animal....Throughout his time in the spotlight, Rafsanjani has famously compromised his principles whenever it was convenient for either the survival or advancement of his political career.[36]

In other words, Hashemi-Rafsanjani was a charter member of that most important Iranian political institution, the *hezb-e-baad* (party of the winds).

---

35. Ibid., 107.

36. Pollack, *The Persian Puzzle*, 249–50.

Describing Hashemi-Rafsanjani's policy toward the United States (and his ability to change that policy when expedient), Pollack writes,

> Since the earliest days of the revolution, he has repeatedly advocated a rapprochement with the United States. It seems to be based on his reading of the practicalities of the situation: Iran needs good relations with the rest of the world, and the United States is most powerful and important in the world, so it is useful to have good relations with the United States. This is not to say that he has not sold that position out whenever it was expedient to do so.[37]

## Enter the Americans (Again)

The American side could not stay away from matters Iranian for long. Officials of the Bush administration, however, were hoping to do things better this time and evade the traps that had ensnared their predecessors. In August 1989, there was an exchange of messengers and messages between Pérez de Cuéllar and President Bush. Eventually National Security Adviser Brent Scowcroft visited Pérez de Cuéllar and told him that the president was prepared to undertake reciprocal measures that would both improve American-Iranian relations and free the hostages in Lebanon. Recalling what had happened in the past with self-interested middlemen, the Americans insisted that their message go directly to President Hashemi-Rafsanjani and that the secretary-general should be the only intermediary.

Pérez de Cuéllar took the president's draft message and told Scowcroft that he (the secretary-general) "would work on the message and have Picco deliver it to the president of Iran." When Picco and his boss discussed the message, they agreed to recast it as a message not from President Bush but from the UN secretary-general. In that way, they intended to protect Hashemi-Rafsanjani from domestic radicals' charges that he had gone against the late imam's long-standing orders and opened negotiations with the United States.[38]

Picco delivered the Pérez de Cuéllar message to Hashemi-Rafsanjani (with only Zarif present) on August 25, 1989, in Tehran. The relevant language was as follows:

> I would like to comment to you on U.S.-Iranian relations. I know George Bush very well. I have known him on a close basis since 1971 and I feel certain that I know how he thinks. I know he would like to see improved U.S.-Iranian relations. Indeed, he has spoken to me on the subject and

---

37. Ibid., 250.

38. Picco, *Man Without a Gun*, 110.

> I call to your attention the statement he made in his inaugural address: "Goodwill begets goodwill." I do know for a certainty, in my own mind, that President Bush has sought the release of the American hostages … [ellipses in original] he would react swiftly by taking action on Iranian monetary assets blocked by the United States and other appropriate gestures. . . . .
>
> You have called in public for the reverse of this sequence of actions. You should know that, in the light of the political realities surrounding the Iran-Contra affair, it would be impossible for President Bush in other than the sequence suggested. I am in a position to assure your Excellency that taking an initiative on the hostages would inevitably elicit a positive response from the United States.[39]

The letter went on to suggest a meeting between the two officials (Hashemi-Rafsanjani and Pérez de Cuéllar) at the Belgrade nonaligned summit scheduled for the next month.

Hashemi-Rafsanjani's reaction was not enthusiastic. He undoubtedly saw through the fiction of the letter's authorship and said that he had accepted the message only out of his personal respect for the UN secretary-general. He also disagreed with the implied connection made in the letter between Tehran and the hostage-takers in Lebanon. The Iranian president insisted on the fact of the latter's separation from Tehran and noted, "They do not have an address. It is difficult to get in touch with them." He also insisted that if the United States was interested in improving relations it should release frozen Iranian assets and "halt their unreasonable animosity toward us."[40]

At this point, Picco says he realized what a difficult and complicated mission he had undertaken. He also realized how important it was for the Iranians to maintain their story that the hostage matter was of no direct relevance to them and that any action on their part would be for purely humanitarian reasons. Despite this apparent setback, however, Pérez de Cuéllar did meet with Foreign Minister Velayati at Belgrade (Hashemi-Rafsanjani did not attend), and the minister told him that a process to release hostages could begin if the United States released 10 percent of the Iranian assets it had frozen after 1979. A few weeks later in New York, Velayati added another condition: that the United States should pay compensation to the victims of the IranAir Airbus passenger plane the Americans shot down in July 1988.[41]

---

39. Ibid., 113.

40. Ibid., 114.

41. Ibid., 114. The 10 percent demand is puzzling. In theory, the Algiers accord of 1981 decided the fate of those assets, either returning them to Iran or putting them into a fund to settle claims on both sides of the dispute. As for the victims of the Airbus, the

The Iranians did not break off their contact through the UN secretary-general. In early 1990, Kamal Kharrazi, Iran's ambassador to the United Nations, repeated Iran's position that it was interested in improving relations with the United States and presented four conditions for such an improvement.

- The United States should release Iranian assets frozen during the 1979–81 hostage crisis.

- The United States should end the embargo on shipping military equipment the shah bought and paid for before his government collapsed in 1979.
- The United States should support the 1975 Algiers agreement between the shah and Saddam Hussein. This agreement, among other things, delineated the border between Iran and Iraq.
- The United States should urge Saddam to withdraw his troops from a small piece of Iranian territory they continued to occupy.[42]

In their demands, the Iranians did not mention the seventeen Dawa movement prisoners in Kuwait. The imprisonment of those Shia militants, who were responsible for attacks on the American and French embassies in Kuwait City in December 1983, had provoked the kidnapping of westerners in Beirut. Although the captors in Lebanon demanded freedom for the Dawa Seventeen, Iranian representatives kept a discreet distance from that issue and continued to act as though what was happening in Lebanon had nothing to do with them.

As UN officials negotiated, they suspected the existence of other channels of communication between Washington and Tehran. Others were claiming that Washington had selected them as intermediaries with the Islamic Republic and there were reports of nonexistent Iranian-American negotiations in Geneva to resolve the hostage issue. Whatever the reality, the American side apparently found the secretary-general's channel to Rafsanjani to be useful and promising. In early March, Thomas Pickering, America's Ambassador to the UN, told Picco and Pérez de Cuéllar that Washington would deal with the hostage issue only through them.[43]

Despite all these difficulties, there were indications in early 1990 that the offer of goodwill begets goodwill might bring results and recognition of

---

American government eventually did pay ex gratia compensation directly to the victims (of all nationalities), although not to the Iranian government.

42. Ibid., 118.
43. Ibid., 123.

common Iranian-American interests. On February 5, the White House received a call from someone claiming to be speaking from President Hashemi-Rafsanjani's office saying that the Iranian president wanted to speak directly to President Bush. Although at first caught off guard by the caller, who asked that the United States make a public declaration that the Iranian president had undertaken such an initiative, the Americans became suspicious that a domestic opponent wanted to discredit and embarrass Hashemi-Rafsanjani. Bush insisted, as a goodwill signal to his Iranian counterpart, that the UN secretary-general inform the Iranian president about the call.

Although there was no explicit Iranian response to this American gesture (see above) and the chorus of anti-American rhetoric in Iran continued, in March Hashemi-Rafsanjani did note that Americans and Iranians had discussed the hostage issue at the Hague, that he was personally interested in settling the issue, that he was optimistic about the crisis being settled in some way, and that he had received messages from the United States on the subject. On April 22, 1990, two more Lebanon hostages—Robert Polhill and Frank Reed—were freed. Hashemi-Rafsanjani confirmed that Iran had been instrumental in arranging the release, claiming that "the Lebanese had decided to release the hostages 'upon Iranian recommendation.'"[44]

## Deus ex Machina: The Problem Simplifies Itself

With the Iranian conditions and the Dawa prisoners on the table, the negotiations to free the remaining hostages promised to be extremely complex. In the fall of 1990, however, thanks to Saddam Hussein—an actor neither Lebanese, Iranian, nor American—the problem became simpler and the negotiation agenda much shorter. Saddam cut the hardest of Gordian knots when on August 2, 1990, his troops entered Kuwait City, opened the gates of the central prison, and allowed the seventeen Dawa prisoners to escape and eventually return to Lebanon. He further simplified the problem when, seeking to protect his eastern flank, he unilaterally offered Iran much of what it was asking for in a settlement of bilateral issues. In a series of letters in late July and early August 1990, he informed Hashemi-Rafsanjani that Iraq was, in effect, abandoning its original demands that had led to the Iran-Iraq War. Finally, in a letter of August 14, Saddam accepted Iranian demands to confirm the 1975 Algiers accord (which had settled the Shatt al-Arab boundary

---

44. Menashri, "Iran," 362–63. Woods, *The Mother of All Battles*, 105.

dispute according to Iran's position) and agreed unilaterally to withdraw Iraqi forces from all occupied Iranian territory in three days.[45]

Just because the agenda was less complicated, however, did not mean that freedom for the remaining hostages would come quickly or easily. In March 1991, after the Persian Gulf War ended, the UN intermediaries resumed serious work. The Americans had provided assurances to Pérez de Cuéllar and Picco that they were Washington's only channel to Iran on the hostage case. In reality, Washington was also using the Swiss channel—that is, communicating with Iran through the Swiss government as the protecting power of American interests in Iran. In March, Iranian deputy foreign minister Vaezi told Picco in Tehran that he had discussed an exchange of American hostages for Arab prisoners of Israel with the Swiss undersecretary of state for foreign affairs. Picco told Vaezi that the UN would withdraw from the negotiations if doing so would help the Swiss channel make faster progress. Vaezi asked Picco to continue his work on behalf of the UN. Picco writes, "What I suspected was true: the Iranians were attempting to make the United Nations and the Swiss compete, hoping to get a better offer by playing one off against the other."[46]

By midsummer, the Iranian side had focused on what became its central demand for freeing Western hostages: that the United Nations carry out the provisions of Paragraph 6 of UN Security Council Resolution 598 (approved July 20, 1987), which, just more than a year later, led to a cease-fire in the Iran-Iraq War. That paragraph had requested the secretary-general "to explore, in consultation with Iran and Iraq, the question of entrusting to an impartial body with inquiring into responsibility for the conflict and to report to the Council as soon as possible." The new political environment that followed Saddam's defeat in the Gulf War now created the possibility that the United Nations could follow through with the commission of inquiry.

According to former NSC officer Bruce Riedel, it was Brent Scowcroft, Bush's adviser for National Security Affairs, who came up with the idea of a UN report blaming Iraq for starting the Iran-Iraq War as a quid pro quo for release of hostages in Lebanon.[47] Wherever the idea came from, Picco and Iranian Ambassador Zarif met in New York on July 27 and decided on what the former called a "deceptively simple swap." He describes the arrangement as follows:

---

45. Menashri, "Iran," 372.

46. Picco, *Man Without a Gun*, 134–35.

47. Cited by Barbara Slavin, *Bitter Friends, Bosom Enemies*, 180.

> Iran would do its level best with the groups in Lebanon to free the
> hostages, and we would deliver Paragraph 6 of UN Resolution 598. If
> we could get more than that—freedom for Lebanese detainees in Israeli
> prisons, information about missing Iranians in Beirut and Israeli airmen
> and soldiers in Lebanon, American "goodwill" reciprocity—it would be
> frosting on the cake. But the game turned on Paragraph 6.[48]

The Iranian concern with justice in the abstract was consistent with their
view of themselves and their situation. During the war, Khomeini had regu-
larly rejected efforts at no-fault mediation, saying that what was important
for Iran was that the guilty party should be recognized and punished. He
reluctantly retreated from that policy, and accepted Resolution 598 (a year
after the UN Security Council had approved it) only when the alternative
appeared to be a complete Iranian military and political collapse. Of course,
the Iranian side also wanted to be certain that the impartial body specified
in the resolution would come to the conclusion that the Iraqi side had been
guilty of unprovoked aggression.

## The Hostages Go Free: No More Goodwill

The arrangement turned out to be anything but simple. While the
UN-sponsored committee of professors worked on their Paragraph 6 report,
there were complex, many-sided negotiations involving the Iranians,
Lebanese Shia groups, the UN intermediaries, the Israelis, the Americans,
the Syrians, the Germans (who were also holding Lebanese Shia prisoners),
and others. Between October and December, their captors released the last
American hostages: Turner, Ciccipio, Sutherland, Steen, and Anderson. On
June 17, 1992, the last two Western prisoners—Germans Kemptner and
Struebig—were released.

Iran did get its favorable report on Paragraph 6. Picco received the report
from the European experts in early November and hid all three copies at his
home. Despite Zarif's requests, he refused to release it until after the hostages
had been released, telling the Iranian representative "the greater the gap between the release of the hostages and the release of the report, the greater the
weight would be accorded a document we both assumed would identify Iraq
as the instigator of the Iran-Iraq war."[49] The UN released its report on December 9, 1991, after the last American hostage had been released. In measured

---

48. Picco, *Man Without a Gun*, 150.

49. Ibid., 234–35.

language, the experts clearly condemned Iraq for an unjustified and illegal attack against Iran. For Tehran, the crucial parts were as follows:

> [From paragraph 5] ... the war between Iran and Iraq ... was started in contravention of international law, and violations of international law give rise to responsibility for the conflict, which question is the center of paragraph 6 [of Resolution 598].

> [From paragraph 6] ... the outstanding event under the violations referred to in paragraph 5 above is the attack of 22 September 1980 against Iran, which cannot be justified under the Charter of the United Nations, any recognized rules and principles of international law or any principles of international morality. . . .

> [From paragraph 7] Even if before the outbreak of the conflict there had been some encroachment by Iran on Iraqi territory, such encroachment did not justify Iraq's aggression against Iran—which was followed by Iraq's continuous occupation of Iranian territory during the conflict—in violation of the prohibition of the use of force. . . .[50]

Slavin describes the UN experts' work as "US-backed."[51] But whether the Americans backed or simply did not obstruct the United Nations' work on Paragraph 6, this action (or inaction) seemed to be the limit of Washington's goodwill toward the Islamic Republic. As events were moving toward a conclusion, President Bush and Scowcroft at first seemed interested in responding further to Iranian efforts on behalf of releasing the hostages. Scowcroft had asked NSC staffer Bruce Riedel to present options for further constructive steps toward Iran. After Iranian dissidents were assassinated in Europe, however, Riedel says he "was told to put the options paper on hold. It never got off the ground again."[52]

By April 1992, Picco had officially received word from Washington— there were to be no positive gestures toward Tehran "anytime soon." The administration would not even allow a NATO ally to sell non-embargoed spare aircraft parts to Iran. Perhaps recent assassinations of Iranian dissidents in Europe had persuaded the Americans that they had gone as far as they could by supporting (or not blocking) the UN experts' work on Paragraph 6. The Americans could claim that they had not bargained with Iran for hostages but had simply allowed the United Nations to do its work. With George H.W. Bush in the midst of his reelection campaign, with memories

---

50. UN Security Council Document S/23723 (December 9, 1991). "Further Report of the Secretary-General on the Implementation of Security Council Resolution 598" (1987). Picco himself describes the report as "academically solid and non-political."

51. Slavin, *Bitter Friends*, 180.

52. Ibid., 180–81.

of the Iran-Contra fiasco still fresh, and with wounds of the 1979–81 hostage crisis still festering, the president and his advisers decided that the time was not propitious for any openings toward Iran.

Picco now realized he had been unable to deliver what he had promised the Iranian side. His last act was to take this bad news to Tehran. When he met President Hashemi-Rafsanjani in the late spring of 1992, the interpreter (Javad Zarif) at first refused to translate Picco's message. When he finally did so, the Iranian president responded,

> My government has always had good relations with you. We have known you for a long time. We have assisted you in Lebanon out of respect for the United Nations secretary-general. We have taken many political risks in our cooperation with you. Not everybody was in favor of such cooperation. Nevertheless, we went ahead. Since we engaged in this effort we have listened carefully to what you told us, including all the various assurances. You understand, Mr. Picco, that you are putting me in a very difficult position. In fact, it may be a very difficult position for both of us.[53]

The Iranian president then expressed his regret for what had happened and advised Picco to leave Tehran as soon as possible before unnamed others learned of the setback and prevented him from doing so.

Despite Hashemi-Rafsanjani's evident disappointment, Iran was not completely shut out in these exchanges. The United States had neither lifted economic sanctions nor made any visible overtures to Iran, but it had (perhaps tacitly) gone some distance in supporting Iran's search for justice in the Iran-Iraq War. It is also unclear just how much Hashemi-Rafsanjani and the Iranians actually did to release the hostages in Lebanon. As noted, those captives had already lost their value as currency for weapons after the collapse of the Iran-Contra dealings in 1986. Of course, Hashemi-Rafsanjani was ready both to claim that Iran had nothing to do with the matter of hostages and Lebanon and, at the same time, to claim credit for having used Iranian influence in a humanitarian effort to free those hostages. What remains unclear, however, is whether he could have done what he did without the unforeseen escape of the Dawa Seventeen from Kuwait in 1990 and without Saddam's sudden yielding to Iranian demands in a desperate effort to secure his eastern flank in his growing confrontation with the Desert Storm coalition. Although he could play the injured party convincingly, Hashemi-Rafsanjani must have had a reasonably accurate idea of the factors limiting George Bush's freedom of action.

53. Picco, *Man Without a Gun*, 6.

## The Lessons: It Will All Be Hard

Freeing the Lebanon hostages was not a simple or elegant process. It involved much improvisation, the fortuitous intervention of Saddam Hussein, many missteps, complex arrangements that were always on the verge of collapse, tacit understandings that could be denied, and a scandal that nearly toppled a popular American president. Even when negotiators believed they had an agreement, it took months before that agreement could be translated into actual freedom for the hostages. The main lessons from nearly a decade of these difficult interactions are as follows:

- **(Once again) the parties had to choose intermediaries with great care.** This principle needs little elaboration. Although no intermediary is completely without self-interest, Manouchehr Ghorbanifarr's pattern of deception and his commercial interests in arranging shipments of arms to Iran should have given clear warnings. His Iranian connections—such as the mysterious Hassan Karoubi and Mohsen Kangarlou—proved mostly concerned with verifying Ghorbanifarr's questionable claims about Iranian factions and Soviet influence—claims that he knew would have a receptive audience among his Israeli and American listeners. Even when the skeptics—such as the ex-CIA official George Cave—were able to have Ghorbanifarr excluded from the negotiation process, the damage was already done. The arms-for-hostages swap was on, and both sides found themselves in too deep to back out.

  After the Iran-Contra fiasco, there were still many would-be intermediaries offering their services to the United States. Each claimed to have excellent contacts at the highest levels inside the Islamic Republic. The Bush administration wisely limited its contacts to the Swiss channel and to UN Secretary-General Pérez de Cuéllar's channel to the Iranian leaders—a channel he had originally established during the difficult negotiations to achieve the Iran-Iraq cease-fire in 1988. Even those channels sometimes collided, and the Iranians were all too ready to play one intermediary against another in the hope of a better deal. In the end, however, the Americans saw the UN channel as the most effective and allowed that one to pursue the hostage negotiations.

- **Negotiators had to deal carefully with harsh domestic political climates and with the legacy of bitterness and hostility between Iranians and Americans.** The toxic political climate in both countries would not permit any basic change in the mutually hostile bilateral relationship that had become central to both Iranian and American foreign policy. Each side felt its grievances, real or imagined, and those grievances created a climate that made the simple complicated and the complicated almost impossible. The American perpetrators of Iran-Contra must have understood that. With the wounds of the 1979–81 hostage crisis still raw, any plan to improve Iranian-American relations, to develop ties with real or imaginary moderates in Tehran, or to help the Islamic Republic resist Soviet encroachment would face strong opposition both from American public opinion and from powerful officials within the Reagan administration—such as Secretaries Shultz and Weinberger. Under such conditions, McFarlane, North, Poindexter, et al., attempted to keep the public and senior officials in the dark and operate in secrecy through dubious intermediaries. Perhaps the American negotiators believed they were being devious and clever; in reality they were being ignorant, clumsy, and amateurish.

Matters were not much different for the Iranian side. President Hashemi-Rafsanjani and others probably realized from the beginning that the fractious political climate in Iran would not allow anything that smelled of rapprochement between Tehran and Washington. Imam Khomeini had warned against such a step and even included the warnings in his will, read after his death in 1989. As illustrated in the bizarre incident of the 1990 fake phone call to the White House, some persons or factions in Tehran were always ready to use anti-Americanism to discredit a rival and scream betrayal of the imam's legacy. That bitter climate paralyzed leaders of the Islamic Republic and prevented them from making the deals and compromises necessary to secure a regular flow of Americans arms and supplies that would have made a real difference in the war against the Iraqis. In that lethal atmosphere, perhaps the Iranian negotiators went as far as they believed they could: a few American weapons bought in exchange for a few American hostages released.

- **The Islamic Republic's priority was its own survival.** As the war with Iraq ground on, the Iranians must have been in desperate straits to enter the original negotiations with the Israelis and Americans. The leaders of the Islamic Republic—although they believed right was on their side— saw the world arrayed against them. Despite their brave rhetoric about sacred defense and war until victory, they knew their regime's survival depended on arms supplies—supplies that they had ended through their own diplomatic incompetence. In the end, the American weapons they managed to buy through Ghorbanifarr and his friends were far too little and too late to affect the course of the war.

Whether victims of their own *mard-e-rendi* thinking, captives of their own rhetoric, or captives of American inability to do more than make a direct arms-for-hostages swap, the Iranians found themselves eventually forced—for the sake of their own survival—to accept a humiliating peace in 1988. By that time, Iraqi forces had returned to the offensive, Tehranis were fleeing Scud missile attacks, and the United States, in a series of military actions in the spring and summer of 1988, had effectively aligned itself with Baghdad. At that time, Khomeini's closest advisers convinced him that Iran could not continue fighting and was on the verge of a complete military and political collapse.

- **A search for justice remained the center of Iran's negotiating position.** With all of the complications in the extended and many-sided negotiations to free the Lebanon hostages, in the last analysis, the Iranian position came down to one central demand: that the international community should, through the process defined in Paragraph 6 of UN Security Council Resolution 598, hold an investigation to identify the guilty party and aggressor in the Iran-Iraq War. In other words, Iranians, above all things, wanted the world community to recognize that they were the aggrieved party in the conflict and that justice was on their side.

As noted before, this concern for justice has deep roots in Iran's political culture. Divine justice (*adalat*) is one of the principles of religion that Shia Islam adds to those three it shares with Sunni Islam (prophethood, monotheism, and the last judgment). Khomeini himself had long insisted on a condition for ending the war that was unacceptable to the Iraqi side: that there could be no settlement until Saddam had been publicly judged an aggressor and suitably punished.[54] In Khomeini's view, which became the Iranian position, anything less than that outcome would have denied Iranians their just rights. It was a measure of Iran's desperation that Khomeini would eventually abandon that position and swallow a United Nations cease-fire resolution that did not include a provision supporting Iran's claim to be the aggrieved party. Paragraph 6 of the 1987 UN resolution was the best the Iranians could get, and even that paragraph remained a dead letter until Saddam, through his own misjudgment, managed to neutralize any Western opposition to carrying out its provisions.

---

54. It is ironic that the United States—Khomeini's great Satan—was to be the ultimate agent of Saddam's punishment.

# 6

# The Lessons
## Fourteen Steps to Success

*At some point, somebody's got to trust somebody.*
—Attributed to Alcibiades (450–404 BCE)
From Steven Pressfield, *Tides of War*

What has history taught us about negotiating with Iranians? The encounters described in these case studies were not all brilliant successes even though many of those involved were intelligent, perceptive, and well-meaning people. All acted out of a very human mix of patriotism, idealism, ambition, opportunism, religious faith, humanitarianism, and cynicism.

Beyond the question of praiseworthy or selfish motives, the history related in these accounts is, for the most part, an uninspiring one. It contains many more don'ts than dos. Too often there is a pattern of leaders acting on impulse, of setting aside their own and others' better judgment, of believing the other side to be stupid, of ignoring long- and short-term consequences, and of not seeing how others will perceive an action or a statement. On the Iranian side, there is distortion of history to suit ideology and the ambitions of those in power; on the American side there is ignorance of history and the belief that somehow Iranian perceptions of the past do not matter.

There are lessons to be learned even from what is often a history of failure. In these cases, negotiators sometimes made judicious decisions that brought agreements beneficial to both sides; more often, however, they did the opposite and made decisions that led to breakdown and to terrible consequences in the long term. American negotiators who in the future are going to deal with Iranian counterparts should consider carefully the successes and failures of their predecessors. They should ask themselves, for example, "Why did United Nations envoy Picco succeed in freeing the Lebanon hostages in 1991 when White House staffer Oliver North had failed in 1985–86?" Those future American negotiators may find themselves dealing with Iranians in many settings. They may be negotiating face-to-face, sitting at a table with other parties, or exchanging messages through intermediaries (as Warren Christopher did through the Germans and Algerians in 1980–81). Their negotiations may be government-to-government, semi-official (track-two), or commercial. In all these contexts, the lessons of history remain valid.

## Fourteen Steps to Success

From these events, from negotiators' earlier successes and failures, I have distilled fourteen suggestions for steps that will raise the chances of success in negotiating with Iranians. Some of these steps require nothing more than applying the basic negotiation techniques taught in dozens of courses and workshops and will work in dealings with representatives of any state counterpart, not just the Islamic Republic. Iran, however, remains a special case, and the American negotiator needs both to apply the basics and then go well beyond them. The persistent, deep, and mutual mistrust that has existed between the two countries since 1979 has meant that negotiators, their judgment too often clouded by real or imagined grievances, have ignored the fundamentals of their craft and have failed to find objective criteria, calculate Best Alternatives to a Negotiated Agreement, and, most important, separate the person from the problem.[1]

Adding to the difficulty is the fact that, in the case of Iran, there are almost no recent positive experiences or store of goodwill that negotiators can use to overcome difficulties of process or substance. Relationships always matter in negotiations, and, in the Iranian-American case, they barely exist. Since the two countries formally broke diplomatic relations in 1980, there has been an almost complete lack of official, bilateral contact. That estrangement has left the field mostly to wheeler-dealers, professional pundits, and self-appointed intermediaries who are often pursuing personal or political agendas. Lacking firsthand knowledge and serious analysis, we are often left with distorted

---

1.  The last principle has been particularly difficult. In the spring of 2007, when Admiral Fallon, the chief of the United States Central Command, asked President Bush about U.S. strategy on Iran, the response was, "These are assholes." Woodward, *The War Within*, 334. Such an opinion is hardly a strategy. The Republican presidential candidate John McCain, in his September 26, 2008, televised debate with Barack Obama, continued the tradition. He rhetorically asked his rival, "How can you sit down with President Ahmadinezhad when he has called for wiping Israel off the map?"

stereotypes about Iranians' basic irrationalism and egoism and with sweeping, questionable assertions such as "Iranians hate negotiations."[2]

Given the burdens of the past, Iranians and Americans who enter negotiations today have a difficult assignment. The setting for their negotiations is unpromising, and the chances of success are uncertain. Even negotiators with infinite patience, the best techniques, the most profound understanding of their craft, and the deepest knowledge of what motivates the other side have no guarantees of success. Yet if there are mutual interests, and if both sides see a benefit in coming to the table—as they did see in 2001–02 about Afghanistan and as they should see today about Iraq—then the suggestions listed below may just help future negotiators and raise their chances of a productive encounter from none to at least slim.

## 1. Establish objective criteria free of legalisms.

Closely reasoned legal arguments may have their place in a negotiation, but for the most part they will not impress the Iranian side. This feature of Iranian negotiating style long predates the Islamic Republic. In February 1946, for example, Iranian Prime Minister Ahmad Qavam, meeting with Stalin on the sensitive issue of Soviet forces remaining on Iranian soil after World War II in violation of international agreements, deliberately avoided arguing the legalisms of the tripartite treaty of 1942 or the 1921 Soviet-Iranian friendship treaty, which gave the USSR the right to intervene in Iran under certain conditions. Instead, knowing he was holding a very weak hand, Qavam referred to Soviet withdrawal as a matter of equity and friendship between the two countries.[3]

The Islamic Republic has had a contentious relationship with the law and legal issues. In its earliest years, the new, revolutionary authorities took drastic steps to eradicate the European-based legal system it had inherited from the Pahlavi era (1925–79) and attempted to replace it with practices the new rulers believed were in accordance with Shia religious law. The new regime also undertook a wholesale purge of judges, lawyers, and prosecutors—especially women—and replaced them with clerics who were sup-

---

2. See chapter 7 for one observer's comment about Iranians' preoccupation with self." See also David Ignatius, "Countering Iran's Distrust," *The Washington Post*, May 27, 2007, B7. The reality is that just about every interaction in Iran—from buying sugar to obtaining a driver's license—involves negotiation. In the documentary "Divorce Iranian Style" (Kim Longinotto and Ziba Mir-Hosseini, 1998), for example, we watch Iranian women negotiate a maze of bureaucracy, family, and religious rules to escape intolerable family situations.

3. See chapter 2.

posed to establish an Islamic and revolutionary legal system. The regime also sacked many members of Iran's diplomatic service, who traditionally had brought strong legal credentials to their work.

In such a setting, it will be vital—although sometimes difficult—for negotiators to establish what experts call mutually acceptable objective criteria in an exchange. The Islamic Republic, particularly in its most revolutionary and ideological moments, has often regarded what others call international law as a pretext for foreigners to cheat Iranians out of their rights. One expert, writing of "the historical distrust Iranians had for Western legalism," asks rhetorically, "Had treaty after treaty not proved that international law was simply a political device to ensure Western control?"[4] For Iranian negotiators, the test of an agreement, therefore, is not whether it conforms to the experts' notions of legality but whether it can be presented as a victory for Islam and for Iran. Such criteria, of course, are subjective and ambiguous, and in a highly charged political arena, what one group claims as victory another will call betrayal.

The American negotiator, therefore, should look for unambiguous, mutually agreeable standards that avoid legal jargon and technicalities. Legal arguments will often carry less weight with Iranians than with Americans. For the American side in a transaction, maintaining the integrity of the process—grounded on legal principles—is often crucial. For the Iranian side, that process is seen only as a means (or an obstacle) to achieving an all-important result. An Iranian visa applicant, for example, will probably have little interest in upholding the integrity of American immigration law. He or she will show genuine confusion if a visa officer protests indignantly ("You lied to me!") on discovering that the applicant misrepresented certain facts in the belief he needed to do so to obtain the visa.

There is an important distinction here. A lack of interest in points of law may suggest that the Iranian side is taking an emotional, subjective view of an issue while ignoring logic and objective factors. The reality is not so simple. The emotional factors may be important, but the true motives of the Iranian side in a negotiation will sometimes be difficult to comprehend. Those motives may be a mixture of the political, personal, financial, and ideological. The American negotiator, lacking clear insight into these motivations, should be wary of taking refuge in the oversimplified and time-honored view of Iranians as emotional and incomprehensible (as opposed to supposedly rational Westerners). In so doing, he risks assuming a self-righteous

---

4. Ansari, *Confronting Iran*, 203.

position and creating a self-fulfilling prophecy. Treated as irrational, the Iranian side in a negotiation is likely to become so.[5]

## 2. The past matters: Be aware of Iran's historical greatness, its recent weakness, and its grievances from decades or centuries before.

Iranians know well that in pre-Islamic times their country was a world power, ruled a vast empire, and on several occasions defeated even the mighty armies of Rome. The friezes of Persepolis show Iranian kings receiving tribute from dozens of subject peoples. The Iranian plateau is covered with such reminders of Iran's ancient glory, even if popular memory now associates those pre-Islamic monuments with mythological heroes such as Jamshid and Rostam rather than long-forgotten historical kings such as Cyrus and Darius. In more recent times—until the eighteenth century—Iran rivaled the neighboring Ottoman and Moghul Empires and could deal with Western nations on equal terms.

Beginning in the 1700s, however, Iran lost its great power status. It progressively surrendered territory and influence to outsiders, notably to Britain, Russia, and (later) the United States. The nineteenth century saw multiple humiliations for Iran: bankruptcy, military defeats, and losses of territory and authority in Afghanistan, central Asia, and Transcaucasia. By means of the notorious capitulations and concessions, foreigners, who enjoyed immunity from Iranian law, gained control of the country's finances and natural resources, including oil, and even its security forces.[6] Iranians escaped overt colonization only because the rival British and Russians checked each other and thus kept the country feeble but nominally independent.

In the twentieth century, the degradations continued. Foreign powers formally divided Iran into spheres of influence (by the Anglo-Russian treaty of 1907), occupied the country (during both world wars), backed provincial separatist movements (in 1945–46), and frustrated Iranians' attempts to gain control of their own destiny by suppressing the Constitutional Movement (in 1906–11) and by overthrowing Prime Minister Mohammad Mosaddegh's nationalist government (in 1953).

---

5. See chapter 3 for a description of how the British fell into the "we are reasonable and they are crazy" trap in 1951–53.

6. "Capitulations" granted foreigners (and Iranians with foreign patronage) legal immunity from Iranian law. "Concessions" were economic privileges and monopolies, which the perpetually bankrupt Qajar monarchs sold to foreign entrepreneurs to raise quick cash.

History, or at least some version of it, will be very much alive for Iranian negotiators. Like all of us, Iranians are captives of their history. In their case, however, that history is a very long and tragic one. What Iranians remember is likely to be some disastrous event that in the retelling has grown and transformed itself into near mythology. With such memories, suggesting that an Iranian interlocutor forget the past or move on is unlikely to meet with much success or response beyond puzzlement or hostility.

Iranian negotiators may never mention history explicitly (unlike Israeli Prime Minister Menachem Begin, whose one-hour meetings famously began with thirty minutes of Old Testament and twenty minutes of Holocaust, or Yasir Arafat, who loved to dwell on past injustices to the Palestinians to the exclusion of anything else). Depending on the Iranian negotiator's cultural orientation, however, one or more of the following events will have shaped his approach to the issue under discussion:

- the Arab invasion and defeat of Iran's pre-Islamic Sassanian Empire in the seventh century CE;

- the civil wars of early Islamic history, climaxing in the martyrdom of the Prophet's grandson, Imam Hussein b. Ali, at Karbala in 680 CE;

- the constitutional revolution and its failure, 1906–11;

- the tripartite Allied (British, Soviet, and American) occupation of Iran, 1941–45;

- the foreign-backed separatist movements in Azerbaijan and Kurdistan, 1945–46;

- the overthrow of Prime Minister Mosaddegh and the restoration of the shah, 1953;

- the exile of Ayatollah Khomeini, 1964, partly because of his public opposition to the law granting immunity to American military advisers and their family members in Iran;

- the Islamic Revolution of 1978–79 and its bloody aftermath, including the Iran-Iraq War of 1980–88; and

- the United States and others' siding with Iraq during the Iran-Iraq War and the downing of an Iranian civilian airliner by the USS *Vincennes* in July 1988.

Most of these events ended badly for Iranians (or at least for some Iranians) and have created a profound sense of national victimization and grievance that still pollutes the country's political atmosphere. Even where the events, in the view of some, did not end badly, the lesson that Iranians often draw from their history is one of "us alone against a hostile world." As a result, Iranian counterparts may come to a negotiation with a view that their nation's history, despite the glories of the distant past, has too often featured defeat, tragedy, victimization, and betrayal.

Because of this history, negotiators for the Islamic Republic will see themselves as holding the weaker position. With that view, and with their reading of Iran's historical experience, they may maintain that the other (stronger) party is not negotiating but attempting to use its superior economic, political, and military muscle to compel Iran to accept an unequal agreement. Official Iranian propaganda, for example, always referred to the Iran-Iraq War as the imposed war. Such language connoted Iranian weakness, suggesting that the country was not acting as an independent and sovereign state but was fighting because larger and stronger foreign powers were forcing her to do so. In such a relationship of perceived inequality, the goal of Iranian negotiators becomes obtaining that ill-defined objective "respect" or at least reaching an agreement that they can present as showing Iran to be any country's equal. Such was the case during the 1951–53 oil nationalization crisis, when Prime Minister Mosaddegh was more concerned with redressing past humiliations than with reaching an economic agreement concerning Iran's oil industry.

Many analysts have noted that Iran's central foreign-policy goal is attaining the respect worthy of its size, population, resources, and historical greatness.[7] At the very beginning of its July 2003 proposal for a dialogue with the United States, the Iranian message mentioned the issue of "mutual respect."[8] As a result, Iranian negotiators may approach a discussion with a combination of grandeur and grievance. Whoever negotiates with Iran should be prepared to deal with these contradictory feelings: the belief that others owe Iran deference for its cultural and political glories and the simultaneous belief that powerful outsiders have betrayed, humiliated, and brutalized a weak Iran and will do so again if given the opportunity. In such a setting, phrases like axis of evil and regime change emerging from Washington have confirmed Iranian suspicions that the American government is determined to rid itself of an assertive Islamic Republic—or at least deprive it of its rights.

---

7. The journalist Barbara Slavin calls Iran the "Rodney Dangerfield of the Middle East." *Bitter Friends*, 13.

8. See appendix for the text of this proposal.

American negotiators should be aware that their Iranian counterparts' pessimistic view of the past can create its own vicious circle, in which the Iranian negotiators come to suspect that any arrangement the other side accepts must ipso facto be unfair to the Iranian side. In that case, the Iranian negotiators—convinced that the foreigners are (again) cheating Iran and that the Iranian side could have gotten more if it had held out—will refuse to close the deal. If the Iranian negotiators do get more, then their original suspicions are confirmed, and they remain suspicious that even the new and better deal is unfair to Iran. If it was not, why would the other side have accepted it?

Can Iranian negotiators escape the burdens of their country's past? Of course they can, if doing so serves some larger interest. As one Iranian-American observer noted, the Iranians, in an effort to mend fences with their Arab neighbors, now appear willing to overlook the fact that Saudi Arabia and most of the Persian Gulf states were strong financial and logistical backers of Saddam Hussein's Iraq throughout the bloody 1980–88 war. The Iranian side could always bring up that history again, but for the moment the need for normal relations with those Arab states dictates putting aside (if not forgetting) historical grievances.

## 3. Choose intermediaries with great care.

In any negotiation, and especially in the absence of formal American-Iranian diplomatic relations, a trusted and skilled intermediary can be very useful. Algerian mediators—to whom each side could talk without making an apparent concession to the other—played such a positive role in the 1980–81 negotiations between the United States and Iran to end the American Embassy hostage crisis. With existing reservoirs of mistrust and suspicion making direct contact so difficult, the right intermediary can allow communication without either side appearing to be the party asking for talks. In the recent Baghdad meetings, for example, the Iraqi government could play that role by issuing invitations to Iranians and Americans, who could then say that they were at the table in response to a request from their Iraqi friends.

In contrast to such official, respectable intermediaries, the last thirty years of American-Iranian contact have also featured self-appointed persons and groups who have acted on their own initiative from more questionable motives. As long as there are no official bilateral U.S.-Iranian relations, there will be no shortage of those volunteering their services as channels to this or that influential person within the murky Iranian political universe. Everything about such persons and their claims, however, should be suspect: their contacts, their motives, their veracity, and their ability to deliver.

Such would-be intermediaries, however, know they have an American audience and often exploit it skillfully. They can use the absence of official contact and the known political leanings of their American listeners. They can tell those listeners what they want to hear and attempt to convince them, for example, that

- Iranians are seething with discontent and are ready to make a new revolution with outside support (especially financial) and encouragement;
- this or that Iranian diaspora group has millions of followers inside Iran who are just waiting for the right moment to launch an uprising;
- a particular ethnic group (e.g., Kurds or Azeris) or region (e.g., Baluchistan) is ready, with outside support, to make trouble for the central government by challenging its authority in an entire province;
- most Iranians would welcome American efforts to overthrow the Islamic Republic, even by force if necessary.; and
- the leaders of the Islamic Republic are ready to moderate their policies and require only a gesture from the United States to show support for policies of some (imaginary) moderate Iranian faction.

U.S.-Iranian relations are littered with the wreckage of ill-judged attempts to use problematic intermediaries. The lawyers Christian Bourguet and Hector Villalon, for example, were doing a profitable business with Iran when they offered their services as intermediaries during the 1979–81 hostage crisis. Eventually, their efforts led nowhere because their Iranian contacts had no power beyond the doors of their own offices. The notorious wheeler-dealer Manouchehr Ghorbanifarr—teamed up with NSC staffer Oliver North—almost brought down an American president (Ronald Reagan) by manipulating and misrepresenting the views of all sides during the notorious arms-for-hostages deal of 1985–86. Despite Ghorbanifarr's well-documented shortcomings as an intermediary, some American officials continued to deal with him as late as 2002.

Such persons should be dealt with warily, if at all. They can and will drag their American contacts into the mud of Iranian political swamps and use their contacts to gain respectability and further their own political and financial fortunes. One should be especially wary if such intermediaries claim purely disinterested or humanitarian motives and declare, "Of course I want nothing for myself. I just want to be of service to both countries." Any variation of the above statement should be a clear warning to stay away.

## 4. Talk to the right people.

The unique and opaque structure of the Islamic Republic—where duplicating and conflicting authorities inhabit a world of contentious and arcane internal politics—can make it very difficult to understand exactly who has authority and responsibility to make agreements. The conventional wisdom in dealing with the Islamic Republic is: "Everyone is in charge; no one is in charge." Rarely will the other side in any negotiation, however, announce that it is not authorized to make an agreement or does not have the power to carry out a commitment. That unpleasant news usually arrives only after one side believes it has reached a deal.

The American negotiator's tempting explanation for such breakdowns may be oriental duplicity, but the reality is that he has probably been negotiating with the wrong people. He should understand that there are parallel and sometimes competing governing structures within the Islamic Republic. There is a republican system with a written constitution, a presidency, ministries, a parliament, and popular elections. Such a system is familiar to us and resembles, at least in appearance, parliamentary and presidential systems in other countries. In this system, titles more or less reflect responsibilities, and fundamental laws limit terms of office and establish mechanisms for accountability. The Iranian parliament, for example, must confirm nominated ministers and can dismiss them by votes of no-confidence.

Alongside this republican system, however, there exists a second, revolutionary or theocratic structure that operates outside and independent of the formal government structure and its legal limitations. At the head of this parallel system is an exclusive men's club of about twenty-five senior clerics who share an ideology and taste for political and economic power. Those within this inner circle have held, with varying titles, the reins of power in the Islamic Republic since its beginnings in 1979.[9] This system emerged from the chaos of 1979–80, when the existing civil administration, police, and military had collapsed and the new regime found itself in a struggle for power with ethnic separatists, armed militias, and dissidents from across the political spectrum. Distrusting the civil and military institutions it had inherited from the monarchy, the victors of the revolution created new, parallel structures, such as the Revolutionary Guards (Iranian Revolutionary Guard Corps [IRGC]) as a private security force, the revolutionary courts to administer summary justice to opponents, and the Ansar-e-Hezbollah (literally, "the supporters of the Party of God"). This last group was to be

---

9.  For further discussion of this elite, see Limbert, *Iran: At War with History*, 145–49.

the new regime's enforcer and goon squad assigned to intimidate opponents and fight the vicious street battles of the time against nationalists, students, women's rights advocates, Marxists, and the hated liberals.[10]

In the provinces, governors (employees of the Interior Ministry) found themselves powerless, dwarfed by the local imam's representative and Friday prayer leader (who was often the same person). During the Iran-Iraq War, the Revolutionary Guards were organized into front-line units, whose role eclipsed that of the regular military. In the March–April 2007 crisis over detained British military personnel, it was clear that the guards' maritime units—not the Iranian navy—were the forces involved in this action. Throughout this crisis, the role and the attitude of the official Iranian government remained unclear.

In a negotiation, these ambiguities will affect how the Iranians will look at the American side. The American government's separation of powers can create similar confusion among Iranians about who speaks with authority for the United States. In the summer of 1979, for example, an ill-timed congressional resolution denouncing summary executions by Iran's new revolutionary authorities negated the effects of more positive statements by executive branch officials. This so-called Javits Resolution—although it had no legal effect—sabotaged American efforts to establish normal working relations with Tehran, including appointing a new ambassador. Twenty years later, after Secretary Albright had made her offer to enter negotiations without preconditions, one heard Iranians complain that they were uncertain about the sincerity of the American offer. Although both President Clinton and Secretary of State Albright had explicitly endorsed the proposal, Iranian analysts continued to see a trap or could not believe that even the president and secretary of state could speak authoritatively. Despite the clear endorsements, the response from Iran was, "But we are hearing conflicting statements, and we're not sure what to believe."[11]

## 5. Understand that the Islamic Republic's priority is survival and its leaders' priority is to stay in power.

Iran's leaders see themselves surrounded by enemies seeking their removal and the Islamic Republic's overthrow. They see American forces in

---

10. In 1979–80 these groups operated under the supervision of the shadowy Revolutionary Council. That body took charge of the government after Mehdi Bazargan's provisional government collapsed in November 1979.

11. Exchange between the author and Professor Sadeq Zibakalam, University of Tehran. Carried by *Radio Azadi* (Radio Free Europe/Radio Liberty), September 6, 1999.

Afghanistan, Iraq, Turkey, and the Persian Gulf; they see hostile Sunnis in Saudi Arabia, Afghanistan, Pakistan, and central Asia; they see hostile Arabs to the south and west; they see hostile Turkic peoples to the west and north; they see nuclear-armed states in India, Pakistan, and Israel; and they see hostile Azeri irredentists to the north, Baluchi separatists to the southeast, and both Kurdish and Arab separatists to the west. When these leaders hear terms like "regime change" and "axis of evil" out of Washington, such rhetoric confirms what they already suspect: that the United States is determined to overthrow the Islamic Republic, using subversion if possible and force if necessary.

Under these conditions, the leaders of Iran will do what they believe they must do to ensure their and their regime's survival. With survival at stake, they will vacillate between extremes of concession and brutality according to which better serves their immediate purpose. Near the end of the Iran-Iraq War, in June 1988, for example, they suddenly executed hundreds of political prisoners—some of whom had already served their sentences—for reasons still unclear.[12] Although willing to sacrifice thousands of their country's young men in the swamps of Khuzistan and southern Iraq during the 1980–88 war, Iran's leaders were not ready to sacrifice themselves and their positions. Thus, in August 1988 they accepted a humiliating cease-fire deal with Iraq when they realized their continuing the war threatened to bring down the whole structure of the Islamic Republic. They have made alliances with the non-Islamic (Armenia), the anti-Islamic (Russia), and the godless (North Korea) at the expense of their fellow Muslims in Azerbaijan, Bosnia, and Chechnya. They have allied themselves with Libya's Muammar Qaddafi and overlooked his role in eliminating Lebanese Shia leader Imam Musa Sadr. They have supported terrorist groups and operations to eliminate dissidents abroad. Believing Iran vulnerable to a Czech-style Velvet Revolution, they have lashed out and arrested, imprisoned, harassed, and murdered domestic opponents, including women, harmless dissidents, and intellectuals whom they somehow see as a threat. Then, when driven to the wall, they have made sudden reversals of policy, as they did when, despite their earlier defiant statements, they accepted the UN cease-fire resolution in 1988 and when, in 2003, they offered to discuss a comprehensive political settlement with the Americans, whose victorious army was camped on their western frontier.

---

12.  For more on these executions, see Abrahamian, *Tortured Confessions*, 209–28.

Facing this wary view of the world from their Iranian counterparts, American negotiators have both a problem and an opportunity. On the negative side, American negotiators will encounter an assumption of bad faith and a wall of suspicion and mistrust from Iranian counterparts. The Iranians will take for granted that America's ultimate purpose in dealing with Iran is not to reach agreement but is to destroy the Islamic Republic and remove its leaders from power. On the positive side, a discussion can progress if negotiators can reassure the Iranian side that agreement will not destabilize the Islamic Republic and may, in fact, allow it to survive.

Tehran's cooperation with the United States during the 2001–02 negotiations on Afghanistan is a case in point. At that time, the Iranians understood very well how they would benefit from the downfall of the Taliban regime and from its replacement by an Afghan government that did not subscribe to a radical anti-Shia and anti-Iranian ideology. Similar considerations should apply in the case of Iraq, where the Islamic Republic, in the interest of its own survival, shares the American aversion to a divided Iraq, an Iraq dominated by Sunni religious extremists, or an Iraq under a militant Arab nationalist—a new version of Saddam Hussein.

## 6. Let the Iranians define what is in their national interest.

Iranians do not appreciate hearing lectures from others on what is logical and what is in their (i.e., Iranians') self-interest. Misreading Iranian interests has led to serious problems in the past. In 1979, for example, American policymakers assumed that Iran's underlying economic and security interests—such as historical animosity to Russia and Iraq—would limit the new leaders' anti-American actions to rhetoric and symbolism. Such an analysis may have been correct as far as it went, but it failed to consider the interests of subgroups and factions in provoking a confrontation and sabotaging any possibility of a normal relationship between Washington and the new government in Tehran. These groups were willing to sacrifice American arms supplies and other Iranian vital interests to serve their own political ambitions and to eliminate their domestic rivals. In 1979–80, such groups ridiculed the whole idea of national interest. By creating an atmosphere of hysteria and fear, they ensured the ultimate victory of radical and absolutist factions in the revolutionary coalition over their nationalist and leftist rivals.

The Iranian negotiator knows very well what serves his national, partisan, family, and personal interests. Such interests may differ from—and may even contradict—what an outsider, largely unaware of the factional infighting in progress, believes is in Iran's national interest, a concept that has been enormously suspect and hotly debated since the 1979 revolution.[13]

The same consideration applies to logic and illogic. American negotiators should be wary of repeating British actions during the 1951–53 oil crisis, when the British representatives portrayed themselves as the only logical party at the table and dismissed the Iranians as hopelessly illogical and emotional. As noted earlier, writing off the Iranians as irrational can become a self-fulfilling prophecy. Assume an adversary is illogical, and he will become so. In some cases, the Iranian side is using logic that the American side cannot penetrate—logic dictated by historical grievances, an instinct for personal survival, a feeling of vulnerability, or by other political and social forces poorly understood by outsiders.

## 7. Understand the Iranian BATNA: Expect actions that may appear (to you) self-destructive.

In negotiation with Iranians, as in all negotiations, it is vital to be aware of the other side's BATNA,[14] as well as one's own. The Iranian negotiators' BATNA may be difficult to predict. In some cases, they may be unwilling to make any agreement lest they come under criticism from political adversaries at home for selling out to the foreigner. Some historians, for example, have argued that Prime Minister Mosaddegh rejected compromise settlements of the 1951–53 Anglo-Iranian oil nationalization dispute out of a desire to benefit from continued political turmoil and out of fear that his domestic political opponents would, using own maximalist rhetoric, accuse him of surrendering to foreign interests. Such an analysis maintains, in effect, that Iranian domestic politics forced Mosaddegh into self-destructive actions.[15]

American negotiators should not convince themselves, "The Iranians will never be so foolish as to do X." In the past, that statement has sometimes become a guarantee that they will do precisely X, driven not by foolishness, but, as noted above, by logic and necessities that the outside observer does not see or understand. In commercial dealings, for example, informants have reported that Iranian negotiators are willing to sabotage an entire deal rather than make some minor concession. Some experts say that Iran's refusal to

---

13. Iranian opponents of President Ahmadinezhad, for example, criticize him for goading the Western countries in a way that does not serve Iran's national interests. For his part, Ahmadinezhad might compare his rhetoric to earlier statements by Imam Khomeini in which he subordinated national interest to pan-Islamic ideals.

14. The term was coined by Fisher, Patton, and Ury in *Getting to Yes*.

15. See chapter 3 for Mosaddegh's comment to Vernon Walters on this subject.

negotiate seriously with foreign partners on oil and natural gas contracts has stopped crucial investments and has damaged that sector's ability to maintain long-term supply and revenues.[16]

In such cases, the Iranian negotiator may not have the power to make any reasonable agreement, and the negotiation becomes an exercise in futility. He may also, in a commercial negotiation, for example, be seeking a bribe, either for himself or on behalf of a patron, to close the deal. Finally, he may be what the Iranians call *mard-e-rendi*, someone who outsmarts himself through pursuing short-term gain with a single-mindedness that blinds him to larger and long-term issues at stake. Iranians often impute this kind of behavior to others on whom they look down. Asked about this trait, a senior Iranian diplomat complained to me that he found being *mard-e-rendi* (sometimes made stronger and called *khar* [donkey] *mard-e-rendi*) was an annoying characteristic of Indians and Pakistanis.

In such circumstances, it will be vital to keep the tone of negotiations professional and serious. If talks break down today, they may resume next month. Iranian-American negotiations can fail for many reasons, but when they do, the American side should resist the temptation to conclude, "The talks broke down because Iranians are irrational, unpredictable, and cannot recognize their own interests." Whatever the reason, maintaining a nonjudgmental tone (or, as Fisher would say, keeping the problem separate from the person) will be essential in preserving the possibility that today's failure can become tomorrow's success.

## 8. Give your Iranian counterparts credit for intelligence.

Iranians have a long history of being treated as simpletons incapable of drawing obvious conclusions from the available evidence. When Britain and Czarist Russia, for example, signed their 1907 treaty that divided Persia into spheres of influence, the preamble stated that both parties pledged to respect Persian independence and territorial integrity. As one contemporary British observer put it, "Such statements are a sure sign that a country is about to lose both its territorial integrity and its independence." More than seventy years later, in October 1979, the American administration thought it could avoid the inevitable and placate Iranian public opinion by announcing that the United States was admitting the deposed shah for purely humanitarian reasons and only for medical treatment. Although someone somewhere may

---

16. See above for a discussion of the roots of such tactics in a "vicious circle of mistrust."

have accepted such an explanation, given the history of Iranian-American relations, no Iranian cognizant of that history would have believed it. Even if true, that rationale, rather than reassure an Iranian audience, inflamed it by insulting its intelligence. For most Iranians, America's admitting the shah confirmed what many, in the highly charged atmosphere of late 1979, already suspected: that the United States was plotting to restage the events of August 1953 to overthrow the new revolutionary regime and restore the Pahlavi monarchy.[17]

In the years before the revolution, most Iranians were perceptive enough to see the reality behind Mohammad Reza Shah's pretensions to power. They saw the regime's flashy parades, expensive military hardware, uniforms, statues, and ceremonies for what they were—the fragile, ornate exterior of a hollow shell. They understood both the emptiness behind the monarchy's splendid façade, and the profound insecurity and simmering anger that lay just below the placid surface.

Although the shah was skilled at deceiving outsiders, he found it difficult to deceive his own people, who were convinced he owed his position to foreign backing and that he depended on continued foreign support to stay in power. Those who saw him as a foreign (i.e., American) puppet could always find evidence to support their belief. In 1963–64, for example, the United States pressured the shah and his submissive parliament into accepting changes in the existing American-Iranian Status of Forces Agreement, expanding the number of resident American military advisers (and their family members) who enjoyed immunity from Iranian legal jurisdiction. At the time, the United States presented the change as no more than a technical adjustment to the existing agreement. To most Iranians, however, the new agreement was just further evidence of their country's degradation and of the shah's complete subjugation of Iranian pride and sovereignty to the will of the Americans. Even the shah's obedient parliament—perhaps responding to the exhortations of the cleric Ruhollah Khomeini—had great difficulty swallowing this particular humiliation.[18]

---

17.  See chapter 4 for the skeptical reaction of Ebrahim Yazdi, Iran's foreign minister at the time.

18.  Ayatollah Khomeini established his nationalist credentials with Iranians by his outspoken opposition to this agreement. His blunt criticism of the SOFA led to the shah's sending him into exile in 1964, where he remained until his triumphant return in early 1979.

## 9. Expect a case based on vague and uncertain claims.

With a shortage of diplomatic expertise and lacking a well-trained cadre of support staff, Iranian negotiators will not always be equipped with facts, figures, maps, and precedents with which to make their case. Instead, they may rely on ill-defined historical claims or on appeals to justice (see point 12 below). Although the Islamic Republic has its own elite—and experts have noted the Iranian elite's ability to reproduce itself despite political turmoil— Iran has yet to recover from the anti-intellectual policies and purges of the republic's early years. At that time, the new regime openly distrusted its experts, whom it saw as insufficiently ideological (*maktabi*) and tainted by their associations with the West. The new authorities deliberately encouraged much of the country's intelligentsia—unable to adapt to the nation's new and harsh realities under a theocratic system—to emigrate. Those who stayed, the new order stripped of influence. In the place of expertise remained slogans, a cultural revolution, and a lingering mistrust of intellectuals and technocrats who somehow represented alien, decadent, and non-Islamic values.

The Islamic Republic has often associated technical expertise with the old regime. In October 1979, for example, one heard the cry at Tehran's Friday prayer ceremonies, "As for those carping intellectuals, we will break their pens!" (or their shinbones, depending on one's translation of the Persian *qalam*). The new, revolutionary regime preferred to put trusted ideologues in charge of ministries, where true belief in the new theocracy outweighed training and qualifications. The result was a social and cultural revolution in which a generation of inexperienced new men took positions of influence and marginalized those infected by travel, foreign education, and association with the old regime. The Islamic Republic quickly purged the Iranian foreign ministry, for example, of its experienced professionals, and replaced them with inexperienced radicals, including some who had learned the practice of diplomacy by capturing and holding the staff of the American Embassy in 1979–81.

## 10. Expect grandstanding, political theater, and flamboyant gestures.

Much of what happens in Iran's political life includes a large element of theater. During the 1980–88 Iran-Iraq War, for example, the media would show ordinary citizens donating jewelry and other valuables for the war and mothers saying how happy they were to have their sons martyred for the cause. During political conflict, partisans will parade purportedly martyred bodies through the streets in noisy processions to stir up pride and anger.

The mourning ceremonies marking the holiest days of Shia Islam often feature music, costumes, animals, and elaborate displays and reenactments. When students seized the U.S. Embassy in November 1979, they saw themselves making a gesture against the United States without much thought about consequences or what came next. When President Ahmadinezhad announced the release of the British military captives in April 2007, he described the action as a gesture of friendship to the British people.

In such a setting, the pose, the appearance, and the grand gesture can replace substance, and American negotiators need to sort out which is which. The equivalent of bumper stickers can replace policy. Iran's political discourse often features fiery rhetoric, slogans, and words like "never," "to the death," and "not one inch." Sometimes the speaker, carried away by his own bombast, loses his grasp on reality. In October 2008, for example, Iranian Vice President for Media Affairs Mehdi Kalhor, discussing U.S-Iranian relations, struck such a defiant pose when he claimed, "It is the Americans who are in dire need of reestablishing ties with Iran" and said Tehran's two preconditions for holding talks with Washington were withdrawal of American forces from the Middle East and ending support for Israel.[19]

Even the feeble and bankrupt Qajar monarchs of the nineteenth century, while presiding over their country's collapse into a collective coma, portrayed themselves as mighty conquerors and heirs to the great Iranian kings of history and mythology with titles such as "he to whom the world directs its prayers" (qebleh-ye-alam). Fath Ali Shah (1797–1834) defaced the pre-Islamic rock carvings at Taq-e-Bustan with a poor rendering of himself as a Sassanian emperor. During the turmoil of the early twentieth century, fiery telegrams and petitions flew around the country as citizens pledged to defend the new Iranian constitution to the death. When matters got difficult, however, many of the thousands of would-be defenders of the constitution weighed their options and made themselves scarce, preferring to join what Iranians call the "party of the winds" (hezb-e-baad).

Khomeini himself was a master of defiant rhetoric. During the 1979–81 hostage crisis, his memorable statement, "America can't do a damn thing" (a polite translation of a much cruder Persian original) immediately appeared on hundreds of walls and banners throughout the country. In 1981, in a fit of anti-British pique, the Iranians renamed Tehran's Churchill Avenue near the British Embassy for martyr Bobby Sands, the IRA operative who starved himself to death in a British prison. In an ironic sequel to that incident, in

---

19. Fars News Agency, October 12, 2008.

2007 a British reporter in Tehran described having a meal at the Bobby Sands Snack Bar near the British Embassy.[20]

With such gestures, the Iranians will paint themselves into political corners. These rhetorical flourishes can become policy and lock the Iranians into uncomfortable and self-destructive positions. The 1980s slogan "war, war, until victory" meant that thousands of Iranians became victims of their leaders' rhetoric and died pursuing a pointless conflict with Iraq—after Tehran had rejected the opportunity for a favorable settlement in 1982. In the late-1980s, as revolutionary fervor cooled, the reminder, "Don't forget 'Death of America' " would appear on Tehran walls, a tacit admission of the end of revolutionary enthusiasm. The Islamic Republic had to spend years untangling itself from the effects of Khomeini's 1989 famous ruling ordering the death of the British writer Salman Rushdie for the heretical views expressed in his novel *The Satanic Verses*.

## 11. Remember that power is respected, weakness despised.

Iranians may fear Aesop's merciless King Stork, but they detest his quiescent King Log. A recurring theme of Iranian history is the respect accorded strong leaders—even bloodthirsty ones—who are able to check the powerful centrifugal forces in the society. Iranians see *fetneh* (disorder) as their worst calamity, far worse than a despot's arbitrary or harsh rule. Public order has always been very precarious in Iran, and a powerful ruler is seen as the only safeguard against the anarchy that is always lurking below the surface, always ready to emerge and shatter that order. Iran has seen recurring social and economic collapse when there is no strong ruler in charge. Tribes, ethnic groups, the clergy, urban mobs, external enemies, and ambitious, opportunistic politicians are always ready to challenge current authorities. The pious, weak, and ineffective last ruler of the Safavid dynasty (1502–1736), Shah Sultan Hussein (1694–1722) is still Iranians' proverbial King Log, the feeble leader who brings the country to ruin and collapse. Shah Sultan Hussein's opposite (Iran's King Stork) is the seventh-century Caliph Omar, who, although hated by Shia Muslims for usurping the rights of the Prophet's family, earns respect as a strong, harsh, decisive, and effective ruler. Both of these rulers' names have entered the common language as symbols of weak and strong leadership.

---

20. See a picture of this establishment in Majd, *The Ayatollah Begs to Differ*, following 148.

Connected to the above view is another recurring theme of Iranian history: leadership is always personal and always charismatic. Ayatollah Khomeini drew a huge personal following when he was seen as a savior of Iran and Islam. Although some convinced themselves he would withdraw to his mosque to teach and study after the victory of the revolutionary forces in February 1979, the realities of Iran's political culture demanded otherwise. He could never leave to others—particularly to the technocrats—the business of governing. As long as he was alive, he remained the final authority, and no one—not a president, prime minister, or anyone else—could exercise any meaningful power. In such an environment, American attempts in 1979 to deal with revolutionary Iran through the Western-educated technocrats of the provisional government were doomed to failure; it soon became obvious that the real power in Iran did not lie with officials carrying ministerial titles.

Similarly, after the soft-spoken and scholarly Mohammad Khatami became president of Iran in 1997, many Iranians saw him as their country's savior after almost twenty years of post-revolutionary austerity and violence. When President Khatami proved unable to fulfill those high expectations, however, his prestige plummeted as Iranians felt they had been deceived into electing a new version of Shah Sultan Hussein. By the end of his second term in 2005, many Iranians dismissed not only Khatami but the entire reform movement as a collection of feckless, squabbling intellectuals who were no match for those tough ideologues who had cut their teeth in the street battles, political infighting, and gang warfare of the 1980s and 1990s. The latter group, although it could not match its opponents in formal education, at least understood how to gain, hold, and use power.

The Iranian respect for power, however, does not mean that American negotiators can rely on threats and intimidation to make his case. That respect does mean that Iranian negotiators will well understand the multiple pressures—internal and external—which impel them to accept or reject a particular offer. In response to an American proposal, the Iranian side will analyze—rightly or wrongly—how much pressure (of all kinds) lies behind the proposal. That degree of pressure will become part of the calculation of response.[21]

---

21.   There is an often-quoted statement (of uncertain origin) that says, "Iranians will never give in to pressure. They will give in only to a lot of pressure."

## 12. Understand that justice, often in a harsh version, in the abstract is extremely important.

From ancient times Iranian history has abounded in references to *daad* and *adl*, two words for "justice," both closely associated with *din* (religion). The medieval Islamic historians and moralists gave the Sassanian ruler Khosrow I Anushiravan (531–579 CE) the label "the just" and presented him to their patrons as the ideal of kingship. The writers urged Islamic rulers to follow Anushiravan's example by upholding the circle of justice to preserve social order and peace. One early twelfth-century Islamic historian expressed this ideal of the just ruler as follows: "There is no kingdom without an army, no army without wealth, no wealth without material prosperity, and no material prosperity without justice."[22] Shia Muslims uphold this Iranian emphasis on justice, and add divine justice (*adl*), along with the imamate, to the three fundamental elements of religion—monotheism, prophethood, and resurrection—that they share with Sunnis.

In a negotiation, Iranian representatives may frame their demands, not in specific or quantitative terms but in terms that claim, "All we are seeking is justice" or "We want our rights." For Ayatollah Khomeini, for example, such justice meant assigning blame and punishing the guilty party in a dispute. In this spirit, he told a visiting Non-Aligned Movement team seeking to mediate a settlement to the Iran-Iraq War that the team members' true mediation mission was to visit both Iran and Iraq, examine what had happened, and determine which of the warring parties had right and justice on its side. "If we are wrong, then condemn us. But if they are wrong, then condemn them. *Justice demands you do this*" (author's emphasis).[23]

In the Iranian setting of precarious social balance, justice is often harsh and not always tempered by mercy. The Persian proverb says, *Zolm bessaviyeh adl ast*, "Injustice equally applied means justice." With a fragile society, a violent history, and foreign and domestic enemies always ready to take advantage of weakness, many Iranians believe that justice should be quick, decisive, and visible. After the victory of the 1979 revolution, there was little interest among the victors in long and carefully prepared trials for the malefactors of the old regime. Despite an international outcry against the rapid verdicts and procedural shortcuts of the revolutionary courts, justice—in

---

22. Lambton, "Justice in the Medieval Persian Theory of Kingship," 100. Garthwaite in *The Persians* also discusses this idea, 91–92, 113, 144.

23. Cited in Limbert, *Iran: At War with History*, 141. See chapter 5 for a discussion of how in 1991 the Iranians insisted on international condemnation of Iraq as the price for their cooperation in freeing the foreign hostages in Lebanon.

that context—demanded swift and visible punishment of the guilty (or even the innocent). A nationalist minister in the Iranian provisional government of 1979 rejected the American chargé's argument that the summary justice and harsh verdicts of the new revolutionary courts were harming Iran's image abroad. The minister replied, "If we had had faster trials and more executions in 1953, then maybe the CIA could not have staged the coup that overthrew Mossadegh."[24]

## 13. Remember that conspiracy theories have great currency—and are sometimes true.

Iranians may seem reluctant to accept simple and straightforward explanations of events. They often prefer more complex accounts, if only because those are more interesting and creative. Behind the surface of events, Iranians often see hidden hands pulling strings and manipulating the world to some subtle and malevolent purpose. To some royalist Iranians, for example, Iran's 1978–79 Islamic Revolution was the product of foreign conspiracies to remove a shah who had become too powerful and too independent-minded for the taste of his Western friends. According to one version of this theory, President Carter and his allies no longer believed the shah could be a reliable buffer against Soviet expansion and sought to replace him and make Iran part of a green belt of Islamic regimes, which could use religion to resist the godless Communists.

Although some of the conspiracy theories may appear absurd, behind them lies a deeper reality. Outsiders, from brutal Mongols in the thirteenth century to manipulative British and Russians in the nineteenth and twentieth, have often subjected Iranians to forces beyond their control or comprehension. Those outsiders who applied such forces were never benevolent and always unscrupulous. In search of power, profit, and security, they were willing to use violence, terror, bribery, and subversion—including recruiting Iranian agents to betray their compatriots—in pursuing their ends and in frustrating Iranians' attempts to control their own destiny.

The archetype of modern conspiracies for Iranians turned out to be true. The American CIA and British intelligence did manipulate and bribe Iranians to bring about the downfall of the nationalist Prime Minister Mosaddegh in August 1953. Although historians still argue about the details of what happened during those events, no one disputes that Western security services played a central role in toppling the popular prime minister and restoring the

---

24. Author's recollection of Laingen-Foruhar meeting, Tehran, October 1979.

weakened Pahlavi monarch. Given that history, it was hardly surprising that twenty-six years later Iranians found it hard to accept the American explanation that in October 1979 the exiled Mohammad Reza Shah was coming to the United States only for medical treatment. In the postrevolutionary hysteria of 1979 and in the prevailing turmoil inside Iran, those Iranians predisposed to seeing conspiracies could easily find signs of a new U.S.-sponsored plot to create instability and restage the events of 1953.

## 14. Expect hands to be overplayed.

The Iranian side may push a small or momentary advantage to a point beyond calculations of gain and loss. Many Iranians attach a negative connotation to the adjective *hesabgar* (calculating), which implies that someone is willing to sacrifice principles, friendships, or feelings for material gain. At times of political stress, Iranians can appear to discard calculation of advantage and disadvantage and become captives of unrealistic, rigid positions and extremist rhetoric.

During the 1979–81 hostage crisis, for example, the Islamic Republic felt that detaining the American Embassy staff gave it an advantage over a U.S. government determined to destroy the revolutionary regime and replace it with either a restored monarchy or something else more friendly to American interests. Rather than calculate their country's long-term interests—which would have demanded a quick end to the crisis and would have reinforced the international credentials of the new Islamic Republic—the country's leaders, bolstered by mass demonstrations of support for the students' action, felt themselves able (or perhaps compelled) to defy the world. Many of the former hostage-takers have since said that they lost control over events and have explained their actions as products of the revolutionary fury that gripped Iran in those days. It is worth noting, however, that during the anti-shah disturbances of 1978–79, the revolutionaries were usually very careful to avoid targeting foreigners. At that time, at least, they knew the value of favorable press in Europe and the United States—a press that could enlist world opinion on their side.

After a student group had captured American personnel, the Iranian leaders pushed their temporary advantage so far that they nearly destroyed the country and wasted hundreds of thousands of Iranian lives. Ten months later, when Saddam Hussein's forces invaded Iran, Tehran found itself, thanks to having overplayed its hand and alienated potential supporters, with very few friends willing to admit that, in all fairness, Iran was the victim and Iraq the aggressor. Thanks to this political ineptitude, Iran's potential friends became explicit or tacit supporters of Saddam. In 1982, after Iranian forces won a major victory and expelled the Iraqis from the port at Khorramshahr, Saddam offered Iran a peace based on the status quo ante. Urged on by Imam Khomeini's rhetoric and by visions of occupying the Shia holy sites, however, the Iranian side once again overplayed its hand. It believed it could press its momentary advantage to bring about the final defeat of the enemy. The results were six more years of missile attacks, frontline carnage, and poison gas warfare. In the end, to avoid a complete political and military collapse, Iran had to forget about its brave rhetoric and accept a humiliating UN-brokered cease-fire in 1988.

In such an atmosphere it will be crucial for American negotiators to be patient, remain focused on the issues under discussion, and not be drawn into rhetorical dead ends. If one sees the Iranian side overplaying its hand, the best response is to ask, "Please explain why you are demanding this." "On what basis are you asking for that?" "I need to understand how you came to that figure." In such a setting, establishing objective criteria that both sides can accept without appearing to surrender—such as agreeing that the Algerians are creditable mediators—will be vital. For mediation or arbitration by an impartial body (such as the Hague Tribunal for adjudicating financial claims) can be a useful mechanism to counter what may appear to be unreasonable demands. In late 1980, when Deputy Secretary of State Warren Christopher received a message from the Iranians that tripled their monetary conditions for the release of the American hostages to $24 billion, he persevered in the negotiations and eventually the Iranians dropped those demands.[25]

## Defining Success

Negotiators who apply the above principles can reach an agreement—but they still may not. Even the above guidelines are no guarantee of productive results.[26] Both Americans and Iranians too often arrive at the negotiating table burdened with assumptions, grievances, ignorance, resentment, and the opinion—based on their special readings of history—that the other side is deceptive, infinitely crafty, overbearing, and will, in the end, reveal its true nature in hostility, treachery, and lies. Americans may be too full of ideas

---

25.  Warren Christopher, "Welcome to the Bazaar," *Los Angeles Times*, June 13, 2006.

26.  Even that master of negotiation Professor Roger Fisher (the author of *Getting to Yes*) admitted to his Harvard Law School class in January 1992 that his contacts with Iranian senior officials during the crisis were fruitless. He said he had the impression that the Iranian's BATNA was too good. See Fisher's detailed analysis in chapter 4.

about Iranian duplicity and irrationality; and Iranians—recalling Khomeini's statement about "What do the sheep and the wolf have to negotiate?"—too full of ideas about American arrogance and America's desire to humiliate Iran in the guise of negotiations. It may be difficult pass up the temptation to score points on the opponent, but the most important step for both countries' negotiators will be to focus on the issues at hand and not to worry about the faults and virtues of the other side.

What works in any negotiation—being prepared, building relationships, exercising patience, knowing both one's own and the other side's BATNA, understanding the other side's real interests—will work in negotiations with the Islamic Republic. Such was the experience of Americans and Iranians in 2001–02 during negotiations over the future of Afghanistan after the fall of the Taliban. Both sides have described the other as professional, businesslike, and, most important, free of the negative preconceptions that have sabotaged other attempts at initiating a dialogue.

In that particular case, historical baggage and preconceptions did not prevent Iranian and American negotiators from holding productive talks and reaching agreements that served the interests of both sides. In the future, whenever the two sides decide (at the same time) that they have more to gain by talking than by shouting and threatening, American negotiators who sit down with Iranians should add to their stock of basic tradecraft the specific guidance this chapter has offered. When the two sides do come to the negotiating table, of course all the negative caricatures and all the festering hostility and grievances will not disappear, even in the midst of smiles and handshakes. In those unpromising circumstances, negotiators should expect that progress will be slow, achievements will be modest, and success, at least initially, may consist of no more than the fact that the two nations are finally sitting down to discuss their common concerns.

# 7

# Overcoming Mutual Myth-Perceptions

Why should we bother thinking about Iranian-American negotiations when, for the last three decades, the two countries' dealings, whether open or secret, direct or indirect, have been mired in futility?[1] In all this interaction, one side has usually felt itself cheated, deceived, or disappointed and has blamed the other for this failure. Even promising moves, such as the Clinton administration's offer of unconditional talks in 1998 and the 2001 Bonn negotiations over Afghanistan, have led nowhere and ended with one side telling itself, "Well, we tried, but they are so (stubborn, deceitful, duplicitous, and so on) that we could never reach agreement." In September 2008, Defense Secretary Robert Gates put it this way:

> Every administration … has reached out to the Iranians in one way or another and all have failed. Some have gotten into deep trouble associated with their failures, but the reality is that the Iranian leadership has been consistently unyielding over a very long period of time about having a different and better kind of relationship.[2]

In such an atmosphere, it will be difficult to apply the negotiating advice and the lessons from the earlier chapters. For how does one negotiate with someone who is not even willing to come to the table or does so only to deceive and humiliate?

Hard as it may be, negotiating with Iran is still worth doing. After three decades of uninterrupted Iranian-American hostility, some American observers argue that the rulers of the Islamic Republic are so evil, irrational,

---

1. An abbreviated version of this chapter appeared in the June 2007 *Foreign Service Journal* under the title "The United States and Iran: Mything the Point."

2. Speech at the National Defense University, Washington, D.C., September 29, 2008.

and mendacious that there is nothing to gain from negotiations except more sterile rhetoric, absurd accusations, and blatant untruths. In this view, the Islamic Republic today is the equivalent of Nazi Germany in 1938, and negotiating with it ignores its true nature and will only give it a legitimacy it does not deserve.[3] These observers claim that this member of the axis of evil is a worthy target only for regime change or that, at a minimum, Iran must change its behavior—that is, do all that we demand of it—before any kind of discourse can begin. In this analysis, the regime in Tehran is beyond the pale. It is so brutal, benighted, and paranoid that there is no point in opening a dialogue unless its subject is the terms of Iran's surrender.

The problem with this Manichean view—regarding Iran as a manifestation of pure evil—is that it is likely to become a self-fulfilling prophecy. When we approach the Iranians (or any counterpart in a negotiation) as though they are the malevolent beings described above, they will quickly perceive how we look at them and adapt their tactics accordingly. If we approach Iranians as irrational, dissimulating cheats, they are quite likely both to perceive and then to fulfill our expectations. This dark and absolutist view of Iran and Iranians also ignores the possibility that negotiating, although it will not change the nature of the Islamic Republic, could be one method of changing what has been a thirty-year destructive U.S.-Iranian relationship of mutual grievance, hostility, and suspicion into something more productive. During that period, mutual recrimination, name-calling, finger-pointing, posturing, and sermonizing have had few results. The Islamic Republic still exists, remains hostile and suspicious, and, in 2007–08, reminded us of its antagonism by high-profile arrests of Iranian-American researchers whose mission was to encourage dialogue and scholarly investigation. The United States, for its part, has imposed more and more sanctions, encouraged others to do likewise, and issued barely veiled threats of military action.

The point is that the United States should be talking to Iran not because the Islamic Republic is friendly and democratic or because talking is easy or even likely to produce immediate and positive results. Americans and Iranians should be talking because both sides will find significant common interests in doing so. Talking to Iran, hard and disagreeable as it might be, is likely to be more productive than continuing almost three decades of noisy and sometimes violent confrontation. We should have no illusions. Discussions with the Islamic Republic are unlikely in the short run to have

---

3.   Such was the view of Norman Podhoretz, as expressed on PBS's *NewsHour*, October 29, 2007.

the kind of positive outcomes we might wish for. Iran is not going to change its behavior immediately and stop all of its misdeeds in the areas of terrorism, Middle East peace, human rights, and nuclear development. Yet serious negotiations—even with a regime we dislike and mistrust—we may discover areas of common interest that lurk behind walls of hostility and suspicion.

## The Hard Road to Realism

The last thirty years of Iranian-American relations have been years of futility. Both sides have turned their backs on considerations of national interest and the obvious reality that decades of name-calling, threats, and insults have been a poor substitute for reasoned policy. When one side makes an approach, the other pulls back on the assumption that some deception or trap must lurk behind the offer. The United States and the Islamic Republic of Iran continue to denounce each other as "mad mullahs" and "great Satans" (to use the title of Professor Bill Beeman's 2005 study).[4] The rhetoric has remained bellicose since 1979. What has changed in the last five years is the volume of saber-rattling that accompanies these exchanges of stale and predictable epithets. Carrier battle groups are moved in the Persian Gulf; missiles are test-fired, war games are performed; quasi-diplomats and scholars are detained under various pretexts; captured weapons are displayed; accusations of high-level complicity are made; insulting, dehumanizing caricatures are drawn; and defiant and threatening speeches are delivered.[5]

Each side's chest-thumpers push the case for confrontation, oppose any move toward discussions, and accuse questioners at home of appeasement and worse; officials from Tehran and Washington visit the other's neighbors to build alliances and counter the (Iranian or American) threat; and Presidents Bush and Ahmadinezhad filled their speeches with denunciations of Iran or the United States as the source of world misfortune.[6] All these moves and harsh rhetoric tell us that American-Iranian relations remain about where they have been for the past thirty years: locked in a downward

---

4.  Beeman, *The "Great Satan" vs. the "Mad Mullahs."*

5.  See the cartoon in the September 4, 2007, *Columbus (Ohio) Post Dispatch* that showed Iran as a sewer from which swarms of loathsome cockroaches infest the region.

6.  The exchanges sometimes reach the point of absurdity. For example, see below for the remarks of an American Defense Department official.

spiral of mutual hostility and suspicion—a downward spiral that neither side seems able to reverse.[7]

## Two Seminal Events

The bases of all this mutual demonization are difficult to explain. How has it happened that both Iranians and Americans simultaneously view the other so negatively? How have Americans and Iranians come to expect the worst and perceive almost nothing but malevolence in each other? How have both sides concluded that the evidence of history proves, beyond any reasonable doubt, that the other side is devious, irrational, arrogant, bullying, and so on—in short, the very personification of wickedness? And why, after almost thirty years, are Americans and Iranians unable to get beyond these caricatures of each other and admit that the denunciations, accusations, finger-pointing, and sterile rhetoric—presented with the rationality of second-graders exchanging insults on the playground—have accomplished nothing?

One answer to the above questions lies in decades of two-sided mythmaking. Americans and Iranians have constructed their reciprocally negative views based on distorted versions of two recent events, both described in earlier case studies. The accepted versions of these events have mixed reality with fantasy to create a picture of pure evil in the other side. In the Iranian case, the critical event was the August 1953 American-backed coup d'etat that toppled the nationalist Prime Minister Mohammad Mosaddegh and restored the power of Mohammad Reza Shah Pahlavi. By so doing, the Americans did what the Russians and British had been doing for decades—frustrating Iranians' efforts to free themselves of foreign tutelage, reverse three centuries of political decline, and take control of their country's petroleum, its greatest source of wealth.

In the American case, the formative event was the seizure of the U.S. Embassy in Tehran and holding (with the connivance of the Iranian authorities) mission staff members hostage for fourteen months in 1979–81. The nightly television images of screaming crowds and burning flags, the hysterical rhetoric, the weeping hostage family members, the threats, the refusal to negotiate, the failed rescue mission, and the Iranians' unwillingness to recognize either accepted norms of international behavior or their own responsibilities toward persons under their protection, all ensured that Ameri-

7. As far as I know, it was the late Professor Richard Cottam of the University of Pittsburgh who, in the early 1980s, gave currency to the term "downward spiral" in describing American-Iranian relations.

cans, unable to understand such happenings, would dismiss Iranians as crazies, as victims of a national temper tantrum, and label them with all the negatives noted above.

Although I was too young to participate in the events of 1953, I was personally involved in the latter episode. Along with fifty-one of my colleagues, I spent the months from November 1979 to January 1981—nine of them in solitary confinement—as an unwilling guest of the Islamic Republic. Although none of my student captors were old enough to have any personal memory of the Mosaddegh era, they linked their action to the events of 1953. They knew for certain that the perfidious Americans, in league with Iranian traitors, had instigated the prime minister's downfall and were thus responsible for all of Iran's subsequent misfortunes—as well as the rest of the world's miseries. Ignoring the absurdity of their question, they demanded that I describe in detail my role in the events of August 1953. I could answer them honestly: "My role was a very minor one. I was ten years old at the time."[8]

In fact, neither Americans nor Iranians should be proud of their country's actions in this sorry history. The American side has justified its 1953 actions by the necessities of the Cold War and fear of Soviet expansion into an unstable Iran; the Iranian side has justified its actions in 1979–80 by the postrevolutionary hysteria and prevailing chaos.[9] Whatever momentary advantage anyone gained turned out to be illusory, and both sides, despite their rationalizations, eventually paid a heavy price for their irresponsible and unwise acts.

However either side rationalizes its actions, these two events continue to cast long shadows over American-Iranian relations and have come to assume mythic importance far beyond their reality. They have shaped each side's view of the other in the most negative way and have proved a formidable barrier to building a more constructive relationship. From those two events—

---

8. One of my colleagues, Vice Consul Donald Cooke, fed up with our captors' harangues on the evils of America, finally responded, "You know, Abbas, you're right. Even before I was born my parents decided that what they wanted me to do was to become a ruthless exploiter of the oppressed people of the third world. And from the time I was small I can remember them teaching me how to be a ruthless exploiter of the oppressed people of the third world. And when it came time for me to decide what kind of job I was going to get, I said to myself, I know what I want. I want to become a ruthless exploiter of the oppressed people of the third world. And here I am. I got a job with the United States government as a ruthless exploiter of the third world, and my parents, they're so proud of me, they thank God every day. They get up in the morning and say, thank you Lord for making our son a ruthless exploiter of the oppressed people of the third world." Even Abbas got the point. Cited by Bowden, *Guests of the Ayatollah,* 542.

9. The more conspiratorially minded, such as former Iranian deputy PM Amir-Entezam, have claimed that the whole hostage episode was a CIA plot.

and from much that followed them—have come the distorted and mutually destructive views that lie at the heart of the downward spiral of our difficult and mutually destructive bilateral relationship. Those events of 1953 and 1979 have provided each side with the assumption and certainty of the other's enmity. With these events as starting points, subsequent history, poured into an existing mould of suspicion, has provided both Iranians and Americans with the evidence they need to prove that the other side is a demonic enemy determined on our destruction.[10]

## Through Warped Lenses

In this confrontation, both Iranians and Americans are convinced of their own rightness, have come to view each other through pairs of badly warped lenses. As a result, in exchanges between the two countries, mythology, distortion, grievance, and stereotype have become accepted wisdom, replacing both reason and reality.

For Americans, the caricatures predate the hostage crisis. In August 1979, for example, in the midst of the upheavals of postrevolutionary Iran, an American Embassy officer in Tehran composed a message to Washington advising his audience on negotiating with Iranians. He told his readers that recent events had shown "there are several lessons for those who would negotiate with Persians. . . ."

- First, one should never assume that his side of the issue will be recognized, let alone that it will be conceded to have merits. Persian preoccupation with self precludes this. *A negotiator must force recognition of his position upon his Persian opposite number.* [author's emphasis].

- Second, one should not expect an Iranian readily to perceive the advantages of a long-term relationship based on trust. He will assume that his opposite number is basically an adversary. In dealing with that adversary, he will ignore a long-term relationship and attempt to maximize the benefits to himself that are immediately obtainable. (Author's note: this trait is the *mard-e-rendi* noted earlier.)

---

10. To perpetuate the stereotype, each side deals with these events in a way, calculated or not, that infuriates the other. Official Washington is largely ignorant of the August 1953 coup or considers it ancient history. Official Tehran holds demonstrations every November 4 and issues commemorative stamps as though its actions in 1979 were something to be proud of.

- Third, interlocking relationships of all aspects of an issue must be painstakingly, forcefully, and repeatedly developed. Linkages will be neither readily comprehended nor accepted by Persian negotiators.

- Fourth, one should insist on performance as the sine qua non at each stage of negotiations. Statements of intention count for almost nothing.

- Fifth, cultivation of goodwill for goodwill's sake is a waste of effort. The overriding objective at all times should be impressing upon the Persians across the table the mutuality of the proposed undertakings. He *must be made to know* that a quid pro quo is involved on both sides [author's emphasis].[11]

So there you have it, our embassy reporter believes. He has, based on his negative experiences in Iran, written a guide to negotiation that tells us Iranians, because of their inherent egoism, will fail to understand links or see the other side's point of view. Furthermore, the writer advises Americans not to bother establishing a positive relationship with Iranian counterparts. Because they will always see the United States as the enemy, building such a relationship will be of no use in a negotiation, and seeking common ground with Iranians will be a waste of time. Instead, the author recommends applying the style of *diktat*. His choice of words connotes compulsion: in a successful negotiation, we learn, the American side must "force" acceptance of its position and the Iranian side must "be made to know" about mutual benefit.

That message, written more than two months before the November 1979 American Embassy seizure, was just an early—and perhaps mild—example of the parade of distortions to follow. The writer has assembled a collection of negative stereotypes produced before relations completely collapsed. The caricatures that came after the final breakdown of the relationship following November 1979 were even worse—decades of demonization characterized by multiplying oversimplifications and misreadings.

## The Incomprehensible Iranian

For the American side, the embassy seizure laid the foundations of the subsequent myths. The students' action, and the accompanying images of mass hysteria, seemed to confirm that Iranians were crazies with all the attributes noted above. Throughout the crisis, Iranians seemed impervious to reason,

---

11. "Message from Iran: Aug. 13, '79," *New York Times*, January 27, 1981. The text of the telegram is given in the appendix.

obsessed with real or imagined past grievances, and determined to follow their leader's most extreme rhetoric even if it led their nation to destruction. Seen through that prism, events that followed the hostage crisis—the Khobar Towers attack in Saudi Arabia, the Beirut Embassy bombings, the Lebanon hostage-takings, the arms-for-hostages deal, the attack on the Buenos Aires Jewish centers, President Ahmadinezhad's bizarre public statements, and his December 2006 pseudo-scholarly Holocaust conference in Tehran— provided further confirmation that Americans' original opinions were correct. Haven't Iranians' own actions and words proved that they—or at least those in charge in Tehran—are just as bad as we thought: devious, mendacious, fanatical, violent, and incomprehensible?

The reality of what happened in 1979–81, however, turned out to be both more complex and more tragic than the myth. The traumatic and prolonged embassy seizure convinced most Americans that, in the case of Iran, they were dealing with a nation of screaming and unreasoning fanatics. The United States felt helpless, and Jimmy Carter lost the election of 1980 in large part because of his apparent inability to resolve the issue. For Iranians, however, the results of the embassy seizure went much deeper. It became a national catastrophe that was much worse than feeling helpless or losing a political office.

Although fourteen months' captivity may have been harsh and difficult for the American prisoners and their families, and may have been a collective nightmare for the American people, for Iranians the event's consequences were many times worse. Its effects were profound and have lasted for decades. The embassy seizure set the Iranian revolution—which up to that time had featured many opposing factions engaged in open, raucous debates over the country's future—on a path to authoritarian, self-destructive rule by the most brutal, bigoted, and narrow-minded faction of the coalition that had made the original revolution.

Iranian analysts, including some of the hostage-takers themselves, have since maintained that their country's national outburst of rage during the embassy seizure led directly to the bloody internecine street battles of the early 1980s, the mass slaughter of the 1980–88 Iran-Iraq War, and the victory of brutal extremism and obscurantism over moderation and tolerance in Iranian domestic politics. The event, they maintain, enthroned a narrow ruling clique, established a harsh and intolerant social system, decimated Iran's educated middle class, and all but ruined the country's economy. With the hostage-taking disappeared any hope that the Islamic Revolution might bring the Iranian people something better than what they had under the monarchy.

# The Treacherous and Arrogant American

For their part, Iranians have created their own set of myths about the United States, based on American actions beginning in 1953. Starting from the CIA-backed coup of that year, Iranians have concluded that the American government remains determined to dominate and exploit Iran, preferably by subversion and other indirect means, but by force if necessary. In the early 1950s Prime Minister Mosaddegh insisted that Iran must reassert its wounded pride and precarious independence. Many Iranians had hoped that the United States would sympathize with Mosaddegh's nationalism and be a counterweight to Iran's traditionally domineering colonial powers (Britain and Russia). Washington's decision-makers, however, eventually concluded that they, like the British, could not tolerate so much independence from a small, third-world country, especially one that bordered the Soviet Union and possessed important oil resources. As a result, instead of supporting Iranian hopes, the United States turned against the country's nascent democracy and betrayed Iranians' hopes that America would back their struggle to become, at long last, masters in their own house.[12]

From that unfortunate beginning, subsequent American actions (or Iranians' perceptions of those actions) have confirmed the image—first created in 1953—of Americans determined to bend Iranians to their will and prepared to crush their aspirations for dignity and independence. Americans now seemed no better than Iran's historical enemies, the British and Russians. These actions included

- lavish public support for the shah and his policies;

- pressing the Iranian government to grant immunity for American military advisers and their families in the 1964 Status of Forces Act debate;

- appointing Richard Helms, former head of the CIA, as ambassador to Iran in 1973. Until then, the United States had at least maintained the pretence of respecting Iranian sovereignty;[13]

---

12. Until 1953, many Iranians had seen the United States in a positive light. Americans had supported Iranian health and education in the nineteenth and early twentieth centuries, had supported the Iranian constitutionalists in 1906–11, and had supported Iran's efforts to maintain its territorial integrity after WWII.

13. Helms himself (and certainly President Nixon) appeared unaware or unconcerned about the symbolism of his appointment for Iranians. After firing Helms as head of the CIA in November 1972, Nixon asked him if he would be ambassador in Moscow. Helms responded that, in light of his past, he did not think such a posting was a good idea. In

- tacit and open support for Saddam in the eight-year Iran-Iraq War, including the sinking of Iranian naval vessels in the Persian Gulf and the 1988 downing of an Iranian civilian airliner (IranAir Flight 655);
- the "axis of evil" rhetoric in President Bush's 2002 State of the Union message;
- the increased American military presence in countries on Iran's periphery; and
- public talk about military action and regime change in Tehran.

## In a Downward Spiral

In the spiral described, each side sees every move of the other in the worst light possible and responds accordingly. That view—assuming the worst about the other—has also driven both Iranians and Americans to acts that eventually create self-fulfilling prophecies. Assumptions of hostility create more hostility. They lead to preemptive actions against real or imagined threats; those actions in turn provoke hostile responses; and those hostile responses provoke further antagonism from the other side, which thus justifies its original action ("We told you they were evil"). Hostility begets hostility, and both sides find themselves in a stubborn cycle of provocation and counterprovocation. As Beeman describes this situation,

> This state of affairs leads to the conclusion that the American conflict with Iran as it continues today is a true postmodern culture conflict. It centers not on substantive differences or real conflict, but rather on symbolic discourse. In this discourse both nations construct the "other" to fit an idealized picture of an enemy.[14]

In other words, hostile intent is assumed, and both sides find the evidence to fit their assumptions. When discussing Iran in 2007, a senior career foreign policy official said privately that the sad reality is many in Washington simply hate Iran and Iranians. As if to confirm his view, the same year a senior Department of Defense official reportedly told a visiting British delegation, in a discussion of Iran, that she hated them all.[15] Reacting to the December 2007 release of a National Intelligence Estimate (NIE) reporting that Iran had

---

the case of a posting to Tehran, however, apparently such attention to appearances did not apply. Weiner, *Legacy of Ashes*, 323.

14. Beeman, "Iran and the United States," 672.

15. That is, all Iranians, not all members of the British delegation. The remarks by Deputy Assistant Secretary of Defense Debra Cagan received wide press coverage. See for example, "I Hate All Iranians, U.S. Aide Tells MPs," *The Daily Mail*, September 29, 2007.

stopped its nuclear weapons program, a former Defense Department official could respond only, "I don't trust them [the Iranians]."[16]

Both the United States and Iran assume the "other" will act in accordance with its enmity and malignant nature. If the United States anticipates the Islamic Republic will be consistently hostile in its policies, then an aggressive American faction will urge Washington to take preventive action against Tehran before an unfriendly Iran can carry out its intent to commit a hostile act—or even before it is capable of doing so. President Bush, for example, argued that Iran should not even have the knowledge that would allow it to build a nuclear weapon.[17] It will come as no surprise that in this situation the officials of the Islamic Republic see American actions in the same negative way. They will react—egged on by their homegrown neoconservatives—on the assumption that Iran is facing relentless hostility from an American enemy determined to destroy it.[18]

Caught in these assumptions, each side believes (or has convinced itself) that it is peaceful and is acting defensively against unprovoked, hostile, and offensive moves by an aggressive other. Presidents and other officials on both sides deliver this rhetoric to their respective electoral bases. They thus feed the downward spiral. According to this view of the other, the United States believes the Islamic Republic is guilty of harboring and supporting terrorists, of secretly building nuclear weapons to threaten Israel and other U.S. friends in the region, and working to make itself—under the banner of a militant Shia ideology—the dominant power across the Middle East. From the Iranian perspective, the United States has shown that it cannot tolerate an independent and defiant Islamic Republic that does not submit to American commands. Iran believes the United States, unable to dominate Iran, has embarked on a policy of subversion, economic warfare, support for dissidents, all amounting to a strategy of regime change—that is, restaging the events of August 1953 and overthrowing a government it does not like.

## How Do I Despise Thee? Let Me Count the (Many) Ways

The depths of mutual hostility, ill will, and suspicion that have prevented dispassionate and reasoned discussions of policy for almost thirty years are

---

16.   Statement by Peter Rodman on PBS, *The NewsHour,* December 3, 2007.

17.   George W. Bush, press conference, October 17, 2007.

18.   In a curious bit of mirror-imaging, Iranian analysts often refer to their homegrown ideologues as neoconservatives.

obvious even to those new to the subject of American-Iranian relations.[19] I recently asked my political science students—who had been studying U.S.-Iranian relations for only a few months—how they believed, on the basis of the recent history they had learned in the class, the United States and Iran viewed each other. In their responses, the students went straight to the heart of the matter of how mutual antipathy has clouded judgment. Based on the last thirty years of history, and our disastrous relations with the Islamic Republic, they believed most Americans saw Iran and Iranians as

- Emotional. Iranians let their hearts rule their heads. Even Iran's leaders cannot calculate their country's interests and had become captives of their own fiery rhetoric.

- Devious. Iranians have lived up to the stereotype of the mendacious oriental. They will cheat and deceive if it suits their purpose—or sometimes even to no apparent purpose.

- Obsessed with the past. Iranians cannot put past events behind them. They are still fixated on events of fifty or sixty years ago (particularly the 1953 coup) and even on seventh-century conflicts in Islamic history.

- Obsessed with religion. Iranians are attempting to establish a theocratic state in the twenty-first century based on a version of Mohammad's seventh-century community in Arabia. They are using religion as a pretext to mistreat their own women and religious minorities.

- Unreliable. Iranians cannot be trusted to keep their word. They will tell you anything to gain a short-term advantage even if the long-term result is a complete loss of confidence.

- Incomprehensible. Many Iranian actions are inexplicable. One cannot begin to understand or predict how they will act in a given situation.

- Vindictive. Iranians will harbor grudges for decades and even for centuries. They overreact against opponents or critics, imprisoning and even murdering those who think for themselves or ask embarrassing questions.

---

19. In the following exercise, I used the generalized terms "Iranian" and "American" for the sake of simplicity. The reality of these stereotypes is more complicated. If questioned, each side (with the possible exception of the U.S. official cited in footnote 15 above) would say it has nothing against individual Iranians or Americans but has serious problems with their respective governments and their policies. In the last analysis, however, it is often difficult to separate criticism of government policies from a distorted view of an entire people.

- Fanatical. Inspired by the stories of their martyred saints, Iranians will embark on suicidal missions. During the mourning days of the Shia calendar, Iranians will work themselves into a frenzy of self-flagellation.

For these students this part of the exercise was easy. They had only to repeat many of the caricatures the popular American media have been propagating for the past three decades. With most American audiences, a simple word-association test of "Iran" and "Iranian" would have yielded about the same results.

I then gave the students a more difficult problem and asked them to put themselves into the place of the other. I turned the original question around, and asked them how they thought Iranians, in light of that same history, might view Americans and American policy. Their answers included

- Belligerent. Americans cannot tolerate opposition and will react violently when they believe their country's hegemony is being challenged. The American government is always looking to teach someone a lesson and to make other nations change their behavior.
- Sanctimonious and hypocritical. Americans deliver sermons to others on upholding human rights and democracy, yet their government has supported many corrupt, undemocratic, and oppressive regimes.
- Calculating. Americans are forever weighing the material profit from courses of action, without regard to any ethical or religious scruple. Americans are always willing to sacrifice humanity for some strategic advantage.
- Godless and immoral. Americans export and glorify a corrupt culture that transforms women into sex objects and undermines family, religion, and tradition.
- Exploitive. Americans are constantly looking for sources of oil and other resources that it can steal or buy cheaply in exchange for the trash—especially military trash—that they make.
- Materialistic. Americans have no spiritual values. They believe that human beings are ruled only by their desires for material goods and have no interest in higher ideals other than the latest fashion or electronic gadget.
- Bullying. If Americans cannot get their way, they will resort to threats, subversion, and direct intervention. The American government has never stopped bullying the Islamic Republic because Iran has chosen its own independent path and has refused to submit to Washington's demands.

- Arrogant. The United States insists that all parties must play by its rules. Iranians thus label the United States as "global arrogance" (*estekbaar-e-jahaani*). Americans claim that their political, economic, and cultural system is the only valid one for humanity.

- Meddling. Americans have been meddling in Iranian affairs for decades. The Bush administration labeled Iran a member of the axis of evil and decided to overthrow the bothersome Islamic Republic and install a more compliant regime in Tehran.

## Endless Enemies?

The cumulative effect of all this mythmaking—so obvious even to outsiders such as my students—has been to build an enormous wall of distrust between our two countries. In such a setting, Washington's simply sending a representative in July 2008 to join multilateral talks about Iran's nuclear program became in the press a huge, symbolic reversal of policy, even when the American representative apparently neither met with an Iranian counterpart or even participated in the multilateral discussions.[20] Even when one side makes a tentative offer to explore a way out of the impasse, the other side assumes the worst, reacts with suspicion, and immediately asks itself, "What do they mean by doing that? Why are they making this offer now? What trap are they laying for us? What devious plan have they devised? Are they admitting a weakness that we can exploit?"

These suspicions and preconceptions have led both sides to make short-sighted decisions and to miss opportunities. In 1998–99, for example, the Iranians rejected the Clinton administration's offer of talks without preconditions on all issues in dispute to create (as Secretary of State Albright put it) "a road map to better relations." At the same time, she addressed a basic Iranian grievance by expressing regret for American actions in 1953. Not to be outdone, in April 2003 the Bush administration, while riding a wave of illusory triumph in Iraq, ignored a proposal from the Iranians to open talks on all subjects of mutual interest.[21]

---

20. Depending on the commentator's place on the ideological spectrum, this small step was either a positive realization of the need to engage with the Islamic Republic or evidence of appeasement of a stubborn and hostile Iranian regime. See, for example, Barbara Slavin's commentary, "Wising Up on Iran" (National Interest Online, July 16, 2008; www.nationalinterest.org/Article.aspx?id=19412), and Michael Rubin's "Now Bush is Appeasing Iran," *Wall Street Journal*, July 21, 2008, A11.

21. The text of this Iranian proposal is in the appendix. The aborted exchange left both sides attempting to rationalize their positions. Some American officials have claimed the

If Washington and Tehran ever do undertake serious negotiations, this propensity of both Iranians and Americans to project the most evil motives on the other side will be a major obstacle to the talks' success. Each side is likely to come to the table handicapped by the strong suspicion (or the certainty) that the other side's only purpose in talking is to cheat and deceive. Many Iranians will ask (repeating Khomeini's famous metaphor), "Why should [we] the sheep negotiate with [them] the wolf? What's in it for us? The Americans have already shown us their treacherous character." For their part, Americans will ask, "What do we have to negotiate about? Didn't we learn anything about 'them' from the disastrous Iran-Contra affair [of 1985–86]? The mendacious Iranians have played us for fools in the past and will do so again if we give them the opportunity. They are so clever and devious (and we are so guileless) that at the end of the day by dealing with them we will lose everything and gain nothing."

Why should both sides remain stuck in this downward spiral? How can they escape it? The United States and Iran—if one applies a reasoned analysis to the two countries' interests— should not be condemned to be endless enemies. Despite the myths and rhetoric, the number of actual casualties in our three-decade-old conflict—in Beirut, the Persian Gulf, and even in the suburbs of Washington, D.C.—has so far been relatively small, in the hundreds on each side. If we compare those numbers with the hundreds of thousands of victims on both sides of the Vietnam War, for example, it is hard to understand how the United States can today enjoy normal diplomatic relations with the Republic of Vietnam while the United States and the Islamic Republic can think only of new ways to insult and punish each other and appear helpless to find a way out of a quagmire of myths, stereotypes, and festering grievances, both real and imagined.

## Have Low Expectations, Have High Expectations

Given this unhappy history of accusation and counteraccusation, it will be very difficult to fulfill one of the first conditions of negotiations: understand the other side's position, even if you do not accept it. The U.S.-Iran relationship has fed for too long on accumulated grievances, reciprocal negative views, self-righteousness, and a stubborn refusal to admit that the unwel-

---

offer came not from representatives of the Islamic Republic but from the Swiss ambassador in Tehran. On the Iranian side, the government now denies that such a message was ever sent.

come viewpoint of the other—distorted as it might be—may have some basis in reality.

There is a possible escape, however, from the American-Iranian downward spiral. That escape is an apparent paradox. In any negotiation with the Islamic Republic, we should keep our expectations low and high at the same time. On the low side: years of accumulated bitterness and the mountain of perceived grievances will make achieving any progress very difficult and very slow. We will have to measure advances in small steps, in nuances, and in symbolic positives. An accomplishment may be only a shift in tone, a handshake, or something not said. For in any Iranian-American encounter, both sides are still too weighed down by their ghosts, by the poet George Seferis' "stones sinking into time" for them to put aside easily all of the pent-up suspicion and hostility.[22]

In such an inauspicious setting, we should keep our expectations realistic. We should not permit temporary setbacks, intemperate statements, unexpected reversals, inexplicable delays, and other problems to distract us and to declare negotiations useless or a failure because we and the Iranian side have not reached immediate agreement on issues that have divided us for years. Because of the unfortunate past, in future Iranian-American meetings, symbols will be as important (if not more important) as substance for a very long time. Perhaps we need to recognize that—given all the bitterness and the mythmaking of the past—symbols will be the substance of at least our first encounters.

At the same time we keep expectations low, in another sense we need to keep them high. We first need to check our negative preconceptions about the other at the door.[23] If we allow these stereotypes of the other side to control our actions and attitudes, then we will remain stuck in the same futile exchanges that have characterized Iranian-American encounters for three decades. If American negotiators expect nothing but unreasoned hostility from Iranians and persuade themselves that only egoism, paranoia, and perceived grievances drive the other side's representatives and have blinded

---

22. Seferis writes, "These stones sinking into time, how far will they drag me with them?" From "Mythistorema." *George Seferis: Collected Poems*. See also his poem "Mycenae," cited in chapter 1 for the burden of a magnificent past.

23. In this area, it is worth noting President Obama's statement to Al-Arabiya TV (January 26, 2009), "And so what we want to do is … set aside some of the preconceptions that have existed and have built up over the last several years. And I think if we can do that, there's a possibility of at least achieving some breakthroughs." Although Obama was speaking specifically about Arab-Israeli matters, the idea clearly has broader application.

them to their own interests (as was the argument of our embassy reporter above), then we have created a formula for permanent failure.

Expectations, assumptions, and perceptions matter. In the early 1950s, Mosaddegh and the British had the lowest possible expectations of each other. Each side concocted myths grounded in distortions of history, half-truths, and simultaneous feelings of superiority and inferiority. The results were catastrophic. Each side came to perceive it was despised by the other. When Mosaddegh looked at the British government and Anglo-Iranian Oil Company officials, he saw contempt, arrogance, and a refusal to recognize Iranians as full members of the human race. When the British looked at Mosaddegh and his followers, they saw dangerous xenophobia and irrationality. These negatives reinforced each other and each side felt, in light of the other side's low opinions, it was justified in taking the extreme position that it did. As long as these low expectations continued, there would be no settlement of the dispute until one side had thoroughly humiliated the other.

Such are the lessons of history. When entering negotiations with Iranians, we should follow the wise counsel of the thirteenth-century Persian poet Sa'adi, who, in his stories in the *Golestan*, advised,

> *Har kera jameh-ye-parsa bini, parsara dan va nikmard engar*

Whomever you see in the dress of an ascetic,
Consider him an ascetic and assume he is virtuous.

In the same vein, the poet tells us to be wary of assumptions:

> *Ta mard sokhan nagofteh bashad, eib va honarash nohofteh bashad*
> *Har piseh gaman mabar nahali, shayad palang khofteh bashad.*

Until a man speaks, his faults and virtues are hidden.
Do not assume that every strand of hair is a sapling;
it could well be a sleeping panther.[24]

In other words, in our encounters with Iran and Iranians, we should keep our expectations realistic—and anticipate progress will be difficult and slow. At the same time, however, we should put aside those prejudices that have convinced us—before a dialogue has even begun—that no accommodation (short of surrender) will ever be possible. Expect negotiations to fail through the fault of the other side and they probably will. Expect better and success becomes possible.

---

24. Author's translation.

# Bibliography

Abrahamian, Ervand. *Iran between Two Revolutions*. Princeton: Princeton University Press, 1982.

———. *The Iranian Mojahedin*. New Haven: Yale University Press, 1989.

———. *Tortured Confessions: Prisons and Public Recantations in Modern Iran*. Berkeley: University of California Press, 1999.

———. *A History of Modern Iran*. Cambridge, UK: New York: Cambridge University Press, 2008.

Afkhami, Gholam Reza. *The Life and Times of the Shah*. Berkeley: University of California Press, 2009.

Alam, Asadollah. *The Shah and I: Confidential Diary of Iran's Royal Court, 1969–77*. London: I.B. Tauris, 1991.

Ansari, Ali M. *Confronting Iran: The Failure of American Foreign Policy and the Next Great Crisis in the Middle East*. New York: Basic Books, 2006.

Armstrong, Scott, Malcolm Byrne, Tom Blanton, and the National Security Archive. *The Chronology: The Documented Day-by-Day Account of the Secret Military Assistance to Iran and the Contras*. New York: Warner Books, 1987.

Atabaki, Touraj. *Azerbaijan: Ethnicity and the Struggle for Power in Iran*, rev. ed. London, New York: I.B. Tauris, 2000.

Beeman, William O. "Iran and the United States: Postmodern Culture Conflict in Action." *Anthropological Quarterly*, 76, No. 4 (Autumn 2003): 671–91.

———. *The "Great Satan" vs. the "Mad Mullahs": How the United States and Iran Demonize Each Other*. Westport: Praeger, 2005.

Bill, James A. *The Eagle and the Lion: The Tragedy of American-Iranian Relations*. New Haven: Yale University Press, 1988.

Bowden, Mark. *Guests of the Ayatollah: The First Battle in America's War with Militant Islam*. New York: Atlantic Monthly Press, 2006.

Christopher, Warren, et al. *American Hostages in Iran: The Conduct of a Crisis* (A Council on Foreign Relations Book). New Haven: Yale University Press, 1985.

Chubin, Shahram. *Iran's Nuclear Ambitions*. Washington, DC: Carnegie Endowment for International Peace, 2006.

Cottam, Richard W. *Nationalism in Iran*. Pittsburgh: University of Pittsburgh Press, 1964. Updated 1979.

———. *Iran and the United States: A Cold War Case Study*. Pittsburgh: University of Pittsburgh Press, 1988.

Dobbins, James F. *After the Taliban: Nation-Building in Afghanistan*. Washington, DC: Potomac Books, 2008.

Draper, Theodore. *A Very Thin Line: The Iran-Contra Affairs*. New York: Hill and Wang, 1991.

Eagleton, William Jr. *The Kurdish Republic of 1946*. London: Oxford University Press, 1963.

Farmanfarmaian, Manuchehr, and Roxanne Farmanfarmaian. *Blood and Oil: A Prince's Memoir of Iran from the Shah to the Ayatollah*. New York: Random House, 2005.

Fisher, Roger, Bruce M. Patton, and William L. Ury. *Getting to Yes: Negotiating Agreement Without Giving In*. New York: Houghton Mifflin, 1981.

Garthwaite, Gene R. *The Persians*. Malden, MA: Blackwell Publishing, 2005.

Gasiorowski, Mark J., and Malcolm Byrne, eds. *Mohammad Mosaddeq and the 1953 Coup in Iran*. Syracuse: Syracuse University Press, 2004.

Harris, David. *The Crisis: The President, the Prophet, and the Shah—1979 and the Coming of Militant Islam*. Boston: Little, Brown and Company, 2004.

Herodotus. *The Landmark Herodotus: The Histories*. Edited by Robert Strassler. Translated by Andrea Purvis. New York: Pantheon Books, 2007.

Herz, Martin E. *A View from Tehran: A Diplomatist Looks at the Shah's Regime in June 1964*. Washington, DC: Institute for the Study of Diplomacy, Georgetown University, 1979.

Jordan, Hamilton. *Crisis: The Last Year of the Carter Presidency*. New York: G.P. Putnam's Sons, 1982.

Kamrava, Mehran. *The Political History of Modern Iran: From Tribalism to Theocracy*. Westport: Praeger, 1992.

———. "Iranian National-Security Debates: Factionalism and Lost Opportunities." *Middle East Policy* 14, No. 2 (Summer 2007): 84–100.

Karabell, Zachary. *Architects of Intervention: The United States, the Third World, and the Cold War, 1946–1962*. Baton Rouge: LSU Press, 1999.

Katouzian, Homa. *Musaddiq and the Struggle for Power in Iran*. London and New York: I.B. Tauris, 1999.

Kazemzadeh, Firuz. *Britain and Russia in Persia, 1864–1914; a Study in Imperialism*. New Haven: Yale University Press, 1968.

Khomeini, Ruhollah. *Islam and Revolution: Writings and Declarations of Imam Khomeini*. Translated and annotated by Hamid Algar. Berkeley: Mizan Press, 1981.

Kinzer, Stephen. *All the Shah's Men: An American Coup and the Roots of Middle East Terror*. Hoboken, NJ: John Wiley, 2003, 2008.

Kornbluh, Peter. *The Iran-Contra Scandal: The Declassified History (The National Security Archives Document)*. Edited by Malcolm Byrne. New York: The New Press, 1993.

Ladjevardi, Habib. "The Origins of U.S. Support for an Autocratic Iran." *International Journal of Middle East Studies* 15, No. 2 (May 1983): 225–39.

Lambton, A.K.S. "Justice in the Medieval Persian Theory of Kingship." *Studia Islamica*, No. 17 (1962): 91–119.

Limbert, John. *"Nest of Spies: Pack of Lies." Washington Quarterly*, 5:2 (Spring 1982*)*: 75–82.

———. *Iran: At War with History*. Boulder: Westview Press, 1987.

Majd, Hooman. *The Ayatollah Begs to Differ: The Paradox of Modern Iran*. New York: Doubleday, 2008.

Marshall, Jonathan, Peter Dale Scott, and Jane Hunter. *The Iran-Contra Connection: Secret Teams and Covert Operations in the Reagan Era*. Boston: South End Press, 1987.

Menashri, David. "Iran." *Middle East Contemporary Survey*, vol. 14 (1990). Tel Aviv University, Moshe Dayan Center: Westview Press, 1992.

Milani, Abbas. *Eminent Persians: The Men and Women Who Made Modern Iran, 1941–1979*. 2 vols. Syracuse: Syracuse University Press, 2008.

Millspaugh, Arthur C. *Americans in Persia*. Washington, DC: Brookings, 1946.

Mokhtari, Fariborz. "Iran's 1953 Coup Revisited: Internal Dynamics versus External Intrigue." *The Middle East Journal* 62, No. 3 (Summer 2008): 457–88.

Moslem Student Followers of the Line of the Imam. *Documents from the U.S. Espionage Den*. Multiple vols. Moslem Student Followers of the Line of the Imam: Tehran, n.d.

O'Donnell, Terence. *Seven Shades of Memory*. Mage Publications, 1999.

Parsi, Trita. *Treacherous Alliance: The Secret Dealings of Israel, Iran, and the United States*. New Haven: Yale University Press, 2007.

Pechatnov, Vladimir O. "'The Allies Are Pressing on You to Break Your Will…' Foreign Policy Correspondence between Stalin and Molotov and Other Politburo Members, September 1945–December 1946." Translated by Vladislav M. Zubok. Woodrow Wilson Center, *Cold War International History Project*, Working Paper No. 26. September 1999, www.wilsoncenter.org/topics/pubs/ACFB29.PDF.

Picco, Giandomenico. *Man Without a Gun: One Diplomat's Secret Struggle to Free the Hostages, Fight Terrorism, and End a War.* New York: Random House, 1999.

Pollock, Kenneth M. *The Persian Puzzle: The Conflict between Iran and America.* New York: Random House, 2004.

Pressfield, Steven. *Tides of War: A Novel of Alcibiades and the Peloponnesian War.* New York: Doubleday, 2000.

Ross, Dennis. *Statecraft and How to Restore America's Standing in the World.* New York: Farrar Straus Girroux, 2007.

Seferis, George. *Collected Poems. Revised Edition.* Translated, edited, and introduced by Edmund Keeley and Philip Sherrard. Princeton: Princeton University Press, 1995.

Segev, Samuel. *The Iranian Triangle: The Untold Story of Israel's Role in the Iran-Contra Affair.* Translated by Haim Watzman. New York: The Free Press, 1988.

Shawcross, William. *The Shah's Last Ride: The Fate of an Ally.* New York: Simon and Schuster, 1988.

Slavin, Barbara. *Bitter Friends, Bosom Enemies: Iran, the U.S., and The Twisted Path to Confrontation.* New York: St. Martin's Press, 2007.

Tale, Hooshang, with Farhad Tale. *Iran in the Claws of the Bear: the Failed Soviet Landgrab of 1946.* Lincoln: iUniverse Inc., 2007.

Walters, Vernon A. *Silent Missions.* Garden City, NY: Doubleday, 1978.

Weiner, Tim. *Legacy of Ashes: The History of the CIA.* New York and London: Doubleday, 2007.

Wilber, Donald. "The Overthrow of Premier Mossadeq of Iran, November 1952–August 1953." CIA report prepared March 1954. Reprinted as "The Secret CIA History of the Iran Coup, 1953." Edited by Malcolm Byrne. Updated November 2000. National Security Archive Electronic Briefing Book No. 28. www.gwu.edu/~nsarchiv/NSAEBB/NSAEBB28/ (accessed March 8, 2009).

Woods, Kevin M. *The Mother of All Battles: Saddam Hussein's Strategic Plan for the Persian Gulf War.* Annapolis: Naval Institute Press, 2008.

Woodward, Bob. *The War Within: A Secret White House History 2006–2008.* New York and London: Simon and Schuster, 2008.

# Appendix

## American Embassy Message of August 13, 1979, on Negotiation with Iranians*

Recent negotiations in which the embassy has been involved here, ranging from compound security to visa operations … highlight several features of conducting business in the Persian environment. In some instances, the difficulties we have encountered are a partial reflection of the effects of the Iranian Revolution, but we believe the underlying cultural and psychological qualities that account for the nature of these difficulties are and will remain relatively constant. Therefore, we suggest that the following analysis be used to brief both USG [United States Government] personnel and private sector representatives who are required to do business with and in this country.

Perhaps the single dominant aspect of the Persian psyche is an overriding egoism. Its antecedents lie in the long Iranian history of instability and insecurity which put a premium on self-preservation. The practical effect of it is an almost total Persian preoccupation with self and leaves little room for understanding points of view other than one's own. Thus, for example, it in incomprehensible to an Iranian that U.S. immigration law may prohibit issuing him a tourist visa when he has determined that he wants to live in California. Similarly, the Iranian central bank sees no inconsistency in claiming force majeure to avoid penalties for late payment of interest due on outstanding loans while the Government of which it is a part is denying the validity of the very grounds upon which the claim is made when confronted by similar claims from foreign firms forced to cease operations during the Iranian revolution.

The reverse of this particular psychological coin, and having the same historical roots as Persian egoism, is a pervasive unease about the nature of the world in which one lives. The Persian experience has been that nothing is permanent and it is commonly perceived that hostile forces abound. In such an environment each individual must be constantly alert for opportunities to protect himself against the malevolent forces that would otherwise be his undoing. He is obviously justified in using almost any means available to exploit such opportunities. This approach underlies the so-called "bazaar mentality" so common among Persians, a mindset that often ignores longer

---

* See Chapter 7.

term interests in favor of immediately obtainable advantages and countenances practices that are regarded as unethical by other norms.

Coupled with these psychological limitations is a general incomprehension of causality. Islam, with its emphasis on the omnipotence of God, appears to account at least in major part for this phenomenon. Somewhat surprisingly, even those Iranians educated in the Western style and perhaps with long experience outside Iran itself frequently have difficulty grasping the inter-relationship of events. Witness a Yazdi*[Ebrahim Yazdi, who was foreign minister until November 1979] resisting the idea that Iranian behavior has consequences on the perception of Iran in the U.S. or that this perception is somehow related to American policies regarding Iran. This same quality also helps explain Persian aversion to accepting responsibility for one's own action. The deus ex machina is always at work.

The Persian proclivity for assuming that to say something is to do it further complicates matters. Again, Yazdi can express surprise when informed that the irregular security forces assigned to the embassy remain in place. "But the central committee told me they would go by Monday," he says. There is no recognition that instructions must be followed up, that commitments must be accompanied by actions and results.

Finally, there are the Persian concepts of influence and obligation. Everyone pays obeisance to the former and the latter is usually honored in the breach. Persians are consumed with developing *parti bazi*—the influence that will help get things done—while favors are only grudgingly bestowed and then just to the extent that a tangible quid pro quo is immediately perceptible. Forget about assistance proffered last year or even last week; what can be offered today?

There are several lessons for those who would negotiate with Persians in all this.

First, one should never assume that his side of the issue will be recognized, let alone that it will be conceded to have merits. Persian preoccupation with self precludes this. A negotiator must force recognition of his position upon his Persian opposite number.

Second, one should not expect an Iranian readily to perceive the advantages of a long-term relationship based on trust. He will assume that his opposite number is essentially an adversary. In dealing with him he will attempt to maximize the benefits to himself that are immediately obtainable. He will be prepared to go to great lengths to achieve this goal, including running the risk of so alienating whoever he is dealing with that future business would be unthinkable, at least to the latter.

Third, interlocking relationships of all aspects of an issue must be pains-takingly, forcefully, and repeatedly developed. Linkages will be neither read-ily comprehended nor accepted by Persian negotiators.

Fourth, one should insist on performance as the sine qua non at each stage of negotiations. Statements of intention count for almost nothing.

Fifth, cultivation of goodwill for goodwill's sake is a waste of effort. The overriding objective at all times should be impressing upon the Persian across the table the mutuality of the proposed undertakings. He must be made to know that a quid pro quo is involved on both sides.

Finally, one should be prepared for the threat of breakdown in negotia-tions at any given moment and not be cowed by the possibility. Given the Persian negotiator's cultural and psychological limitations, he is going to resist the very concept of a rational (from the Western point of view) nego-tiating process.

# Iranian Proposal for Talks, July 2003*

### Iranian aims

The U.S. accepts a dialogue "in mutual respect" and agrees that Iran puts the following aims on the agenda:

- **Halt in U.S. hostile behavior and rectification of status of Iran in the U.S.:** (interference in internal or external relations, "axis of evil," terrorism list)

- **Abolishment of all sanctions:** commercial sanctions, frozen assets, judgments (FSIA), impediments in international trade and financial institutions.

- **Iraq:** democratic and fully representative government in Iraq, support of Iranian claims for Iraqi reparations, respect for Iranian national interests in Iraq and religious links to Najaf/Karbala.

- **Full access to peaceful nuclear technology, biotechnology, and chemical technology.**

- Recognition of **Iran's legitimate security interests** in the region with according defense capacity.

- **Terrorism:** pursuit of anti-Iranian terrorists, above all MKO and support for repatriation of their members in Iraq, decisive action against anti-Iranian terrorists, above all MKO and affiliated organizations in the U.S.

---

* See Chapter 1. Emphases as in original.

## U.S. aims

Iran accepts a dialogue "in mutual respect" and agrees that the U.S. put the following aims on the agenda.

- **WMD:** full transparency for security that there are no Iranian endeavors to develop or possess WMD, full cooperation with IAEA based on Iranian adoption of all relevant instruments (93+2 and all further IAEA protocols).
- **Terrorism:** decisive action against any terrorists (above all Al Qaida) on Iranian territory, full cooperation and exchange of all relevant information.
- **Iraq:** coordination of Iranian influence for activity supporting political stabilization and the establishment of democratic institutions and non-religious government.
- **Middle East:**
  1. Stop of any material support to Palestinian opposition groups (Hamas, Jihad, etc.) from Iranian territory, pressure on these organizations to stop violent action against civilians within borders of 1967.
  2. Action on Hizbollah to become a mere political organization within Lebanon.
  3. Acceptance of the Arab League Beirut declaration (Saudi initiative, two-states approach).

## Steps

I.  Communication of mutual agreement on the following procedure

II. Mutual simultaneous statements: We have always been ready for direct and authoritative talks with the US/with Iran in good faith and with the aim of discussing—in mutual respect—our common interests and our mutual concerns based on merits and objective realities, but we have made it clear that such talks can only be held if genuine progress for a solution of own concerns can be achieved.

III. A first direct meeting on the appropriate level (for instance in Paris) will be held with the previously agreed aims.

    a. Of a decision on the first mutual steps

- **Iraq:** establishment of a common group, active Iranian support for Iraqi stabilization, U.S.-commitment to actively support Iranian reparation claims within the discussions on Iraq foreign debts.
- **Terrorism:** U.S.-commitment to disarm and remove MKO from Iraq and take action in accordance with SCR 1373 against its leadership, Iranian commitment for enhanced action against Al Qaida members in Iran, agreement on cooperation and information exchange.
- Iranian general statement "to support a peaceful solution in the Middle East involving the parties concerned."
- U.S. general statement that "Iran did not belong to the 'axis of evil.'"
- U.S.-acceptance to halt its impediments against Iran in international financial and trade institutions.

b. Of the establishment of three parallel working groups on disarmament, regional security and economic cooperation. Their aim is an agreement on three parallel road maps, for the discussions of these working groups, each side accepts that the other side's aims (see above) are put on the agenda:

- **Disarmament:** road map, which combines the mutual aims of, on the one side, full transparency by international commitments and guarantees to abstain from WMD with, on the other aside, full access to western technology (in the three areas).
- **Terrorism and regional security:** road map for above mentioned aims on the Middle East and terrorism.
- **Economic cooperation:** road map for the abolishment of sanctions, rescindings of judgments, and un-freezing of assets.

c. Of agreement on a time-table for implementation.

d. And of a public statement after this first meeting on the achieved agreements.

# Index

Abrahamian, Ervand, 43, 47, 51, 64, 76,
   136n29
Abu Bakr (caliph), 26
Achaemenian Persian Empire, 19, 24, 25
Acheson, Dean, 72, 73n26
*adalat* (divine justice), 152, 173
adaptability, as element of Iranian character,
   23–24
Afghanistan, 155, 165, 177, 179
Ahmadinezhad, President, 8n3, 166n13, 170,
   181
Ahura Mazda, 25
AIOC. *See* Anglo-Iranian Oil Company
Ala, Hossein, 67
Ala, Hussein, 46, 48
Alam, Asadollah, 33
Al-Arabiya TV, 194n23
Albright, Madeleine, 10, 163, 192
Algerian mediation, during hostage crisis,
   118, 119, 154, 160, 176
Algiers accord (1975), 144, 145
Algiers accord (1981), 143n41
Ali, Imam, 16, 26
Ali b. Abu Talib, 26, 27n14
Allen, George, 46, 49, 49n29, 51, 54
*Al-Shiraa* story, 136–37
Amini, Ali, 78
Amir-Entezam, Abbas, 99, 183n9
Anderson, 147
Anglo-Iranian Oil Company (AIOC), 53, 59,
   195
   boycott, 67, 68n16, 76
   compensation for assets of, 72–74, 78–79,
      79n40
   Gass-Golshayan Agreement, 62, 65–67
Anglo-Persian Oil Company (APOC), 60, 61,
   61n3, 83
Anglo-Russian treaty (1907), 2n2, 37, 37n1,
   117, 157, 167
Ansar-e-Hezbollah, 162
antiaircraft weapons, 128, 129–30, 132, 137
anticlericalism, 29–30
APOC (Anglo-Persian Oil Company), 60–61,
   61n3, 83
Arabic script, 24
Arafat, Yasir, 158

ARAMCO, 61
Aristotle, 20
arms-for-hostages. *See* Iran-Contra scandal
art cinema, 25
Ashura, 27
assassinations of Iranian dissidents, 148
Atabaki, 48
Attlee, Clement, 72
authority, establishment of, 162–63
awareness, of Iranian history and culture, 6,
   15, 153, 168, 177
axis of evil, 180, 188, 192
Azerbaijan crisis (1945–47), 7, 35–57, 158
autonomy agreement, 48–50
   conclusions, 55–57
   oil concessions law and, 38, 41, 50, 52,
      54–55, 63
   Soviet involvement in, 39–40, 40n6, 42, 43
   UN Security Council case, 46–47
Aziz, Tariq, 123

Baghdad meetings, 10, 160
Baha'i faith, 29
*bahar-e-azadi* (spring of freedom), 95
Bahremani, Mehdi, 135, 136
Baku-Cayhan oil pipeline, 106
Baluchistan, 47
Bani Sadr, Abu Al-Hassan, 103, 104, 112, 113
Baqa'i, Mozaffar, 64, 75
*bâtiniyya* (esotericism), 29
BATNA (Best Alternatives to a Negotiated
      Agreement), 4–5, 177
   Iranian, 5, 154, 166–67
Bazargan, Mehdi, 49, 96, 99–101, 100n20.
      *See also* provisional government
Beeman, Bill, 123, 181, 188
Begin, Menachem, 158
Behbehani, Ayatollah, 77
Beheshti, Mohammad, 5, 103, 107, 113
Berthoud, Eric, 70
Bevin, Ernest, 42
Bill, James, 11n7, 56, 71–72, 79, 80, 139
Bolshevik Revolution (1917), 32
Bourguet, Christian, 110–12, 118, 161
boycott, AIOC, 68, 68n16, 76

British Persianists, 69–70. See also United
    Kingdom
British Petroleum (BP), 78, 79n40
Brzezinski, Zbigniew, 91, 97, 99n18, 100n20
Bush, George H.W., 122, 139–40, 142–49
Bush, George W., 10, 154n1, 181, 189, 192
Byrnes, James, 46

Cadman, John, 61
capitulations, *versus* concessions, 157n6
Carter, Jimmy
    conspiracy theories and, 174
    decision to admit shah, 2, 99
    hostage question, 99, 99n16
    hostage release and, 116, 118, 186
    letter to Khomeini, 102–03
    reaction to embassy takeover, 109
    refusal of shah's visit, 97
    Tehran visit (1978), 90
Cave, George, 134, 136, 150
cease-fire negotiations, Iran-Iraq war,
    137–40, 146, 149–51, 164
Christopher, Warren, 115, 116, 118, 119, 135,
    154, 176
CIA, Iran-Contra scandal and, 124, 125, 131
CIA coup (1953), 31–32, 75–77, 75n30
long-term effects of, 81, 85–86, 117, 157, 158,
    174, 182, 187
Ciccipio, Joseph, 135, 137, 147
cinema, 25
Clark, Ramsey, 102–03
clergy, attitude toward, 29–30
Clinton, Bill, 163, 179, 192
Cold War, 36–37, 91, 183
    Iran-Control scandal and, 125–26, 134, 151
communication, through public speeches,
    123
communication channels, between
    Washington and Tehran, 10–11, 144
Communist Party (Tudeh), 39, 42, 43, 49–50,
    49n29, 56, 76
Compagnie Française des Pétroles, 78
compensation
    for AIOC assets, 72–74
    to IranAir Airbus victims, 143, 143n41
concessions. See also oil concessions
    *versus* capitulations, 157n6
consortium of oil companies, 78–80
conspiracy theories, 174–75
Constitutional Movement (1906–11), 35,
    157, 158

Cooke, Donald, 183n8
Cottam, Richard, 44, 46, 66, 75, 182n7
coup (August 1953), 32, 75–77
long-term effects of, 81, 85–86, 87–88, 117,
    157, 158, 174, 182, 187
coup attempt (July 1980), 113
CREEP (Committee to Reelect the
    President), 33
Crocker, Ryan, 10, 11n6
cultural openness, as element of Iranian
    character, 23–24
culture (Iranian), 6, 15–32
    tension between religion and, 30, 30n17
culture (U.S.), Iranian fear of, 12
Cutler, Walter, 92
cynicism, in Iranian political culture, 60, 81
Cyrus the Great, 19, 157

D'Arcy concession (1901), 60, 83, 117
Dawa Seventeen, 144, 145, 148
de Cuéllar, Pérez, 139–50
Democratic Party of Azerbaijan (DPA),
    39–40, 48, 49, 52, 57
Democratic Republic of Kurdistan, 40n8
Democrat Party, 49, 49n29, 52, 64
diaspora (Iranian), 12, 161, 169
diplomatic relations (U.S.-Iranian), lack of,
    10–11, 154, 160
diplomatic service
    American, 11
    Iranian, 11–12, 156, 169
distrust, 192–93
    for legalism, 155–56
    during oil nationalization crisis, 70–73,
    84–85
"Divorce Iranian Style," 155n2
*Documents from the U.S. Espionage Den,* 104,
    104n23
Douglas, William O., 127n12
"downward spiral," 182, 182n7, 184, 188–89
    escape from, 193–95
DPA (Democratic Party of Azerbaijan),
    39–40, 48, 49, 52, 57
Draper, Theodore, 129, 135

Eisenhower, Dwight, 74n29, 75
elections (Majles)
    December 1946, 52
    hostage negotiations and, 113
    October 1949, 65–66
embassy hostage crisis (1979–81), 8, 87–119

conditions preceding, 92–101
events during, 1–4, 101–02, 117
Iranian foreign relations and, 105–07
Iranian negotiating stance, 103–08,
    175–76, 176n26
Iranian political battles during, 103–04
lessons learned, 4–5, 117–19
Limbert's role in, 1–4, 183
long-term effects of, 87–88, 119, 151,
    182–83, 186
Miller-Clark mission, 102–03
rescue mission, 110, 113
resolution of, 113–16
U.S. misunderstanding of situation and,
    100, 117
U.S. negotiating stance, 107–09, 117–18
emigration, 12, 95, 156, 169
Eradeh-ye-Melli (National Will) party, 41
esotericism (bâtiniyya), 29
expectations, realistic, 193–95

Falle, Sam, 69
Fallon, Admiral, 154n1
Farland, Joseph, 33, 33n20
Farmanfarmaian, Manuchehr, 78
Fatemi, Hossein, 77
Fath Ali Shah, 170
fatwa (religious opinion), 140, 171
Feda'iyan-e-Islam, 67
Fesharaki, Feridoun, 80
fetneh (disorder), 171
Firuz, Mozaffar, 42, 48, 49, 49n29
Fisher, Roger, 4–5, 62–63, 68, 84, 97, 176n26
    on hostage negotiations, 5, 107–08, 108n28
Flandrin, George, 98
folklore, 28, 157
foreign innovations, Iranian adoption of,
    24–25
foreign relations, embassy hostage crisis
    and, 105–07
Forqaan, 95, 95n10
Fortier, Donald, 125
Foruhar, Dariush, 64
Fraser, William, 72, 72n24, 78
frozen assets, 143

Gasiorowski, Mark, 74
Gass-Golshayan Agreement, 62, 65–67
Gates, Robert, 179
geographic vulnerability, 23

German intermediaries, in hostage crisis,
    115, 119, 154
Getting to Yes (Fisher), 4–5
Ghorbanifarr, Manouchehr, 124–39, 152, 161
goodwill
    Bush's statement on, 122, 139
    limits of, 146–47, 185
Gulestan treaty (1813), 117

Hafez of Shiraz, 30n17
Hague Tribunal, 176
Hakim, Albert, 133, 135, 136
Harriman, Averell, 68–69, 73, 83
Harvard Law School, 4
Hashemi, Ali, 137
Hashemi, Hadi, 135
Hashemi, Mehdi, 136, 136n29
Hashemi-Rafsanjani, Ali Akbar, 114, 118, 140
    1990 fake telephone call from, 122, 143, 151
    Iran-Contra deals and, 136
    Lebanan hostages and, 123, 141–49
    policy toward United States, 142
    on UN mediation, 147
Hashemi-Rafsanjani, Mahmoud, 135
Hashemi-Rafsanjani, Mohsen, 135
Hawk antiaircraft missiles, 128, 130, 131n20,
    133, 134, 137
Helms, Richard, 118, 187, 187n13
Henderson, Loy, 74
heresy, 28–29
Herodotus, 19, 23
hesabgar (calculating), 175
hezb-e-baad (party of the winds), 141, 170
Hezb-e Zahmatkeshan (Toilers' Party), 64, 75
Hezbollah, 123
Hidden Imam, 27
hijacking, TWA Flight 847, 123
historical background, 15–32
historical monuments, 31, 157, 170
history
    importance of, 6, 12, 83, 117, 153, 157–60,
        195
    Iranian case based on, 169
    political, 17–18, 22–23
    seminal events in, 182–84
Hoover, Herbert, Jr., 78
hostages
    in Lebanon (See Lebanon hostages)
    TWA Flight 847, 123
    U.S. embassy (See embassy hostage crisis)
hostility, 189–92

during oil nationalization crisis, 70–73, 84–85

Howland, Michael, 1

humanitarian grounds
Lebanon hostage release on, 143, 148
U.S. admission of shah on, 98, 100n19, 100, 117, 167, 175

Hussein (son of Ali), martyrdom of, 27

Hussein, Imam, 16, 158

Hussein, Saddam, 106
Lebanon hostage crisis and, 8, 144–46
Persian Gulf War, 144–45, 148
UN Resolution 598 and, 152, 152n54

Hussein, Shah Sultan, 171

Ibrahimian, Ibrahim, 133

intelligence, crediting negotiators with, 167–68

intermediaries, 154
choice of, 160–61
during embassy hostage crisis, 110–12, 110n30, 115–16, 119, 154, 160–61, 176
during Iran-Contral deals, 131, 148, 161
during Lebanon hostage crisis, 140, 141, 144, 146, 150, 161
during oil nationalization crisis, 68–73, 83, 85

international opinion
embassy hostage crisis and, 105–07
Iranian negotiating stance and, 175–76

Internet, 25

IranAir Airbus, 143, 143n41, 158, 188

Iran-Contra scandal (1985–86), 8, 121, 123–39
arm shipments, 128, 136
collapse of deals, 133–39
events during, 128–32
hostage releases, 128, 134, 136
involvement of Reagan administration in, 131–32, 137
Iranian goals during, 138–39, 151–52
lessons learned, 150–52
long-term effects of, 137–38, 150
political misjudgments, 137
U.S. goals during, 125–28, 138–39, 150–51
U.S.-Iranian relations preceding, 121–22

Iranian Communist Party (Tudeh), 39, 42, 43, 49–50, 49n29, 56, 76

Iranian dissidents, assassinations of, 148

Iranian Revolutionary Guard Corps (IRGC), 128, 162

Iranian-Soviet treaty (1921), 37n1, 45, 53, 55, 155

Iran-Iraq war (1980–99), 106, 158
cease-fire, 137–40, 146, 149–51, 164
international opinion of Iran and, 175–76
Iran-Contra scandal and, 123–39
Iraqi blame for, 145–48, 152, 159–60, 173, 173n23
media coverage during, 169–70
outbreak of, 114
political prisoner executions, 164
U.S. alliance with Iraq, 138, 152, 188

Iran Party, 49, 50, 49n28, 64, 65

Iraq, 10, 160, 165
U.S. alliance with, 138, 152, 188

Iricon, 78

Islamic Republic
authority and responsibility within, 162–63
legal issues and, 155
motives of, 163–64

Islamic Republican Party (IRP), 113

Islamic Revolution, 90, 158
August 1953 coup and, 82, 86
conspiracy theories and, 174
internecine battles during, 94–95, 102, 103–04, 186
Iranian foreign relations and, 105–07
U.S. attitude toward, 91

Ismaili Assassins of Alamut, 29

Israel, Iran-Contra scandal and, 123–39

Jacobsen, David, 135, 137

Javits Resolution, 92, 92n7, 163

*Jebheh-ye-Melli. See* National Front

Jenco, Lawrence Martin, 135, 137

Jews, 21, 31n18

Jordan, Hamilton, 99, 110–11, 110n30, 119

*jujeh-komunist* (mini-commies), 102

justice, Iranian insistence on, 152, 169, 173–74
after Iran-Iraq War, 146–47, 149
during oil nationalization crisis, 83–84

Kalhor, Mehdi, 170

Kangarlou, Mohsen, 130, 132, 135, 150

Karoubi, Hassan, 127–28, 129, 150

Karoubi, Mehdi, 127, 127n13

Kashani, Ayatollah, 64, 67, 75, 77

Katouzian, Homa, 22, 82, 86

Kavtaradze, Sergei, 38

Kazemi-Qomi, Kazemi, 10

Kean, Benjamin, 98
Kemptner, 147
Khamene'i, Ali, 104, 134, 140
Kharrazi, Kamal, 144
Khashoggi, Adnan, 124, 127
Khatami, Mohammad, 105, 105n25, 172
Khomeini, Ahmad, 102, 114n35, 113, 114, 135
Khomeini, Ayatollah
    August 1953 coup and, 81
    death of, 140, 141, 151
    disorder encouraged by, 105, 105n24
    on economic stability, 93–94
    exile of, 158, 168n18
    hostage negotiations, 103, 109, 111–14,
        114n35, 118
    Iranian respect for, 30, 172
    justice sought by, 173
    return from exile, 90
    rhetorical statements, 12, 170, 193
    support for embassy takeover, 101–02, 119
Khomeini, Ruhollah, 7
Khorrām-Dīnān of Azerbaijan, 29
Khosrow (Chosroes) I Anushiravan, 20n4,
    173
Khuzistan, 60
Kimche, David, 124, 128, 132
Kish Island, Iran-Contra meetings at, 132–33
komitehs (local vigilantes), 93
Kurdistan, 37, 40n8, 50, 57, 158
Kuwait, Dawa Seventeen in, 144, 145, 148

Laingen, Bruce, 1, 92
    on Iranian reaction to shah in U.S., 99,
        99n18
    on shah's request to visit U.S., 97, 98
    on Yazdi's UN visit, 96n11
Lambton, Ann, 69–70
language, 11, 11n7, 20–21, 20n6, 24–25
lawlessness, climate of, 105, 105n24, 171
leadership, respect for, 172
Lebanon hostages, 8. See also Iran-Contra
    scandal
    lessons learned, 150–52
    negotiations, 140–45
    releases of, 128, 134, 136, 143–44, 147–48
Ledeen, Michael, 126, 126n11, 128, 130, 132
leftist groups, embassy hostage crisis and,
    102, 104, 118
legalism
    avoidance of, 155–57
    Soviet-Iranian treaty and, 55

Levy, Walter, 68, 78
lob-e-matlab, 8
Louis, William Roger, 62, 69–70

Ma'adikhah, Abd al-Majid, 95n10
Mahabad autonomous regime, 50
Mahdi, Mohammad al-, 27, 28n16
Mainz meeting, 136
Majles
    dispute with Mosaddegh, 76
    elections (See elections)
    elections law regarding foreign troops, 51
    hostage negotiations, 116
    oil concessions law, 38, 41, 51, 53, 63
    oil nationalization law, 67
Makki, Hossein, 75
maktabi, 169
Malek, Redha, 116
Manichaeism, 29, 180
Mansur, Ali, 65
mard-e-rendi behavior, 103, 105, 138, 152, 167,
    184
Martyrs Fund, 127
Matin-Daftari, Hedayatollah, 65
Mazdakism, 29
McCain, John, 154n1
McFarlane, Robert, 124–26, 126n11, 134, 135,
    136n29, 151
McGee, George, 73, 73n26
Medes, 19
middle class, Islamic Revolution and, 95
military defeats, contrast between past
    history and, 32, 157
Miller, William Green, 89n2, 96n12, 102–03
Millspaugh, Arthur, 38
mob rule, 105, 105n24, 171
Mohammad, death of, 26
Moharram, 30
Mohtashemi-Pour, 123
Mojahedin-e-Khalq Organization, 102, 104,
    113, 118
Molotov, Vyacheslav, 45
monarchy. See also Pahlavi shahs; specific
    monarch
    collapse of, 90
Montazeri, Hossein Ali, 136, 136n29, 140
monuments, 31, 157, 170
Morrison, Herbert, 70, 72
Mosaddegh, Mohammad, 41, 43
    British view of, 71

as center of oil nationalization crisis, 62–65, 84
coalition formed by (*See* National Front)
foreign oil concessions law, 38
Iran Party and, 49n28
Islamic Revolution and, 94–95
meeting with Harriman, 68–69
negotiating stance, 74, 166
overthrow of, 32, 75–77, 75n30, 87, 117, 157, 158, 174, 182, 187
personal characteristics of, 64–65
political background of, 63
as prime minister, 67
view of British, 68, 68n17, 84
Moslem Student Followers of the Imam's Path, 1
motives
of foreign powers, 41–42
of Hashemi-Rafsanjani, 141
Iranian, 156, 163–64
of Islamic Republic, 163–64
of U.S., during embassy hostage crisis, 99, 99n18, 119
Mousavi, Mir Hossein, 128, 130, 134, 136
multiethnic empire, history as, 18–21
Murray, Wallace, 46
Muskie, Edmund, 114
myths. *See also* stereotypes
overcoming, 179–95

Nabavi, Behzad, 114n35
Nasiri, Ne'matullah, 77
Nasseri, Cyrus, 140, 141
national character (Iranian), 6, 17–18, 23–25. *See also* stereotypes
British view of, 62, 69–71, 84, 195
U.S. view of, 9, 154n1, 155, 184–86, 190–91
National Front (*Jebheh-ye-Melli*), 63
formation of, 49n28, 63–64, 64n7
Islamic Revolution and, 95
opposition to Gass-Golshayan agreement, 67
National Intelligence Estimate (NIE), 188
national interest, Iranian control of, 165–66
National Iranian Oil Company (NIOC), 79–80
nationalism, oil industry and. *See* oil nationalization crisis
National Party, 64
national referendum (July 1953), 76

National Security Decision Document (NSDD), 125
national unity, Azerbaijan crisis and, 56
National Will (Eradeh-ye-Melli) party, 41
negativity, 189–92
during oil nationalization crisis, 70–73, 84–85
negotiations
effect of history and culture on, 15–32, 157–60
reasons for pursuing, 179–81
neoconservatives, 189n18
New Iran (Iran-e-Novin) Party, 49n28
Newsom, David, 98
Nicaraguan Contras, 137
NIE (National Intelligence Estimate), 188
Nimrodi, Yaacov, 124, 127, 130
NIOC (National Iranian Oil Company), 79–80
Nir, Amiram, 132, 133
Nixon, Richard, 33, 187n13
nonjudgmental tone, 167
North, Oliver, 130–39, 151, 153, 161
Nowruz, 30
NSDD (National Security Decision Document), 125
nuclear weapons, 189

Obama, Barack, 154n1, 194n23
objective criteria, establishment of, 155–57, 176
oil agreements
APOC (1933), 60–61, 83
consortium (1954), 78–80
nationalization (1954), 78–80
oil boycott, AIOC, 67, 68n16, 76
oil concessions
Anglo-Russian treaty and, 37, 37n1
versus consortium agreement, 80
D'Arcy Group (1901), 60, 83, 117
1944 law concerning, 38, 41, 50, 53–55, 63
Soviet requests for, 38–40, 42, 46, 51, 61
Iranian rejection of, 52–54
UK interest in, 42
U.S. requests for, 37, 47, 77
oil nationalization crisis (1951–53), 7, 59–84
agreement ending, 78–80
Gass-Golshayan agreement, 62, 65–67
international dimension of, 68–70
lessons learned, 81–85
long-term effects of, 59–60, 87

Mosaddegh as center of, 62–65, 84
oil concessions laws and, 53
outlines of, 60–62
psychological side of, 62, 65–71, 83–85,
   159, 195
rigidity of opponents in, 70–73
U.S. attempts to mediate in, 68, 71–74,
   82, 84
Omar, Caliph, 171
Operation Eagle Claw, 110, 113
Owen, Roberts, 116
Ozymandias factor, 31–32, 157

Pahlavi Foundation, 92n7
Pahlavi shahs. *See also specific monarch*
   APOC and, 60
   attempts to separate religion and politics,
      25–26
   Iranian discontent with, 22–23, 23n11, 90
   U.S. support for, 32, 44n15, 54n40, 89, 89n2,
      91–92
Pakistani mediation, in Lebanon hostage
   crisis, 141
Panamanian mediation, during hostage
   crisis, 110–12, 110n30, 118, 161
Paniranist Party, 64
Parsi, Trita, 126
Party of Ali (Shiat Ali), 26
Patton, Bruce M., 62–63
Peres, Shimon, 124, 126
Persian Empire, 19, 24, 25, 30, 158
Persian Gulf War, 146, 148
Persianists (British), 69–70
Persian language, 11, 11n7, 20–21, 20n6,
   24–25
petroleum. *See* oil concessions
Pezeshkpour, Mohsen, 64
Phoenix missiles, 128, 130
Picco, Giandomenico, 140–49, 153
Pickering, Thomas, 144
Pirnia, Hosein, 78
Pishavari, Jafar, 48, 52
Poindexter, John, 132, 134, 151
Polhill, Robert, 145
political battles
   during embassy hostage crisis, 103–05
   Iran-Contra scandal and, 151
   during Islamic Revolution, 94–95, 102
   oil nationalization crisis and, 59
   post-WWII, 41, 55
political culture, cynicism in, 60, 81

political ideology, religion in, 25–28
political system (Iranian)
   authority and responsibility within,
      162–63
   historical background, 17–18, 22–23
political system (U.S.), Iranian confusion
   about, 163
Pollack, Kenneth, 141
positional bargaining, 68
power, Iranian respect for, 171–72
pre-Islamic history, 17–18, 28, 30, 157, 170
pressure, degree of, 172
pro-shah party, 49, 49n28
provisional government
   collapse of, 101, 102, 163n10
   inability to protect U.S. embassy, 2, 100
   Islamic Revolution and, 95
public speeches, communication through,
   123

Qaddafi, Muammar, 164
*qahr*, 109
Qajar rulers, 32, 60, 157n6, 170
Qashqa'i, Naser Khan, 50, 56
Qavam, Ahmad, 43, 63, 74
   coalition government formed by, 49, 53
   meeting with Stalin, 44–45, 46, 155
   role in Soviet withdrawal, 43, 56
   UN Security Council case, 46–47
Qazi Mohammad, 40n8
*Qiyam-e-Iran* (newspaper), 52
Qotbzadeh, Sadeq, 96, 103
   hostage negotiations, 110–12, 118
   resignation of, 113

Raja'i, Mohammad Ali, 114n35, 118
Rashidian brothers, 75
Razmara, Ali, 65, 67
Reagan, Ronald
   Cold War mentality, 125–26, 134, 151
   embassy hostage release and, 116
   involvement in Iran-Contra deals, 131–32,
      138, 161 (*See also* Iran-Contra scandal)
   on Iran, 122
   Lebanon hostages and, 109n29, 129, 138
   Nicaraguan Contras and, 137
Reed, Frank, 135, 137, 145
Reed, Joseph V., 98
religion, 15–32. *See also* Shia Islam; *specific
   religion*
   anticlericalism, 29–30

centrality of, 25–28
as element of Iranian identity, 21, 24
tension between culture and, 29–30, 29n17
religious diversity, tradition of, 21, 21n7
religious minorities, 21, 21n7
republican system, 162
responsibility, establishment of, 162–63
revolutionary authority structure, 162
Revolutionary Council, 1n1, 93, 112, 163n10
revolutionary courts, 93, 174
Revolutionary Guards (Iranian
   Revolutionary Guard Corps), 128, 162
Reza Pahlavi, Mohammad
   admission to U.S., 2, 100, 117, 167, 175
   1953 coup and, 77, 158
   death of, 114
   departure from Iran, 90
   extradition requests, 110, 110n30
   illness of, 89, 89n3, 98–99, 98n15
   insecurity of, 33, 168
   interest in U.S. visit, 97
   Iranian dissatisfaction with, 22–23, 23n11
   Soviet withdrawal and, 51, 54
   U.S. support for, 89, 89n2, 91, 182
   viewed as American puppet, 60, 168
Reza Shah Pahlavi
   deposition of, 32, 36–37, 41
   modernizing reforms of, 35, 41n9
rhetoric, 170, 181, 193
Riedel, Bruce, 146, 148
rigidity
   Iranian stance of, 175
   during oil nationalization crisis, 70–73
Roosevelt, Kermit, 32, 77
Royal Dutch Shell, 78
Rushdie, Salman, 140, 171
Russia. *See also* Soviet Union
   Anglo-Russian treaty (1907), 2n2, 37, 37n1,
      117, 157, 167
   WWI occupation of Iran, 32, 36, 157

Sa'adi, 195
Sadchikov, Ivan Vasilivich, 46, 48, 50, 53, 54
Sadr, Imam Musa, 164
Sa'ed, Mohammad, 38
Safavid dynasty, 25, 171
Saleh, Allahyar, 49, 65
Samii, Ali, 136
Sands, Bobby, 170
Sarell, R.F.G., 69
Sassanian Empire, 19–20, 25, 158, 173

Saudi Arabia, 61, 160
Saunders, Harold, 96, 97, 107, 109, 111
Sazegara, Mohsen, 114n35
schismatic movements, 29
scholarships, 80
Schwimmer, Adolph, 128, 130
Scowcroft, Brent, 142, 146, 148
Secord, Richard, 133, 135, 136
Seferis, George, 194, 194n22
Segev, Samuel, 127n13, 128, 132
Seyyed Zia al-Din Tabatab'i, 41
Sha'ban Ja'fari, 77
*The Shah and I* (Alam), 33
Shepherd, Francis, 69
Shia Islam. *See also* Twelver Shia Islam
   adoption of, 18, 24
   centrality of, 25–28
   divine justice, 152, 173
   as element of Iranian identity, 16, 21, 24,
      173
   origins of, 29
Shia religious law, 155, 173–174
Shiat Ali (Party of Ali), 26
*sholugh*, 3
Shultz, George, 124, 137, 151
Sibuyeh the Grammarian, 24
Sidewinder missiles, 128, 130
Sinclair, 37
Slavin, Barbara, 10, 106, 148, 159n7, 192n20
Smith, William French, 131
SOFA (Status of Forces Agreement)
   controversy, 7, 32, 33n19, 81, 168, 168n18
   long-term effects of, 117, 158
Soviet-Iranian oil company, proposal for, 46,
      52–54
Soviet-Iranian treaty (1921), 37n1, 45, 53, 55,
      155
Soviet Union
   Iran-Control scandal and, 125
   objectives in Iran, 42–43, 51
   oil concessions sought by, 38–40, 42, 43,
      46, 51, 61
   Iranian rejection of, 52–54
   support for Azerbaijani separatists, 39–40,
      40n6, 42, 43
   UN Security Council case, 46–47
   withdrawal from Iran, 41–43, 46, 50–51,
      55, 61
   WWII occupation of Iran, 36–41, 155, 157,
      158
spheres of influence, 2n2, 157, 167

spring of freedom (*bahar-e-azadi*), 94
Stalin, Joseph, 44–45, 46, 54, 155
Standard Vacuum, 37
Status of Forces Agreement (SOFA)
    controversy, 7, 32, 33n19, 81, 168, 168n18
long-term effects of, 117, 158
Steen, 147
stereotypes, 9, 154n1, 155, 184–88. *See also*
    national character
    overcoming, 179–95
    perpetuation of, 184n10, 190–92
Stokes, Richard, 72
street fighting
    during hostage crisis, 101, 113
    during Islamic Revolution, 93–94, 105,
        105n24, 186
Struebig, 147
success, defining, 176–77
Sullivan, William, 90n5, 97
Sunni Islam, 26n13, 28n16, 29, 152, 173
Sunni Kurds, 21
Sutherland, 147
Swiss channel, 11, 146, 150

Tabataba'i, Sadeq, 114, 115, 117, 119, 135
Taliban, 165, 177
tanker war (Persian Gulf), 122, 188
Taqizadeh, Hassan, 60
Tehran
    atmosphere in, during Islamic Revolution,
        93–94, 105
    hostage crisis in (*See* embassy hostage
        crisis)
    Iran-Contra meetings in, 133–34
Teicher, Howard, 125, 134
Teymurtash, Abdul Hussein, 61
theatrical element, in Iranian negotiating
    style, 169–71
theocratic structure, 162
*The Times*, 67
Toilers' Party (*Hezb-e Zahmatkeshan*), 64, 75
Tomseth, Victor, 1
TOW antitank missiles, 128–29, 129, 132, 137
Tracy, Edward, 135, 137
treaties
    Anglo-Russian (1907), 2n2, 37, 37n1, 117,
        157, 167
    Gulestan (1813), 117
    Iranian-Soviet (1921), 37n1, 45, 53, 55, 155
    tripartite (UK-USSR-Iran), 36, 39, 117, 155,
        158

Turkmanchai (1828), 7, 117
Truman, Harry S., 68, 72
Tudeh party, 39, 42, 43, 49–50, 49n29, 56, 76
Turkey, WWI invasion of Iran by, 36
Turkish Empire, 25
Turkish language, 20
Turkmanchai treaty (1828), 7, 117
Turner, 147
TWA Flight 847, 123
Twelver Shia Islam, 24
    as element of Iranian identity, 21, 24
    origins of, 27, 27n15

United Kingdom
    Anglo-Russian treaty (1907), 2n2, 37, 37n1,
        117, 157, 167
    Iranian view of, 66–69, 69n17, 71, 84–85
    objectives in Iran, 42
    occupation of Iran
    during WWI, 32, 36, 157
    during WWII, 36–41, 117, 157, 158
    oil interests, 42 (*See also* Anglo-Iranian Oil
        Company)
    pro-monarchy coup supported by, 32
    view of Iranians in, 62, 66–72, 84–85, 166,
        195
United Nations
    AIOC case, 72
    embassy hostage negotiations, 110–12,
        110n30, 118
    Iran-Iraq cease-fire negotiations, 138–40,
        146, 149–51, 164
    Lebanon hostage negotiations, 139–50
    Yazdi's visit to, 96, 96n11, 96n12
United Nations Security Council, 36
    Azerbaijani case submitted to, 46–47
    Resolution 2, 44
    Resolution 3, 47–48
    Resolution 598, Paragraph 6, 146–48, 152
United States
    attempts to mediate in oil nationalization
        crisis, 68, 71–74, 82, 84
    August 1953 coup and, 75, 81, 87, 157, 174,
        182, 187
    Azerbaijan crisis and, 46–48, 51–52
    first major role in Iran, 36
    hostage crisis (*See* embassy hostage crisis)
    as Iranian enemy, 60, 81–82, 85–86, 87–88,
        121–22
    Iranian view of, 9, 187–88, 187n12, 191–92
    Iraqi alliance with, 138, 152, 188

Islamic Revolution and, 91, 95
lack of formal diplomatic relations with
    Iran, 10–11, 154, 160
objectives in Iran, 42
oil concessions sought by, 37, 47, 78
Pahlavi network in, 92n7, 97n13
pro-monarchy stance, 32, 44n15, 55n40, 89,
    89n2, 91–92
view of Iranians in, 87–88, 117, 121, 184–86
    (*See also* stereotypes)
visas for, 12, 95, 156
unorthodox ideas, 28–29
Ury, William L., 62–63
USSR. *See* Soviet Union
USS *Stark*, 122
USS *Vincennes*, 158

Vance, Cyrus, 2, 96, 96n12, 97, 98
Velayati, Ali Akbar, 123, 141, 142
Venezuela, 61
Versailles peace conference (1919), 45
victimization, Iranian sense of, 158–59
Villalon, Hector, 110–12, 118, 161
Voice of America, 75, 114n35

Waldheim, Kurt, 111
Walters, Vernon, 69, 69n17, 73
weakness, Iranian despisal of, 171–72
Weinberger, 151
Weir, Benjamin, 129, 137
World Bank, 73, 74
World War I, invasion of Iran during, 32, 36
World War II
    Allied occupation during, 32, 36–41, 117,
        155, 157, 158
    Iranian political battles following, 41, 55

Yazdi, Ebrahim, 98
    embassy takeover and, 102
    UN meetings, 96, 96n11, 96n12
    on U.S. motives, 100, 100n19, 117
Yazid (caliph), 26
yellow ribbons, 125

Zaehner, Robin, 69–70
Zahedi, Fazlollah, 77
Zarif, Javad, 141, 146, 147, 151
Zoroastrianism, 21, 25

# About the Author

John Limbert was appointed Distinguished Professor of International Affairs at the U.S. Naval Academy in August 2006 after a 33-year career in the United States Foreign Service. Ambassador Limbert holds the Department of State's highest award—the Distinguished Service Award. He holds his PhD from Harvard University in history and Middle Eastern studies and has taught in Iranian high schools and at the University of Shiraz. He has written numerous articles on Middle Eastern subjects and has authored *Iran: At War with History* and *Shiraz in the Age of Hafez*.

# United States
# Institute of Peace Press

Since its inception, the United States Institute of Peace Press has published over 150 books on the prevention, management, and peaceful resolution of international conflicts—among them such venerable titles as Raymond Cohen's *Negotiating Across Cultures*; *Herding Cats* and *Leashing the Dogs of War* by Chester A. Crocker, Fen Osler Hampson, and Pamela Aall; and I. William Zartman's *Peacemaking and International Conflict*. All our books arise from research and fieldwork sponsored by the Institute's many programs. In keeping with the best traditions of scholarly publishing, each volume undergoes both thorough internal review and blind peer review by external subject experts to ensure that the research, scholarship, and conclusions are balanced, relevant, and sound. As the Institute prepares to move to its new headquarters on the National Mall in Washington, D.C., the Press is committed to extending the reach of the Institute's work by continuing to publish significant and sustainable works for practitioners, scholars, diplomats, and students.

VALERIE NORVILLE
DIRECTOR

# Negotiating with Iran

*Text:* Palatino Lt Std
*Display Text:* Optima
*Cover Design:* Katie Sweetman
*Interior Design and Page Makeup:* Cynthia Jordan
*Copyediting:* Jane Sevier
*Proofreading:* Amy Thompson
*Indexing:* Mary Coe